BOOKTALKING BONANZA

Ten Ready-to-Use Multimedia Sessions for the Busy Librarian

Betsy Diamant-Cohen and Selma K. Levi

AMERICAN LIBRARY ASSOCIATION
Chicago   2009

Dr. Betsy Diamant-Cohen is the children's programming specialist at the Enoch Pratt Free Library in Baltimore, Maryland, and the creator of the *Mother Goose on the Loose* early literacy program. She is the author of *Mother Goose on the Loose* as well as many articles on early literacy and public library programming. In 2004, she was named a Mover and Shaker by *Library Journal*. Diamant-Cohen earned her doctorate in communications design from the University of Baltimore and her master's degree in library science from Rutgers University. Diamant-Cohen is often accompanied on her travels by a giant stuffed frog.

Selma K. Levi has been the supervisor of the Children's Department of the Central Library of the Enoch Pratt Free Library in Baltimore, Maryland, since 1987. She is a professional storyteller and has even taken her "Storytelling for Non-tellers" workshop into the Maryland correctional system, where she inspired prisoners to tell stories to their children when they came to visit. Levi earned her master's degree in library science from Indiana University and served on the 1987 Newbery Award Committee. She reads constantly, including while walking her dog, while brushing her teeth, and while navigating stairs (albeit while holding onto the banister with the other hand).

The paper used in this publication meets the minimum requirements of American National Standard for Information Sciences—Permanence of Paper for Printed Library Materials, ANSI Z39.48-1992. ∞

Library of Congress Cataloging-in-Publication Data

Diamant-Cohen, Betsy.
Booktalking bonanza : ten ready-to-use multimedia sessions for the busy librarian / Betsy Diamant-Cohen and Selma K. Levi.
     p.   cm.
Includes bibliographical references and index.
ISBN 978-0-8389-0965-2 (alk. paper)
1. Book talks—United States. I. Levi, Selma K. II. Title.
Z1003.15D53 2009
021.70973—dc22   2008015371

ISBN-13: 978-0-8389-0965-2

Printed in the United States of America

13   12   11   10   09   5   4   3   2   1

For Jay, who bought the laptop that brought me, kicking and scream-ing, into the twentieth (not twenty-first) century, and who is worth much more than all the money he lavishes on everyone else.

For Adam, who troubleshoots all of my computer crises with aplomb, and who will always be, despite his mensch-iosity, my little boy.

For Mom and Dad, Henry and Wendy, who have always been proud of every little thing I've done . . . well, this is slightly bigger.

For Banistre, Cooper, and Peyton, who are the right ages for most of these books . . . get reading and let me know what you think!

For Brett, Marisa, Sarah, David, Michael, and Miranda, who are a bit too old now, but thanks for letting me practice giving you the right book(s) way back when.

For Selma and Bill, my biggest Baltimore boosters.

SKL

For Stuart, who made Selma and me endless cups of herbal tea on cold winter days, even while leaving the door open by mistake!

For Yoella, who spent countless hours checking and rechecking websites.

For Alon, who fixed the computers whenever they went on the blink.

For Maya, who offered to help whenever she could.

For Celia, who drew everything I requested and who explained over transatlantic telephone how to use Adobe Photoshop.

To Dad, who encouraged me to spend time on the book even when he would have preferred my company.

BDC

CONTENTS

FOREWORD

THE BEDROCK OF LIBRARY SERVICE TO CHILDREN AND YOUNG adults is to connect the right book to the right person at the right time. This is the essential purpose of most of our work as children's librarians and young adult librarians. It is the words of authors we admire that speak to us as we guide new readers from new generations to great books.

The advent of technology has changed the way young people view the world and their expectations of entertainment and information seeking. We despair that everyone is reading less. We read articles that speak to the death of the book, but those of us who have made books our life seek a new way to weave the words and stories we love back into the fabric of the world of our children.

I have had the honor of working with both Selma and Betsy during my career as a children's librarian. Their energy and passion for their work have been an inspiration to me. I am delighted by their latest endeavor. Like most things these two ladies do, it is fresh and fun and speaks to the passion for books and stories. Using technology to make books more accessible to children of this time, children who have grown up with the Internet and instant information, is a stroke of true genius. It brings together the time-honored mission of the library and the creative use of the best the new technology offers us. As you will see from these pages, books come alive in a new way. In the end, it is all about giving the next generation the power to imagine and hence to change their lives.

Ellen Riordan
Coordinator of Children's Services
Enoch Pratt Free Library

ACKNOWLEDGMENTS

FIRST AND FOREMOST WE THANK BLANE HALLIDAY AND Michael Rios, our partners in crime, for the first two live incarnations of "Booktalking with Pizzazz." Blane helped originate the idea and, when he moved to Florida, joined us in Orlando at our ALA presentation. (He also kept the white carnation alive and turned it brilliantly green to boot!) Michael took over after Blane departed the Sights and Sounds Department and put his own spin on things when we presented our live Pizzazz show around Maryland.

We also acknowledge the Sights and Sounds Department of the Enoch Pratt Free Library as a whole and Michele Ringger-Weil and Tom Warner in particular for suggesting lists of songs, films, and Internet connections for us to consider.

Thank you to Renee Vaillancourt McGrath, who encouraged us to write a book for ALA Editions, and to the other folks at ALA, including Patrick Hogan and Eugenia Chun. Thank you to Celia Yitzhak, illustrator extraordinaire, who was generous with both her time and her talent, drawing anything we asked.

In order to reproduce screenshots, cite websites, and use lyrics for songs and poems, a certain amount of detective work is required: Who needs to be asked for permission, and how can they be contacted? Sometimes obtaining permission was easy, but more often than not it required sending an e-mail to one person who directed us to another, who directed us to another. We gratefully acknowledge all of the people who responded to our e-mails and letters:

San Le for graciously sending images of tetrahedrons; Cindy McFarlane from August House; Mike Morrison from the Museum of Science, Boston; Nathan Kells from the Miami Science Museum; Jerry and Sabrina from Grossi and Anubis Productions; Dan Robinson; George Tselos from the Statue of Liberty–Ellis Island Foundation; Jeff Dosik, librarian at the National Park Service, Statue of

Liberty National Monument; the Learning Page Reference Team/ LD; Pete Guoba, VP marketing, EMI Music Incorporated; Todd J. Biederman; Sandy Yaguda (Jay and the Americans); SoloSong; Marcy J. Gordon, Betsy's wonderful cousin, and Bryan-David Kee for taking a digital picture of the Statue of Liberty for our chapter on immigration; Wendy Hogan from Kids' Turn Central; Lara Sissell, publicist, William B. Eerdmans Publishing Company; Marcia M. Soward, program coordinator, Office of Management, National Institute of Environmental Health Sciences (NIEHS); David Balihar; Michael Paul Moore; the Sanatan Society; Jim Bumgardner, Krazydad.com; Natalie Reynolds; Molly McElroy; Bob Hirshon, senior project director, AAAS; Jennifer Thomson, community history curator, Walsall Museum, Walsall, U.K.; Patrick Sterno, Caricature Zone; Jenny Beard, Walters Art Gallery; Ellen Freedman; Dan Smythe, Canadian Museum of Nature/Musée canadien de la nature; Janine Hanson and Gail Vold Greco, directors of communications and public relations, Science Museum of Minnesota; Eric Mueller, Science Museum of Minnesota; Jordan LeBaron; Felice Holman; Jim Derosiers, Boston Book Company; Scott Oldeman; Alec Long, photographer; Harvey Kirsch, Children's Literature Research Collections; Michelle Thibodeau; Dan Crow; Martha C. Craft, assistant vice president, public relations and corporate communications, Orkin, Inc.; George Shannon; Tony Ihrig, InfoPoint, University of Minnesota Libraries; Julie A. McComb, Make-A-Wish Foundation of America; Laura Mihalick, publicity assistant, Abrams Books for Young Readers/Amulet Books; Mo Smith, keeper's secretary, World Museum Liverpool; Patricia Garfield, PhD, author of *Creative Dreaming;* Agneta Wallin Levinovitz, executive editor of Nobelprize.org; Diane L. Saltzman, director of institutional stewardship, United States Holocaust Memorial Museum, for granting us permission to use photographs from their archives; and Laura Pelehach, who got the ball rolling.

Thanks are due to the following authors, musicians, publishers, publications, and agents for permission to use their materials in this book:

All chapter-opening illustrations are copyright © 2009 by Celia Yitzhak.

Lyrics from "Only in America," sung by Jay and the Americans/ Rock-Away Music Enterprises, used courtesy of Rock-Away Music Enterprises.

Quotations from *True Lies: 18 Tales for You to Judge,* by George Shannon (Beech Tree, 1998), copyright © 1982 by George W. B. Shannon. Used by permission of the author and HarperCollins Publishers.

"The Child Who Cried," from *I Hear You Smiling and Other Poems,* by Felice Holman (Charles Scribner's Sons, 1973). Used with permission of the author.

Untitled limerick on p. 71, author unknown, from *Bring Me All of Your Dreams,* edited by Nancy Larrick (M. Evans and Company, 1980).

Parody of McDonald's song from *Greasy Grimy Gopher Guts: The Subversive Folklore of Childhood,* by Josepha Sherman and T. K. F. Weisskopf (August House, 1995), used with permission of the publisher.

Lyrics from "Homonyms," from *The Word Factory,* by Dan Crow (Allshouse, 2000), used courtesy of the artist (http:// dancrow.com).

INTRODUCTION

THE GENESIS OF *BOOKTALKING BONANZA* CAN BE TRACED INNO-cently enough to a day Selma was driving down the highway, listening to National Public Radio (NPR) on her car radio. She had been pondering off and on how she could pep up her booktalks. It dawned on her that NPR was doing what she wanted to do, including clever and timely snippets of music that enhanced and even extended the news and entertainment pieces. In fact, she often found herself even more intrigued by the subject when she identified with the music. Why couldn't we do the same with our library audiences?

She took the idea back to the library and immediately began brainstorming with Betsy and Blane Halliday (the former supervisor of the Enoch Pratt Free Library's Sights and Sounds Department). We each came up with ideas that fit our own personalities and interests. Betsy had been the manager of a small library branch that had almost more computers per square inch than written materials for children, and her instant response was, "We have to do something using websites!" Blane knew his video collection inside and out and could identify segments from longer videos that would instantly transform a typical booktalk into a multimedia extravaganza.

Selma had done traditional juvenile booktalks for years; Betsy had two teenage children and was interested in keeping up with young adult (YA) literature. Blane added the very important adult component to counterbalance all our experience with children's literature. In addition, Betsy loved the topic of food, Blane kept up with social commentary, and Selma was fascinated by science experiments and magic tricks.

Because the Enoch Pratt Free Library both maintains the State Library Resource Center at its central branch and serves as the Baltimore city public library system, we were all highly aware that our collection was unusual in its depth. As a state repository for books, we had a large collection of oldies but goodies that we didn't want to neglect. We decided that we wanted to focus attention on these classics alongside the newer titles.

Selma decided to start with the first book she ever really used music with during a booktalk: Dick King-Smith's *The Fox Busters,* with a take-off on the *Ghostbusters* movie theme song. Our "Fowl Play" section developed from there. Betsy pointed out that the video of *Rosie's Walk,* though intended for young children, was ideal for breaking the ice with all ages due to its catchy music and universal humor. There seemed to be an unending supply of chicken stories, and when one of us attended a wedding where the "Chicken Dance" was played, we knew we had to incorporate that into our program too. This led to egg stories, which led to science experiments dealing with eggs, which culminated in viewing coops of live chickens over the Internet and looking at online science experiments involving floating eggs.

Our next topic was "Mad Scientists." The ultimate video-book combination came to be when Selma's insistence upon booktalking *Shoebag,* by Mary James, met with Blane's amazing ability to link that with a film, *When the Lights Go Out.* Our audiences stared in horrified fascination at the cockroaches crawling out of electrical outlets onto kitchen counters as Selma described the story of a young cockroach who woke up one morning transformed into a human boy. This was outdone only by a perfectly timed reading from Betsy Duffey's book *Coaster,* choreographed to go along with a clip of an actual roller-coaster ride. Audience members went up and down steep hills while hearing about the roller-coaster adventures of Hart and his father. Just as the booktalk ended, the video roller coaster pulled into the station, and viewers sank back into their seats with a mixture of relief and exhilaration.

A number of topics were chosen, and library materials and props were gathered together. Selma, Betsy, and Blane met for the first time to see if they could create a program to inspire others with these wild combinations of ideas. Together they worked on a script, and in 2002 they created the training workshop "Booktalking with Pizzazz." After presenting their workshop throughout Maryland, they presented it at the 2004 American Library Association Annual Conference in Orlando, Florida. When Blane took a new job at a library in Florida, we were pleased to welcome Michael Rios as our expert in the Sights and Sounds Department. Michael suggested we add foreign language films and graphic novels to the mix. We continued offering the workshop and gave our final presentation at the Maryland Library Association Annual Conference in 2005. Follow-up comments and evaluations for all of the presentations were overwhelmingly positive. Due to requests from other librarians for complete multimedia programs, even if they entailed more work than one person could accomplish alone, we felt there was a need for this type of book.

The first ten chapters provide actual, full-length booktalk presentations, with complete scripts from beginning to end. They are geared for children in the upper grades of elementary school. We make a few exceptions for material usually used with younger children that is funny or powerful enough to work for older audiences as well. And at the end of each chapter, we supply a list of additional theme-related materials that can be substituted for audiences of different ages. Our intention is that you will still use books from the body of the chapter, but you might also want to supplement or substitute with some of the additional books. "Additional Books for Younger Audiences" recommends material for children in grades 3 and below, whereas "Additional Material for Older Readers" is intended for students in grades 4 through 6. "Books for Use with Young Adult and Adult Audiences" refers to adults, of course, and to children who are twelve years of age and older.

You might wonder why we've added some adult titles to the mix. Apart from indulging our natural inclination to share our enthusiasm for a good book, we recognize that you may want to do a family program, so we have squeezed in a few good books for adults. Or, if you have sophisticated young adults in your audience, by mentioning material on a higher reading level, you will give them the opportunity to stretch themselves.

Chapter 11 includes a complete description of the "Booktalking with Pizzazz" workshop as presented at the ALA conference. This was not a typical booktalk because it was geared for an audience of adults and the how-to aspect was always present. Its purpose was to give ideas to librarians that they could then incorporate into their own library programs. It did not provide training in basic booktalking skills or a complete script for one booktalk. Rather it gave a sampling of a variety of interconnected ideas and showed how they could be integrated sparingly into the traditional booktalk. We say *sparingly* because the average librarian works alone and cannot be expected to present a booktalk and to run a video projector, a computer, a CD player, and an audio-cassette machine all at the same time. Rather than asking librarians to imitate our program, we emphasized our goal of providing them with examples of what was possible.

A large percentage of our booktalk scripts include a felicitous combination of the book author's own words interwoven with and enhanced by a judicious selection of comments by the presenter. In some cases, paragraphs and even pages are quoted directly from the books. We take this approach because we feel that an author's own words can be the truest gateway to her book, if chosen with care.

When possible, we offer links to established websites. We realize, however, that nothing on the Internet is guaranteed to be permanent. We understand that some sites might no longer be available at the time of this book's publication, but by including sample sites anyway, we are illustrating available options for adding pizzazz to your booktalk. Many of the songs can be found as video clips on YouTube (www .youtube.com) or on online digital music sites such as Rhapsody (www .rhapsody.com), where you can listen to twenty-five songs per month for free. (You may need to download software in order to hear them.) To find the material you need, just go to those or similar sites, type in your search term, and find a version of the song or video clip that will be acceptable for your audience. Make sure to check that your downloads work ahead of time in order to avoid potential dead spots in your program. Being flexible is essential when you incorporate technology into your programs.

Making connections between books, websites, video clips, music, food, creative dramatics, role-playing, puppetry, crafts, poetry, science experiments, and magic is invigorating. We hope this book will help you to jazz up your booktalks and inspire your public to use *all* the materials available at your library.

Lightning

A Bolt from the Blue

The National Weather Service website is a great resource for lightning information, pictures, and activities. Before beginning, download the maze from www.lightningsafety.noaa .gov/resources/Maze%20-%201.pdf. Make copies and distribute it to the children at the end of your program.

If the Harry Potter lightning-bolt temporary tattoos are available, hand them out at the beginning of the program and ask everyone to put them on.

Show the opening shot from *Sweet Home Alabama,* where two children are struck by lightning as they innocently kiss, and the boy says, "Don't worry, lightning doesn't strike twice."

Play the last five lines from the song "Lightnin' Strikes," by Lou Christie, in which "Lightning is striking again" is repeated over and over. Then turn the lights on.

If you were really struck by lightning you'd either be dead . . . or you'd have a life-changing experience like the characters in the following books:

Go to http://science.howstuffworks.com/vdg.htm. Project the picture of the father and child with their hair standing on end and continue talking . . .

In Donna Jo Napoli's *Soccer Shock,* after a particularly bad soccer practice, Adam had few hopes for his chances to make the team. On the way home "the lightning flash came down in front of him with blinding intensity. The thunder sounded at the same time. Adam was hurled to the ground . . . He could feel his arm hairs stand on end" (p. 10). No, he wasn't dead, but he heard a voice say, "He's quite fortunate, you know . . . Ten feet closer and the shock wave would have been strong enough to stop his heart" (p. 12). There were actually two voices, but when Adam struggled to sit up, there was no one there. No, he wasn't insane; after experimenting for a while he realizes that the lightning somehow gave him the ability to hear his freckles talk. Now this may help him play soccer better because the freckles could keep an eye out for the ball, but how can he live his life with freckles that have minds of their own?

> **Show this video clip with the lights down: http://stormhigh way.com/video-sears.shtml. Click on the preview clip of "Lightning Strikes the Sears Tower" and see a close-up of lightning striking the antenna at the top of the building.**

The most unlikely hero of Philip Pullman's *The Scarecrow and His Servant* feels "the lightning [strike] him . . . fizzing its way through his turnip (head) and down his broomstick and into the mud" (p. 3). With a brain the size of a pea—no, excuse me, it *is* a pea—and only the feeling that he needs to find his true place in the world, he sets off, with the help of an orphan named Jack. He survives a shipwreck and the dastardly Buffaloni clan's attempts to murder him with termites, among other hazards; his adventures are as hair-raising as the bolt from the blue that gave him life.

> **Show www.kidslightning.info/sabintro.htm.**

Here is a website written by a real kid who actually did get hit by lightning and survived. She starts out saying, "Hello. My name is Sabrina. I was struck by lightning." After explaining that she and her parents were struck when they were hiking in the Grand Canyon, she describes many aspects of lightning. Then, by following a link, you can get to her "Lightning Safety for Kids" page.

In addition, by following this link (**www.kidslightning.info/lsaftposi.htm**), you can get to Sabrina's lightning crouch page. This shows you how to position yourself to be as safe as possible if you are near lightning and there is no shelter nearby. The lightning crouch is not taught in school because it is safest for you to go inside a building or a car if there is lightning, and professionals don't want people to make the mistake of thinking that they'll be safe doing the lightning crouch rather than running to shelter. However, if there is *absolutely* no indoor place for you to go, the crouch could save your life. There can be no guarantees of 100 percent protection from lightning anywhere. It's good to know that the best thing to do is to seek shelter. In the meantime, let's all practice the lightning crouch!

> **If you are in a tight space, choose a volunteer to come up front to demonstrate the crouch. If space allows, ask every- one to stand up in place. (In a classroom setting, you may need to remind children to step away from their desks.) Pause long enough to give all the children time to see if they can get into the lightning crouch. After a short while, ask them to sit back down.**

We mustn't forget that Harry Potter has a lightning-shaped scar on his forehead or that lightning animated Mary Shelley's Frankenstein . . .

The Miami Science Museum brings alive "Frankenstein's Lightning Laboratory." On this site, you can find experiments or play a game about electrical safety.

> **From this site, www.miamisci.org/af/sln/frankenstein/, click on "Electrical Safety." This will take you to the next website, www.miamisci.org/af/sln/frankenstein/safety.html, where you can click on the characters to find out what they are doing wrong. The Bride of Frankenstein is sticking a fork into a toaster, the Wolf Man is placing something on top of a power cord, Dracula is using a hair dryer near water, the Mummy is putting his bandages near a hot lightbulb, the Phantom is sticking something into the electrical socket, the Hunch- back is flying a kite near power lines, and so forth.**

We have our own horror stories to keep up with Frankenstein . . .

It's too bad that Poppy has such a bad reputation as a liar. "She was halfway across the overgrown lawn when the forked tongue of lightning sprang down from the clouds and licked towards her . . . Cautiously she opened her eyes and raised her head. At the same moment the statue, fallen from its pedestal . . . , raised its head also, and they stared at one another, both so white and motionless that it was difficult to tell which girl was made of stone" (p. 6). The statue of Belladonna disappears and no one, of course, believes Poppy when she explains that the statue moved of its own accord. Meanwhile Belladonna and other renegade statues from graveyards and gardens across the countryside have their own agenda. Poppy and her friend Emma must find a way to undo what the lightning has set in motion. Read *The Stonewalkers*, by Vivien Alcock, and you'll never look at a statue in the same way again.

Who wouldn't be scared of a man with knives for fingers? He's chasing Maddy, a fifteen-year-old Narragansett Indian girl in Joseph Bruchac's *Whisper in the Dark*. Is he the creature from her grandmother's stories who attacks once his prey is paralyzed with fear? Just *before* lightning strikes Maddy sees a "section of the brick walkway [lift] up like there was a secret trapdoor . . . A red-eyed figure wrapped in darkness was rising out of the ground . . . I couldn't see the figure's face, but . . . there was something held in its raised, threatening hand that glistened like steel" (p. 74). When lightning does strike, it clears the air, but Maddy is still at the mercy of an urban/Native American legend come alive.

Maddy might know the answer to this riddle. The Comanches ask, "What is inside you like lightning?" (p. 39) The answer is *meanness*. How about this one: Who is "the old man . . . wrinkling his forehead?" (p. 19) The Chatino people of Oaxaca, Mexico, tell us that it is lightning. *Lightning Inside You, and Other Native American Riddles*, edited by John Bierhorst, is full of unexpected and mysterious brainteasers from over twenty Native American languages and gives suggestions for non-Indians on how to come up with the right answers. Try some of them. Maybe lightning will strike and you'll solve a tricky one!

Fiction is all well and good, but when dealing with the subject of lightning wouldn't you like more factual information? In *Eye of the* he vaporizes his pre-algebra teacher, he realizes that there is more than attention deficit/hyperactivity disorder (ADHD) and dyslexia for him to deal with. Percy discovers that although his mother was a human, his father was the god Poseidon, and consequently he has some incredible powers. Along with his newfound skills comes an introduction to the world of the mythical gods and beasts, where Percy finds himself in the middle of an angry search by Zeus for a missing lightning bolt. While trying to stay alive and solve the mystery, Percy discovers a lot about himself and the world of the gods. For a modern-day view of Hades and Olympus, read *The Lightning Thief,* by Rick Riordan.

Mark Helprin's sprawling, flamboyant, but decidedly decaffeinated novel *Memoir from Antproof Case* includes an intricately plotted bank robbery that commences "when I went into the bank, the electricity I felt crackling around in me was like a thunderstorm viewed from 40,000 feet, in which the lightning never ceases and its flashes dance like raindrops on a sun-saturated pond. I was afraid I would set off the alarm" (p. 377). See how an obsessive hatred of coffee powers this writing tour de force.

And don't forget any romance novels you could possibly think of!

Additional Films and Videos

Francis Ford Coppola's film *Youth without Youth* tells the story of a man in his seventies who is struck by lightning and reborn in his thirties. It may be worth using with an adult audience at the very least, and judicious cutting might make it work for younger audiences as well.

Additional Websites

From the Boston Museum of Science, www.mos.org/sln/toe/staticmenu .html gives some easy experiments to explore static electricity.

Photographs, video of a storm moving in, a quiz to see how much you know about lightning, experiments, a list of how often lightning strikes in your area, and stories by survivors who were struck by lightning can be found at www.nationalgeographic.com/lightning/.

Here's a website that answers the question, Can I get struck by lightning if I am indoors? http://science.howstuffworks.com/question 681.htm.

One website, www.lightningsafety.com, has many pages that would work well in a booktalk presentation. Did you ever wonder what causes memory deficit, sleep deficit, attention deficit, muscle spasms, or hearing loss? Being struck by lightning can cause these and many other changes in a person. Scroll down to see some documented effects of being struck by lightning: www.lightningsafety.com/nlsi_lls/sec.html.

The high number of lightning deaths shown by the statistics on this gruesome website prove that lightning is dangerous: www.lightning safety.com/nlsi_lls/35_years_injuries.html.

The National Weather Service website (mentioned earlier) has links to other useful pages. Here are a crossword puzzle, a hangman game, a coloring book, tips for safety, and survivor stories: www.lightning safety.noaa.gov/kids.htm. Lovely lightning photos can be viewed at www.lightningsafety.noaa.gov/photos.htm. In addition, vivid lightning posters are featured at www.lightningsafety.noaa.gov/multimedia.htm. You might want to order some to publicize your program or to raffle off as prizes at the end of your program.

Additional Activities

In *Exploratopia,* by Pat Murphy, Ellen Macaulay, and the staff of the Exploratorium, you can actually do an experiment to prove how fast it takes sound (i.e., thunder) to travel from place to place and how quickly you will have to get out of the lightning's way! Try "Speed of Sound," on page 351.

RESOURCES CITED

Books

Alcock, Vivien. *The Stonewalkers.* Delacorte, 1983.

Benz, Derek, and J. S. Lewis. *The Revenge of the Shadow King.* Orchard Books, 2006.

Berkeley, Jon. *The Palace of Laughter.* HarperCollins, 2006.

Bierhorst, John, ed. *Lightning Inside You, and Other Native American Riddles.* Morrow, 1992.

Bruchac, Joseph. *Whisper in the Dark.* HarperCollins, 2005.

Bryan, Ashley. *The Story of Lightning and Thunder.* Atheneum, 1993.

Graham, Joan Bransfield, and Nancy Davis. "Lightning Bolt." *Flicker Flash.* Houghton Mifflin, 1999.

Helprin, Mark. *Memoir from Antproof Case.* Perennial, 1996.

Kramer, Stephen. *Eye of the Storm: Chasing Storms with Warren Faidley.* G. P. Putnam's Sons, 1997.

McKay, Hilary. *Caddy Ever After.* Margaret K. McElderry, 2006.

Murphy, Pat, Ellen Macaulay, and the staff of the Exploratorium. *Exploratopia.* Little, Brown, 2006.

Napoli, Donna Jo. *Soccer Shock.* Dutton Children's Books, 1991.

Paulsen, Gary. *Harris and Me.* Harcourt Brace, 1993.

————. *How Angel Peterson Got His Name, and Other Outrageous Tales about Extreme Sports.* Wendy Lamb Books, 2003.

Pullman, Philip. *The Scarecrow and His Servant.* Alfred A. Knopf, 2005.

Riordan, Rick. *The Lightning Thief.* Miramax, 2006.

Rowling, J. K. Harry Potter series. Scholastic.

Shelley, Mary Wollstonecraft. *Frankenstein.* Signet Classic, 1978.

Shepard, Aaron. *The Legend of Lightning Larry.* Skyhook Press, 2005.

Shepard, Aaron, and David Wisniewski. *Master Man.* HarperCollins, 2000.

Skye, Obert. *Leven Thumps and the Gateway to Foo.* Shadow Mountain, 2005.

VanCleave, Janice. *Janice VanCleave's Electricity: Mind-Boggling Experiments You Can Turn into Science Fair Projects.* Wiley, 1994.

Yaccarino, Dan. *The Lima Bean Monster.* Walker, 2001.

Music

Christie, Lou. "Lightnin' Strikes." *20 Best of 60s Rock and Roll.* Madacy Records, 2004.

Floyd, Eddie, and Steve Croppe. "Knock on Wood." *Formidable Rhythm n Blues*. Vol. 9. Atlantic, 1972.

Films and Videos

Sweet Home Alabama. Directed by Andy Tennant. Touchstone, 2002.

Youth without Youth. Directed by Francis Ford Coppola. American Zoetrope, 2007.

Websites

Appalachian Skies Media. "Storm Highway: Video Clips: Lightning Strikes the Sears Tower." http://stormhighway.com/video-sears .shtml.

Green, Dorrit, et al. National Geographic Society. "Lightning: The Shocking Story—National Geographic Kids." www.national geographic.com/lightning/.

How Stuff Works. "Can I Get Struck by Lightning When I'm Indoors?" http://science.howstuffworks.com/question681.htm.

Miami Science Museum. "Frankenstein's Lightning Laboratory." www.miamisci.org/af/sln/frankenstein/.

Museum of Science, Boston. "Theater of Electricity." www.mos.org/ sln/toe/.

National Lightning Safety Institute. "National Lightning Safety Institute (NLSI) Home Page." www.lightningsafety.com.

NOAA, National Weather Service, Office of Climate, Water, and Weather Services. "Lightning Safety." www.lightningsafety .noaa.gov.

Sabrina and Anubis Productions International. "Kids' Lightning Information and Safety." www.kidslightning.info.

Zavisa, John M. How Stuff Works. "How Van de Graaff Generators Work." http://science.howstuffworks.com/vdg.htm.

Immigration

Hello, New Home!

Program begins with the strains of Dvořák's *New World Symphony* **(Symphony no. 9 in E Minor).**

Hello is our greeting here in America. In *Hello World! Greetings in 42 Languages around the World!* by Manya Stojic, you can learn how to greet newcomers in their own language. A welcoming, recognizable word can begin friendships with people from all over the globe . . . so *ciao* (Italian), *jambo* (Swahili), and *konnichiwa* (Japanese)!

Immigrants have come to America to seek a better life or to escape oppression, and then there are those who have been brought here against their will. Let's meet a variety of immigrants from all walks of life, from many parts of the world, and with their own unique stories . . .

"Ruby was quite proud that aliens ran in her family" (p. 57). When her cousin, Flying Duck, emigrated from China, she came to live with Ruby's family. Now Ruby has a new best friend "who [is] an entire foreign country unto herself . . . [one who] ate one-thousand-year-old eggs for breakfast" (p. 7), who used the toilet by standing on the rim and squatting **(act this out!)**, and who, because she is deaf, can teach Ruby Chinese sign language. And such excitement Flying Duck brings! Who else could save the life of Ruby's little brother Oscar when he puts tiny magnets up his nose? Who else could help Ruby get through summer school by trying to fry an egg on the playground slide? With

Flying Duck by her side, Ruby can face learning to swim, getting her first pair of glasses (decorated with rubies, of course), and learning to make up with her former best friend, Emma. And what's the sign for friend? **(Demonstrate: "Interlock pointer fingers, separate, then exchange their positions and come together again as before" [p. 164, from the illustrated sign language glossary].)** Become friends with Ruby Lu and Flying Duck in *Ruby Lu, Empress of Everything,* by Lenore Look. **(This is the sequel to *Ruby Lu, Brave and True,* but stands alone easily.)**

When kids call you doo-doo and you can't speak English well enough to defend yourself, *The Trouble Begins.* **(Hold up the book.)** Du Nguyen has never met his family. When he was a baby, they emigrated from Vietnam to California while he remained with his grandmother in a refugee camp. When Du finally arrives in the United States ten years later, his grandmother is sick, his older brother calls him bad luck, and everything just seems to go wrong. He starts a running feud with the elderly next-door neighbor, taking his lawn mower apart, picking his berries without asking permission, and putting up a sign saying "Free Oranges" so that all who pass take the man's fruit. He is accused of stealing a bicycle, tennis balls, and chickens; he orders more food than the family can afford at the movie theater and drinks and eats from every container; he even tangles with a skunk. At school he is in the "superdumb reading group" (p. 21). Some of his problems come from not understanding how people live in the United States; others result from false accusations made because he seems the easiest person to blame; still others are caused by his ways of venting his frustration with this new and complicated society in which he finds himself. On the other hand Du shows initiative and creativity. He saves his sister's science project from the trash, helps translate for another Vietnamese family in a crisis, helps save his father's business by delivering newspapers at the last minute, and saves a cat and her kittens from a fire. So is Du trouble or is he just growing into a boy who can be proud of himself? Read Linda Himelblau's book and find out.

In this video, an Asian boy moves to a new school and refuses to participate in class. He is picked on by other kids. One child befriends him, and in return he shows him how to do origami, in particular how to make a paper camera. When the Asian boy and his family move away, he leaves the paper camera with his friend.

> Show the clip from *Paper Camera* just after the new boy has been beaten up by the bully, when the other boy helps him and the new boy shows him his paper camera.
>
> Instructions for making an origami camera from www .perfectnow.net/origami/pages/camera.html can be screened with an LCD projector. If you have the time and inclination, give paper to each child and make cameras! A website that has a video showing the actual step-by-step creation of

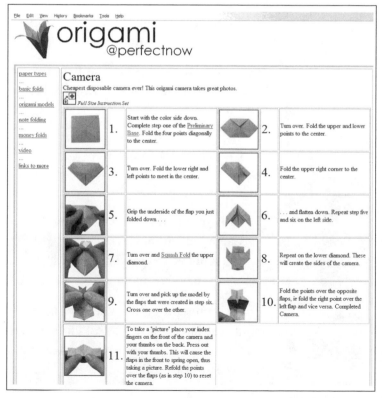

Instructions for making an origami camera from Origami@perfectnow.
Courtesy of Michael Paul Moore.

an origami camera is listed in "Additional Websites" at the end of this chapter.

Would a paper camera be able to capture Drita on film? (**Hold the thumbs and forefingers of each hand up to form brackets around your face as if you are holding an imaginary camera. Bend your right finger and make a clicking noise, as if you are taking a photograph of your audience.**) Maxie's first impression of Drita was that "the new girl is the kind of white person who's so pale, she's like a ghost—you think you can see right through her" (p. 19). When Maxie is rude to Drita, the teacher assigns her to write her social studies research paper on Drita's native Kosovo. Drita speaks little English, so Maxie must spend quality time with her and her family. (**Read excerpts from Maxie's social studies report here [pp. 133–135].**) In alternating chapters you will hear from both girls about their long road to friendship in *Drita, My Homegirl,* by Jenny Lombard.

Photograph © 2009 by Bryan-David Kee. Used with permission.

Background music: Play the first two stanzas from "Only in America," sung by Jay and the Americans:

Only in America
Can a guy from anywhere
Go to sleep a pauper and wake
    up a millionaire

Only in America
Can a kid without a cent
Get a break and maybe grow
    up to be President

Becoming president would be nice, but how about just having a full set of clothes? The year is 1892. The day after thieves steal his pants, nine-year-old Dom's mother gives him his first ever pair of new shoes. Then she walks him to the harbor in their native Italy and tells him,

"Your job is to survive" (p. 23). Dom thinks they are off to find their fortune in the United States, but his mother has paid for his passage alone. He spends his first night in the United States in a barrel. The next few days are taken up with finding food and keeping away from the padroni who "protect" homeless boys in return for the money they make begging. Dom's goal is to make enough money to go back to his mother in Napoli. He starts small by buying a long sandwich for twenty-five cents, cutting it into fourths, and selling them for twenty-five cents each. As his business grows, he makes friends who help him and finds a place to live. But he is still hounded by a particularly vicious padrone who has killed and will kill to keep control of his boys. Will Dom find a way to return to his mother, or will he stay in this new world with its dangers and opportunities? Read *The King of Mulberry Street,* by Donna Jo Napoli, a story partially based on her grandfather.

Some immigrants have no choice in the matter . . .

You are Kofi, the twelve-year-old son of a great chief. It is March 1788, and your whole family is traveling to take part in the yearly ceremony honoring the great Ashanti kings of the past. Betrayed by the family slave, Oppong, you see your father killed and find yourself a captive. In the United States you taste the bitterness of bondage, suffer the feel of the whip against your skin. There are, however, moments of hope. Despite the fact that her husband believes that "God has a plan . . . The African is supposed to be a servant and is too dull to learn much" (p. 131), your mistress secretly teaches you to read and write, skills you use to escape. Your goal is to return to Africa. Fast-forward to 1811 and your name is now Kofi Kwame Paul. You have taken your father's name, Kwame, in remembrance, and the name of the man who you hope will deliver you to your native land, Captain Paul Cuffe. This is a side of slavery rarely seen; you are there in *The Captive,* by Joyce Hansen.

With his whole being, Kofi did not want to be in the United States. But there are many others whose lives depend on coming here. In a popular musical *West Side Story,* characters sing about their desire to be in America . . .

Play "America," from *West Side Story,* as background music, or show a film clip.

Since we are being musical, here are some instruments that music-loving people from Puerto Rico and Cuba have brought to the United States. Let's take this fun quiz and see how many answers you can supply.

Using an LCD projector, screen the website http://memory .loc.gov/learn/features/immig/cuban_voc.html.

Moving from one island in the Caribbean to another . . .

"Some questions steal a person's courage" (p. 25). Paulie lives with her uncle and grandmother. Her uncle builds coffins for a living, but in his spare time he is secretly building a boat to take them to Miami and

Vocabulary activity from the Immigration feature presentation
on the Learning Page, a resource for teachers on the
Library of Congress American Memory website.

freedom. When an American journalist confronts her family and asks if they would like to leave the Haiti of 1993, which has no food, no work, and barely enough wood for her uncle to follow his trade, only Paulie's friend's brother, Jean Desir, speaks the truth. When he faces the ultimate punishment for his answer, "every part of Paulie's own body hurt for [the battered, lifeless husk that was] Jean Desir" (p. 68). Paulie must seek out the journalist and let honesty overpower her fear so that the world may know what the government has done. But Paulie's courage must remain firm; she faces a different kind of fear when she and her family and friends face the open sea in the boat they have named *Seek Life. Tonight, by Sea,* by Frances Temple, brings recent history alive.

Immigrants don't always want to come to the United States. Sometimes, it's just a rest stop on a journey to somewhere else . . .

First, twelve-year-old Felipe is lucky enough to escape being forced to become a Salvadoran soldier. Next, when his dog finds part of a man's arm and hand in the dump, his father explains that it is probably from someone who dared to criticize the government. Then in quick succession Felipe finds a note in their door that reads "Leave and don't come back. If not, you die" (p. 32), and his father's motorcycle is found abandoned outside the city. Felipe and his mother and younger sister immediately *Grab Hands and Run* for Canada. Their escape leads them through Guatemala and Mexico and then through the United States. All the while "the possibility [that their father/husband] is dead [or] the possibility that he is alive and needs [them makes] a crater in the middle of [their] souls" (p. 136). Will they get into Canada, and is their father/husband alive? Frances Temple's story is based on a real Salvadoran family who stayed with her family while they tried to become Canadian citizens.

> Give each child a piece of paper and a pencil. Tell the group that they are going to be immigrating to a new country and only have enough room to fit three personal things inside their suitcase, aside from underwear and other basic stuff. Because they don't have time to think deeply before leaving, give them one minute to write down their choices. Depending on the group, either collect the papers and read a few

of the choices aloud, or call on individual children and ask them to tell the group what they have chosen to take.

And since you've now made this difficult decision, here is a similar problem that's out of this world . . .

What book would you pack to take with you if you could have only one book to read on a trip to a new home? (**Another audience-participation opportunity!**) Here's a story about people leaving a dying Earth, immigrants to a distant planet. They are limited to only one or two personal items and only "one book per voyager" (p. 3). When they arrive they find that there are multiple copies of *Robinson Crusoe* and a variety of technical manuals but nothing to really inspire them and give them hope in this new place that the youngest child names Shine. Quite the opposite, this new world is a dreary place overrun with poisonous gray grass and inhabited by giant moths. It is only through the courage of middle-child Sarah that the people find a chance of survival and a use for the very different kind of book she has chosen to bring with her. Read *The Green Book,* by Jill Paton Walsh, and think again about which one book you would choose to take with you on a voyage of no return.

No matter where you end up, on another planet or closer to home, that land is your land . . .

> **Pass out lyrics to Woody Guthrie's song "This Land Is Your Land" and play a CD or sing together a cappella. Or use an LCD projector to screen the lyrics from the NIEHS website that has musical accompaniment: http://kids.niehs.nih.gov/lyrics/thisland.htm. Sing the first verse together.**

EXPANDING YOUR OPTIONS

Books for Use with Younger Audiences

Why do 219 people from all over the world make their way to downtown New York City on a very snowy day? It's *A Very Important Day,* and Maggie Rugg Herold explains it all to you. (**Suggested activity:**

The oath of citizenship at the back of the book may be too long to read aloud, but the privileges of citizenship that follow are worth sharing.)

A grandmother tells her grandchild how her mother journeyed with her brother alone across the sea to join their parents in the United States. In Riki Levinson's book they *Watch the Stars Come Out* as their lives change forever. (**Suggested activity: Have a star map available, and point out constellations that are recognizable anywhere in the Northern Hemisphere.**)

Hector, the new kid, is from Puerto Rico. He looks like Charles but speaks Spanish. Charles wants to help Hector adjust to the United States in general and school in particular, so he comes up with a very creative way of showing him how to fit in. Open John Steptoe's *Creativity* to find out how.

The tender and evocative drawings by Tom Feelings and the equally expressive poems by Kwame Dawes express their feelings about the African diaspora in *I Saw Your Face*. (**Suggested activity: Show the drawings and read some of the poems aloud.**)

Newly arrived from Russia, Molly is assigned is to create a pilgrim doll from a clothespin. What happens when her mother offers to help? Read *Molly's Pilgrim,* by Barbara Cohen, and the word *immigrant* will take on a whole new meaning. (**Suggested activity: Make pilgrim dolls out of clothes pins or have some already prepared.**)

Mei Mei doesn't want to lose the part of herself that is Chinese. Speaking English makes her feel that she is turning her back on her heritage. No wonder *I Hate English!* is her motto. But all it takes is a teacher who really understands. Ellen Levine will help you understand Mei Mei even if you don't speak Chinese. (**Suggested activity: Have children pick their favorite English words that Mei Mei might enjoy learning.**)

Maylin is the creative genius behind her father's successful restaurant. Her food even sounds tasty. Roses Sing on New Snow—yum—is the name of one of her dishes. When her brothers get all the credit for her cooking, she turns the tables on them in a most deliciously embarrassing scene. Author Paul Yee's *Roses Sing on New Snow: A*

Delicious Tale will make you hungry for Chinese food! (**Suggested activities: Share other unusual Chinese names for food, or have your audience think of creative, tasty descriptions of American food. For example, waffles could be called Small Windows Hold Sweetness.**)

Having recently arrived in the United States, Hassan can't tell his classmates about his feelings for his homeland because he can't speak English well enough, but his pictures of Somalia explain the terrible reason why his family had to leave. Mary Hoffman's *The Color of Home* shows us art as a welcoming and comforting universal language. (**Suggested activity: Ask children to imagine that they can only communicate through their art and to draw a picture of their family, home, etc., from that perspective.**)

A Swedish father, separated from his family, finds his wife and son when he sees them in a silent movie. How can he reconnect with them? Chew your popcorn quietly while you read Avi's *Silent Movie*. (**Suggested activity: Show a real silent movie and narrate that black-and-white gem frame by frame.**)

Where do you keep your memories? Anna's mother helps her remember life in Russia by creating a quilt of memories. Patricia Polacco's homemade *Keeping Quilt* will make you want to have a quilt to keep your own remembrances alive. (**Suggested activity: Have the children draw a memory; fit their pictures together as a paper quilt.**)

Additional Books for Older Readers

When Linda's school history project requires her to question her mother about her heritage and her arrival in the United States from Albania, her mother proves reluctant to tell all. Illegal immigrants need both the courage to leave their home country in the first place and the nerve to risk exposure on a regular basis in their adopted country. *Swimming to America,* by Alice Mead, takes us into the insecure world of the undocumented.

"Oy felt as though she would trade all the rubies in [her beloved] Thailand for the chance to" (p. 41) be part of Liliandra's club. Ever since Oy had moved across town and started at the new school she had yearned for a friend, but the price of admission puts her family's customs and her own precious, delicate, silk Thai dancing dress at risk. At what cost friendship? Read *The Gold Threaded Dress*, by Carolyn Marsden, and find out.

Celiane's diary describes her journey from the mountains of Haiti, where she and her mother are almost killed, to the skyscrapers—the "mountains"—of New York City, where she is reunited with her father. But her new life has its own share of violence, and Celiane struggles with learning difficulties. Read Edwidge Danticat's *Behind the Mountains* and see how even "mountains of obstacles" (p. 159) in any country can be conquered.

We Are Americans, by Dorothy and Thomas Hoobler, is a history of U.S. immigration that includes dramatic first-person reminiscences, including everything from a Japanese bride's arrival in the United States to how Native Americans were "[taught] how to be white" (p. 19). **(Read selections from the book.)**

If there is *Nothing Here but Stones,* why would anyone want to come? In 1882 a group of Russian Jewish immigrants try to start a new life in a bleak and unforgiving landscape. Emma's only comfort is the wonderful horse, Mazel, whose life she has saved. Read Nancy Oswald's book for an immigrant story that defies all the odds.

Books for Use with Young Adult and Adult Audiences

Have you ever wondered what it's like to move to a new place where you don't speak or read the language? What would you do if the customs, the food, and even the animals were totally different from the ones you were familiar with? In the graphic novel *The Arrival*, Shaun Tan puts us in the shoes of a man who leaves his family to come to a new world. As flying ships and strange inventions surround him, we experience an immigrant's bewilderment and discomfort. Working without words, Tan uses only his art to capture the man's initial alienation and slow acclimation process. Will he be ready when his family comes to join him?

Picture Books to Be Used with Adults

Alan Say's autobiographical books *Grandfather's Journey* and *Tea with Milk* have beautiful watercolor illustrations. They document his family's passage from one county to another. It is rituals that bind a people to their past, regardless of where they end up. *Grandfather's Journey* won the Caldecott Award for illustration in 1994. **(Suggested activity: Offer children tea with milk to create an authentic experience that will spark lively discussion. Use *Tea with Milk* with new immigrants to introduce conversation regarding their difficulties in acclimating to their new country and the things they value from their former homes. The book can also be used with a general adult group to encourage sharing of memories.)**

Additional Music

"They've all come to look for America" is a well-known line in Simon and Garfunkel's "America."

"When I First Came to This Land," by Pete Seeger, is another song about the immigrant experience.

Additional Films and Videos

Nightmare: The Immigration of Joachim and Rachel stars a very young Sarah Jessica Parker as one of two sibling who escape from the Warsaw ghetto (filmed in black and white) and end up in the United States (filmed in color). This Holocaust film is to be commended for the sweep of its coverage without showing specific horrors, making it perfect for elementary school children.

Books mentioned in the booktalk that have been made into videos include *Watch the Stars Come Out, The Keeping Quilt,* and *Molly's Pilgrim.*

Additional Websites

You can see someone actually folding a paper camera in less than three minutes at www.metacafe.com/watch/519144/the_camera_origami _tutorial/.

For downloadable patterns and instructions for a complicated Dirkon paper camera created by Martin Pilný, Mirek Kolář, and Richard Vyškovský, go to www.pinhole.cz/en/pinholecam eras/dirkon_01.html.

**Dirkon paper camera.
Courtesy of David Balihar.**

Go to http://memory.loc.gov/learn/ features/immig/irishvoc.html to play a game that involves trying to guess the meanings of Irish words.

Take a virtual tour of a tenement apartment similar to those in which new American immigrants lived at www.thirteen.org/tenement/virtual.html.

The Small Object Big Story project hails from Australia. Find guidelines at www.museum.vic.gov.au/sobs/ for helping people choose an object and find the story surrounding it, especially in relation to their family's immigration.

To look at pictures from Ellis Island, where many families arrived when they first came to the United States, go to www.ellisisland.com.

Take a virtual tour of the buildings on Ellis Island at www.save ellisisland.org/site/PageServer?pagename=SouthSideTour.

Additional Activities

The Vegetable Salad Game

The United States is not a melting pot in which everyone just blends together. Instead, it could be looked at as a salad bowl in which each person retains her identity and contributes her own special flavors. When vegetables in a salad are mixed together, they form a colorful, tasty, fascinating concoction. A salad with red peppers, cucumbers, carrots, lettuce, and sunflower seeds is much more interesting than one made with only lettuce. This game, based on the game musical chairs, illustrates the point that a salad is tastier with a variety of ingredients. Randomly assign players to be immigrants from countries such as those mentioned in the booktalks above. Make sure that at least three children are given the same country. Explain that when you call out a nation-ality, all of the children assigned that nationality must switch places. For example, when you call out "Chinese," all the children who have become Chinese immigrants must get up and change chairs. When you call "USA," everyone must get up and switch places.

Creating an Atmosphere

When the children enter the room, give them the name of the country from which they came, how much money they have in their pockets, whether or not they speak English, whether or not they have any con-tacts at all, or what skills they have.

Or give them simulated passports and take pictures of them with an instant camera to attach to their U.S. passports. Then at the end or your program, when they become full-fledged citizens, have everyone recite the Pledge of Allegiance.

Statue of Liberty Exercise

Ask the children to go online and see how many different images they can find of the Statue of Liberty. Are there cartoon images? Images of the statue when it first arrived in the United States? Images of the statue being put together? Images of the inside of the Statue of Liberty? Images from inside the statue looking down?

RESOURCES CITED

Books

Avi. *Silent Movie*. Atheneum, 2003.

Cohen, Barbara, and Daniel Duffy. *Molly's Pilgrim*. Lothrop, Lee and Shepard, 1998.

Danticat, Edwidge. *Behind the Mountains*. Orchard Books, 2002.

Dawes, Kwame. *I Saw Your Face*. Dial Books, 2004.

Defoe, Daniel. *Robinson Crusoe*. Barnes and Noble, 2003.

Hansen, Joyce. *The Captive*. Scholastic, 1995.

Herold, Maggie Rugg, and Catherine Stock. *A Very Important Day*. Morrow Junior Books, 1995.

Himelblau, Linda. *The Trouble Begins.* Delacorte, 2005.

Hoffman, Mary, and Karin Littlewood. *The Color of Home*. Phyllis Fogelman Books, 2002.

Hoobler, Dorothy, and Thomas Hoobler. *We Are Americans*. Scholastic Nonfiction, 2003.

Levine, Ellen, and Steve Björkman. *I Hate English!* Scholastic, 1989.

Levinson, Riki, and Diane Goode. *Watch the Stars Come Out*. Puffin Books, 1995.

Lombard, Jenny. *Drita, My Homegirl*. G. P. Putnam's Sons, 2006.

Look, Lenore, and Anne Wilsdorf. *Ruby Lu, Brave and True*. Aladdin, 2006.

———. *Ruby Lu, Empress of Everything*. Atheneum, 2006.

Marsden, Carolyn. *The Gold-Threaded Dress*. Candlewick, 2002.

Mead, Alice. *Swimming to America*. Farrar, Straus and Giroux, 2005.

Napoli, Donna Jo. *The King of Mulberry Street*. Wendy Lamb Books, 2005.

Oswald, Nancy. *Nothing Here but Stones*. Henry Holt, 2004.

Polacco, Patricia. *The Keeping Quilt*. Simon and Schuster, 1988.

Say, Allen. *Grandfather's Journey*. Houghton Mifflin, 1993.

———. *Tea with Milk*. Houghton Mifflin, 1999.

Steptoe, John, and Earl Lewis. *Creativity*. Clarion, 1997.

Stojic, Manya. *Hello World! Greetings in 42 Languages around the World!* Scholastic, 2002.

Tan, Shaun. *The Arrival*. Arthur A. Levine Books, 2006.

Temple, Frances. *Grab Hands and Run*. Orchard Books, 1993.

———. *Tonight, by Sea*. Orchard Books, 1995.

Walsh, Jill Paton. *The Green Book*. Farrar, Straus and Giroux, 1982.

Yee, Paul, and Harvey Chan. *Roses Sing on New Snow*. Macmillan, 1991.

Music

Dvořák, Antonín. Symphony no. 9 in E Minor (*From the New World*). EMI Classics. Deutsche Grammophon, 1977.

Guthrie, Woody. "This Land Is Your Land." *This Land Is Your Land: American Favorite Ballads*. Vol. 1. Smithsonian Folkways Recordings, 2002.

Jay and the Americans. "Only in America." *Come a Little Bit Closer: The Best of Jay and the Americans*. Capitol Records, 2005.

Seeger, Pete. "When I First Came to This Land." *American Favorite Ballads*. Vol. 3. Smithsonian Folkways Recordings, 2004.

Simon and Garfunkel. "America." *Bookends*. Sony, 1990.

Sondheim, Stephen, and Leonard Bernstein. "America," from *West Side Story*. Original Broadway cast recording. Sony, 1998.

Films and Videos

The Keeping Quilt. Narrated by Patricia Polacco. Spoken Arts, 1993.

Molly's Pilgrim. Directed by Jeffrey D. Brown. Phoenix Films, 1985.

Nightmare: The Immigration of Joachim and Rachel. Directed by Tom Robertson. Films for the Humanities, 1988.

Paper Camera. Directed by Gregory J. Sinclair. New Dimension Media, 1992.

Watch the Stars Come Out. Directed by Hugh Martin. Great Plains National Television Library, 1986.

Websites

Aramark. "Ellis Island Immigration Museum." www.ellisisland.com.

Balihar, David. "Dirkon—the Paper Camera." www.pinhole.cz/en/pinholecameras/dirkon_01.html.

Jun and Xue. "Metacafe—The Camera Origami Tutorial." www.meta cafe.com/watch/519144/the_camera_origami_tutorial/.

Library of Congress. "Immigration . . . Can You Speak Irish?" http://memory.loc.gov/learn/features/immig/irishvoc.html.

Library of Congress. "Immigration . . . Puerto Rican/Cuban: Transforming a City." http://memory.loc.gov/learn/features/immig/cuban_voc.html.

Museum Victoria: Australia. "Small Object Big Story." www.museum.vic.gov.au/sobs/.

National Institute of Environmental Health Sciences (NIEHS). "Lyrics and Music—This Land Is Your Land." http://kids.niehs.nih.gov/lyrics/thisland.htm.

Perfect Now. "Camera—Origami@perfectnow." www.perfectnow.net/origami/pages/camera.html.

Save Ellis Island. "Save Ellis Island: About Ellis Island—South Side Toursland." www.saveellisisland.org/site/PageServer?pagename=SouthSideTour.

Wolff, David, Ruth Ann Burns, and Barry Levine. "Tenement Museum: Tenement VR Thirteen/WNET New York." www.thirteen.org/tenement/virtual.html.

Wishes

Wishing Well

To prepare ahead of time, bring something made of wood—such as a wooden ruler—and something blue with you. Also, have an index card with the following phrase printed on it: "Be careful what you wish for, you just might get it!"

Show the scene from *The Wizard of Oz* in which Dorothy clicks her heels together three times and says, "There's no place like home," and her wish to return home comes true.

Raise your hand if you know what movie this clip is from. Who can tell me what is happening here? (**Pause and give children a chance to answer.**) Yes, it is Dorothy from *The Wizard of Oz,* clicking her heels and wishing to go home.

Instead of going home, Mags would like to live in a home that's not a trailer so that she could be more like other children and be popular. But you only get three wishes on a unicorn—even, and probably especially, if it's a mangy old stuffed one. Mag's little sister Hannie finds it in a field. And it seems that the first two wishes, Mag's wish for new clothes and her brother Mooch's wish for something to eat, come true with remarkable speed, but what will Hannie wish for? Hannie is different, slower than other children. Other kids make fun of her, especially Brody Lawson. When Mooch is accused by Brody of stealing a whole box of Twinkies, can Hannie understand what to wish for to set things right? Read *Wish on a Unicorn,* by Karen Hesse, and think about which three wishes you'd like to make.

Three wishes from a unicorn! Even better, here's a movie about a girl who gets seven wishes from a very unusual fairy godmother.

> **Show a clip from *The Seven Wishes of Joanna Peabody* video where the fairy godmother comes to the girl on the television screen to fulfill her wishes.**

Wishes can be fulfilled through both magic and realistic effort. Here's a bit of the former . . .

All it costs is fifty cents. When Thaddeus Blinn comes to Coven Tree, he promises he can give anyone anything they want. One wish per customer; but take great care in the wording of your wish, as it "will be granted exactly as you ask for it" (p. 14). For example, fifteen-year-old Rowena wishes that the traveling salesman, Henry, whom she likes, would "put down roots . . . and never leave again" (p. 98), and indeed Henry turns into a tree. Be careful what you wish for, you just might get what Bill Brittain's *The Wish Giver* gives you . . . and you will be stuck with it!

Now, I need a volunteer. Please raise your hands and I will choose one person.

> **Pick a volunteer, have her come up to the front of the room, and hand her the printed index card. Tell your volunteer to recite the phrase, "Be careful what you wish for, you just might get it!" at the same time that you are reciting it, then to touch first the wooden object and second the blue object (both of which you've prepared in advance).**

When two people have said the same thing, "Be careful what you wish for, you just might get it!" each can make a wish, then touch wood, and then touch something blue. According to *The Book of Wishes and Wishmaking,* by Duncan Emrich, if you follow this sequence, your wish will certainly come true.

**Play the first few lines of "When You Wish upon a Star."
If you don't have a recording of it, you can find the music
online at http://solosong.net/wish.html.**

Also in *The Book of Wishes and Wishmaking* the author says that when
you see the first star in the evening and say this traditional rhyme, your
wish will come true.

> Star light, star bright
>
> First star I see tonight,
>
> I wish I may, I wish I might
>
> Have the wish I wish tonight.

When King Midas got his wish that everything he touched would
turn to gold, "he felt a charge like a bolt of electricity shoot through his
fingers and through his hands, stopping short at his wrists. It shocked
him so that he cried out, and everything went black" (p. 15). When
he comes to, everything from the food on his plate to his favorite dog
turns to gold at his touch. But it is his daughter, Delia, whose golden
stillness pushes him to try to reverse the consequences of his greed.
How to remove a permanent spell? The king must wash his hands in
the River Cijam (that's *magic* pronounced backward). But the river has
been blocked by the witch, Wuzzleflump, and Midas must trick her
or live with his condition forever. Read *The Adventures of King Midas,*
by Lynne Reid Banks, for a story that will take you beyond Greek
mythology.

When Melisande is born she is cursed with baldness. In her one
chance to reverse the curse she wishes that she "had golden hair a yard
long and that it would grow an inch every day and grow twice as fast
every time it was cut." If you are good at arithmetic you know that this
will be a big problem. Read *Melisande,* by E. Nesbit, and discover how
to reverse this hairy problem.

Speaking of hair . . . did you know that if you "find an eyelash . . .
that has fallen out, place it on your thumb, make a wish, . . . blow the
eyelash away and the wish will come true" (from *The Book of Wishes and
Wishmaking,* by Duncan Emrich).

Put this image of Ganesh on the screen behind you as you are doing the next booktalk: http://hinduism.about.com/library/weekly/extra/bl-ganeshart3.htm.

Ganesh painting by Pieter Weltevrede.
Courtesy of the Sanatan Society, Afsnee, Belgium.

Maya may have been born in India, but she longs to be fully Canadian. When her beautiful cousin Pinky comes for a visit, she brings with her a statue of the Hindu Elephant God, Ganesh, "who grants wishes and removes obstacles" (p. 63). Pinky lets Maya borrow him. Maya plies him with candy, especially Jelly Bellies, and lays all her problems at his feet, wishing that he will remove her pimples; prevent her family's move to California, where she will be separated from Jamie, whom she dreams will be her boyfriend; and send Pinky back home so that Jamie won't be so fascinated with her. Ganesh agrees to grant her wishes in order for her to "find [her] truth" (p. 106). Immediately Maya's life falls into place: Pinky's uncle happens to fall ill and she returns to India; Jamie follows Maya around like a lovesick puppy; and Maya's parents decide to pass up job opportunities in California. Maya has everything she wished for, but, with everyone around her "trapped inside her wishes" (p. 163), she feels so alone. It takes a trip back to India and another heart-to-heart talk with Ganesh for Maya to find herself. Read *Maya Running,* by Anjali Banerjee, and then learn more about Ganesh.

"Most people say if you tell a wish it won't come true. But . . . I don't believe there's some bad-tempered wish-fairy with a clipboard, checking off whether or not you've told. *Oops! You've told your wish. No new bike for you!* But it's a long shot I'll get my wish, so even if there is a fairy in charge of telling, it won't matter" (p. 190). Twelve-year-old Catherine's brother, David, is autistic. It seems she spends all her time keeping him from embarrassing her and teaching him how to get along in the world. Her list of rules for David and herself keeps getting longer. The rules include

> Say "excuse me" after you burp. (p. 9)
>
> Don't stand in front of the TV when other people are watching it.
> (p. 9)
>
> Flush! (p. 9)
>
> A boy can take off his shirt to swim, but not his shorts. (p. 10)
>
> Looking closer can make something beautiful. (p. 19)
>
> Sometimes people laugh when they like you. But sometimes they
> laugh to hurt you. (p. 30)

Some people think they know who you are, when really they don't.
(p. 178)
A real conversation takes two people. (p. 191)

But even with the rules, David's differences keep getting in the way. With her best friend in California for the summer, Catherine pins her hopes of a normal friendship on the new neighbors, who have a daughter her age; but a different relationship also appears unexpectedly when she meets Jason, a paraplegic. He helps her understand that although her wish that "everyone [have] the same chances" (p. 190) may be impossible to fulfill, breaking the rules for the right reasons will make all the difference. Read *Rules,* by Cynthia Lord, and think about what you would wish for and what rules you would have to make or break to make your wish come true.

Sometimes you don't need magic to make wishes come true, you just need enough money and people who are willing to help. "Wags for Wishes" is a dog show that raises money for the Make-A-Wish Foundation, a foundation that grants the wishes of children with severe and terminal illnesses.

> **Project this website where everyone can see it: www.wags forwishes.com. Put your cursor on "Events" on the left menu, and click once on each event to see pictures of dogs in a variety of poses.**

These dogs help raise money; Wilma's dog accidentally ruins her life. When Wilma's paper, written from the point of view of her dog, is read aloud by her English teacher, Wilma knows all is lost; life as she knew it is over.

"I hear the elevator door open. It is my beloved Wilma coming home from school . . . My beloved Wilma is asleep. From the foot of the bed, I watch her. She is so beautiful . . . I see Celeste, the Dalmatian who is my best friend after my beloved Wilma. She is peeing. I rush to smell her pee. Celeste had chicken for dinner. I lift my leg over her pee" (p. 5). Suddenly, except for a few barks and the occasional comment about finding "any good fire hydrants near school" (p. 7), Wilma is ignored. She becomes a loner, if only out of self-protection. Until, that is, the day on the subway when the old lady to whom she gives up her seat offers to grant her a wish in return for her good deed. The wish, to be the most popular kid in school, finds her with friends fighting over her and forty boys who want to take her to the graduation-night dance. Too bad eighth grade ends three weeks after the wish is granted, at which point Wilma, no longer "in school," will go back to being invisible. Gail Carson Levine's *The Wish* will make you think twice about what *you* wish for too.

And now, I wish you better luck than Wilma with this virtual greeting card:

> **View www.comics.com/webmail/SendAStrip?AppName=E CardsFlash&ComicName=pearls&Attachments=/ecards/ cards/ecard_pearls_slug.swf. This e-card has a funny cartoon that ends with the greeting "Wishing you better luck."**

EXPANDING YOUR OPTIONS

Books for Use with Younger Audiences

Her older brother (four years older!) can run, climb, throw, burp and spit better than Patricia can. When she wishes on a falling star (after spitting on two fingers and slapping her chest, of course—**do so!**) that she can do something better than her older brother, Patricia finds out that older brothers aren't always rotten. (Yes, this is really the author's story, and you can see pictures of her and her brother too!) Her name is Patricia Polacco, and her book is *My Rotten Redheaded Older Brother*. **(Suggested activity: Ask your audience what they would wish they could do better than their older brother or sister.)**

Seppy is the seventh son of a seventh son, and his heart's desire is to be the best fiddler in the country. A mysterious voice tells him to "throw [his] shoe at the moon . . . each night for seven nights" to get his wish. He follows the instructions, but because he has dirtied the moon's face with his shoes, he must go barefoot for seven years, and until he can find the seven shoes again, his little sister must remain mute and the rest of his family remains in the gravest of dangers. Try Joan Aiken's *The Moon's Revenge* and see why it's not a good idea to make the moon mad. (**Suggested activity: Show photos of the moon. You'll find a wide variety on the NASA Goddard Space Flight Center at http:// nssdc.gsfc.nasa.gov/photo_gallery/photogallery-moon.html. Click on a photo to enlarge it and ask, "Do the markings look like dirty shoe prints or something else?"**)

"To make certain that a wish comes true, make it while kissing a dime three times, and then wear the dime in your shoe." In *The Book of Wishes and Wishmaking*, by Duncan Emrich, find that and other funny wish-making formulas, such as

> The first time you wear a new pair of shoes, you may make a wish.
>
> Make a wish before breaking a . . . wishbone . . . The one who holds the longer piece will get his . . . wish. Place your piece of the wishbone . . . over an outside door, and your wish will come true when the bone has decayed.
>
> When you stub your toe, kiss your thumb and make a wish.
>
> If, while it is thundering and lightning during the first storm of Spring, you can catch a glass half-full of rain water and drink it, you may make a wish.
>
> You may make a wish while rubbing a penny over a cat's back seven times.
>
> If you think you are going to sneeze, make a wish quickly. If you do not sneeze, your wish will come true.

> **Suggested activity: Ask your audience what other wish-related superstitions have been handed down in their families.**

Carey's dogs are annoying in ordinary doggy ways. They take up his whole bed when they sleep with him, and all three of them bark constantly at squirrels. Butch loves to chase cars; if there was an Olympic contest for napping, Ed would be in the running; and as for Dee Dee, she lives for food—it doesn't matter whether it's on a plate or in a garbage can. On the day of an eclipse, when Carey accidentally wishes his dogs were people, he finds out that humans who act like dogs can do a lot more damage and are impossible to explain to your mother. After you read Merrill Markoe's *The Day My Dogs Became Guys,* you'll be glad it's only a story.

Additional Books for Older Readers

Did you know that "wishing is the beginning of imagination" (p. 255)? As a raging storm paralyzes the area and creates a state of emergency, Dinah, Zeke, and their little sister, Rebecca Ruth, hunker down with very little food and without their parents or electricity. As they wait out the storm, their twenty-one-year-old cousin, Gage, tries to keep their minds occupied by telling them a story from his childhood. "What-the-Dickens" is an orphan "skibbereen," also known as a tooth fairy. When probationary skibbereen Pepper finds him, he follows her back to her clan. Because "What-the-Dickens" was not born into regular skibbereen society, he is considered an outsider. Although he proves that he is not a spy, he is still asked to leave, and Pepper, on her final provisional assignment, is required to "lose" him. But her mission turns into a harrowing adventure when she is captured by the then ten-year-old Gage. As you listen to the now grown-up Gage's story, you will learn the minutest details of tooth-fairy culture, including what they do with the teeth they collect, how to sing the tooth fairy anthem **(sing it to the tune of "The Battle Hymn of the Republic," p. 118)**, and why the "whole reason that tooth fairies give wishes . . . is to help us practice imagining a better world" (p. 293). Read *What-the-Dickens: The Story of a Rogue Tooth Fairy,* by Gregory Maguire, to find out if the story is the product of Gage's imagination or the result of a wish granted.

Jane, Mark, Catherine, and Martha have been reading the books of E. Nesbit, known for her magical stories **(see above)**, and are walking back to the library to get more books when they find a nickel on the sidewalk. Little do they know that it is a magic coin with peculiar properties. They will get half of everything they wish for, so they have to double their wishes to get what they want . . . quite a tricky proposition. Read *Half Magic,* by Edward Eager—you may have to read it twice to get the full effect!

In *The Chocolate Touch,* by Patrick Catling, magic gives John Midas a special touch much like the touch of the original King Midas, but with more calories!

In *Touch Blue: Signs and Spells, Love Charms and Chants, Auguries and Old Beliefs, in Rhyme,* by Lillian Morrison, you will find all kinds of wish spells from old beliefs. **(Choose selections to read from pp. 3–7.)**

The Hodgepodge Book, collected by Duncan Emrich, is an almanac of American folklore. **(Look for wish "curiosities" on pp. 230–232.)**

Children have contributed their own special ways of wishing in *The Whim-Wham Book,* also collected by Duncan Emrich. **(Pick an assortment to read from pp. 182–195.)**

Additional Music

The music and lyrics to "Swingin' on a Star" can be found at www.smick andsmodoo.com/oldcodgers/oldcodgers.shtml (scroll down to pick the song from the list).

Additional Films and Videos

Seven Wishes of a Rich Kid. Trying to impress at girl a school is not as easy as you might think . . . even if you are rich and have seven wishes from a genie!

There are different versions of *Aladdin* that all have exciting genie scenes.

Enjoy *The Fisherman and His Wife,* a classic tale of wishes and greed.

Screen the part of *Big* in which the main character sees the gypsy in the booth and makes his wish.

In *13 Going on 30,* at her failure of a thirteenth-birthday party, Jenna wishes she were all grown up. Although her wish comes true, her mind hasn't quite caught up with her new body, and things don't go quite according to plan. Screen the clip in which Jenna is in the closet making her wish.

Additional Websites

For more information about Ganesh, including an explanation of his significance, visit http://hinduism.about.com/library/weekly/aa083000a.htm. To see a gallery of Ganesh pictures, visit the Exotic Art Gallery at http://hinduism.about.com/library/weekly/extra/bl-ganeshagallery1.htm.

For poems about and pictures of unicorns, visit www.unicornlady.net/index2.html.

Instead of just wishing on a star, name one and then add a special wish! If you don't mind promoting something that has a fee attached, the site www.starwishing.com shows how you can get a wish, name a star, and purchase the deed to it.

A BBC website for very young children with a story to read online and an easy matching game can be found at www.bbc.co.uk/cbeebies/fimbles/comfycorner/story13.shtml.

Visit the virtual wishing well from the National Autism Association to complement *Rules:* www.nationalautismassociation.org/wish.php. Again, this site requires donations of money to enable online wishes.

There are some wishes that really do come true. Learn about people with serious illnesses who can make a wish and have their dreams come true from the Make-A-Wish Foundation. Go to the website www.wish.org/stories/. Click on the "Wish Stories" tab, then click on "Adventure, Fantasy and Theme Park, Sports and Entertainment" to show the wide variety of things kids wish for.

RESOURCES CITED

Books

Aiken, Joan. *The Moon's Revenge.* Alfred A. Knopf, 1987.

Banerjee, Anjali. *Maya Running.* Wendy Lamb Books, 2005.

Banks, Lynne Reid. *The Adventures of King Midas.* Morrow Junior Books, 1992.

Brittain, Bill. *The Wish Giver: Three Tales of Coven Tree.* Harper and Row, 1983.

Catling, Patrick Skene. *The Chocolate Touch.* Bantam, 1981.

Eager, Edward. *Half Magic.* Thorndike Press, 2005.

Emrich, Duncan. *The Book of Wishes and Wishmaking.* American Heritage Press, 1971.

————, comp. *The Hodgepodge Book: An Almanac of American Folklore; Containing All Manner of Curious, Interesting, and Out-of-the-Way Information Drawn from American Folklore, and Not to Be Found Anywhere Else in the World; as well as Jokes, Conundrums, Riddles, Puzzles, and Other Matter Designed to Amuse and Entertain—All of It Most Instructive and Delightful.* Four Winds Press, 1972.

————, ed. *The Whim-Wham Book.* Contributed by youngsters, college students, mothers, and aunts and uncles from San Jose, California, to Fort Lauderdale, Florida, and from Yarmouth, Maine, to San Antonio, Texas. Four Winds Press, 1975.

Hesse, Karen. *Wish on a Unicorn.* Henry Holt, 1991.

Levine, Gail Carson. *The Wish.* HarperCollins, 2000.

Lord, Cynthia. *Rules.* Scholastic, 2006.

Maguire, Gregory. *What-the-Dickens: The Story of a Rogue Tooth Fairy.* Candlewick, 2007.

Markoe, Merrill. *The Day My Dogs Became Guys.* Viking, 1999.

Morrison, Lillian. *Touch Blue: Signs and Spells, Love Charms and Chants, Auguries and Old Beliefs, in Rhyme.* Crowell, 1958.

Nesbit, E. *Melisande.* Harcourt Brace Jovanovich, 1989.

Polacco, Patricia. *My Rotten Redheaded Older Brother.* Simon and Schuster, 1994.

Music

Crosby, Bing. "Swinging on a Star." Words and music by Johnny Burke and Jimmy Van Heusen. Recorded by Bing Crosby, 1944.

Traditional. "Star Light, Star Bright."

Washington, Ned. "When You Wish Upon a Star." Music by Leigh Harline. Bourne Music Co., 1940.

Films and Videos

Aladdin. Directed by Ron Clements and John Musker. Walt Disney Pictures, 1992.

Big. Directed by Penny Marshall. Twentieth Century Fox, 1988.

The Fisherman and His Wife. Directed by Mark Sottnick and C. W. Rogers. SVS, 1989.

Seven Wishes of a Rich Kid. ABC Afterschool Specials. Directed by Larry Elikann. 1979.

The Seven Wishes of Joanna Peabody. ABC Weekend Specials. Directed by Stephen H. Foreman. 1978.

13 Going on 30. Directed by Gary Winick. Revolution Studios, 2004.

The Wizard of Oz. Directed by Victor Fleming. MGM, 1939.

Websites

BBC. Gauld, Stephanie, ed. "CBeebies—Fimbles—Wishing Upon a Star." www.bbc.co.uk/cbeebies/fimbles/comfycorner/story13 .shtml.

Das, Subhamoy. About.com: Hinduism. Ganesha: Lord of Success. http://hinduism.about.com/od/lordganesha/a/ganesha.htm.

———. "Ganesha Art Gallery—2." http://hinduism.about.com/ library/weekly/extra/bl-ganeshart3.htm.

EcoPlanet. "Star Wishing—Name a Star and Add a Special Wish." www.starwishing.com.

Make-A-Wish Foundation of America. "Wish Stories." www.wish. org/stories/.

NASA Goddard Space Flight Center. "NSSDC Photo Gallery—Moon." http://nssdc.gsfc.nasa.gov/photo_gallery/photogallery-moon.html.

National Autism Association. "Wishing Well." www.nationalautism association.org/wish.php.

Smick and Smodoo. Smick and Smodoo's World, Old Codger's Midi Page. "Swingin' on a Star." www.smickandsmodoo.com/ oldcodgers/oldcodgers.shtml.

Solo Song's Place. "When You Wish Upon a Star." http://solosong. net/wish.html.

Unicorn Lady. Mystical Unicorn. www.unicornlady.net.

United Media. Comics.com e-cards. "Pearls Before Swine by Stephan Pastis." www.comics.com/webmail/SendAStrip?AppName=ECards Flash&ComicName=pearls&Attachments=/ecards/cards/ecard _pearls_slug.swf.

Wags for Wishes. "Events." www.wagsforwishes.com.

4

Lies

Liar, Liar, Pants on Fire

Screen a brief cut from the movie *Pinocchio* showing his nose growing when he lies.

I'll bet you all know who this is! And I'm sure you know why his nose is growing, too. It was easy for Pinocchio's friends to tell when he was lying—all they had to do was look at his nose! Generally, there is no magic sign to tell us if someone is lying or not. Instead, we have to rely on a number of subtle cues to help us decide if a person is being truthful with us or not.

How can you tell if someone is lying? According to Thomas J. Leonard, infopreneur, here are some things to look for to tell if someone is lying to you:

See if they look you in the eye, or if their eyes are cast down. When they speak, are their explanations too long? Do they laugh nervously? Are they pretending not to know something you know they know? Do they ask you to just trust them without giving a logical explanation? Do you have the sense that something is wrong even though you can't put your finger on what it is? When you ask for an explanation or clarification does it seem that they are pausing or stalling while they think up something?

This information comes from the website "The Top Ten Ways to Tell if Someone Is Lying to You" at http://topten.org/Con tent/tt.BG40.htm.

Now I'd like two volunteers to come up here and use the words "I finished all my homework, Mom; I really did" to act out trying to convince their mother of something that is not true. By watching them, we can see if the list on the website is accurate and if we get the sense that they are lying. (**First, one volunteer will be the child and the other will be the parent; after about two minutes the volunteers can switch roles and try it again. There are no prescripted words; this is an improvisational skit that gives children a chance to express how they might feel in this circumstance. By taking turns being the parent, they also get an idea of the other side of the coin.**)

For the next booktalk, show a picture of a big, hairy spider projected from this website: www.chevroncars.com/learn/ wondrous-world/tarantulas/.

"Lying was easy. Simple. You could tell people all sorts of fake stories about yourself, but if you told them with a straight face, well, people would believe you. Especially if you had just moved to town from another state, with no way for people to check whether or not you were telling the truth. This was maybe the only advantage to being the new kid in town" (p. 45). Just like his favorite spiders that lie, or camouflage themselves to survive, Bobby tells one outlandish story after another as he tries to adjust to his new school in New York. Caught in his lies, Bobby must learn to coexist even with the bully who calls him "Spider Boy from Illinois." Ralph Fletcher's *Spider Boy* is full of facts about spiders, including tarantulas, and takes an honest look at being honest.

But Bobby doesn't know things like this: "The Santa Fe [spider] is the most dangerous spider in the whole world. It has one hundred legs with a stinger on each, and a forked tail with two large stingers and fangs bigger than a rattlesnake's. If it stings you with its legs, you might last an hour. If it stings you with its stingers, you might last fifteen minutes. But if it stings you and bites you at the same time, you have only five minutes to live. First you will turn blue, then yellow, then a beautiful bright green. Then your hair will fall out. Then you will drop dead as a doornail" (p. 81). Read *Whoppers* like this in Alvin Schwartz's collection of 145 tall tales and other lies, also known as "windies or gallyfloppers" (p. 11), from American folklore.

And since I just told you a whopper, I'd like to give you a Whopper as well!

Offer them Whoppers candy.

How many lies have you told in your life? Josh McBroom claims he has told only one lie. Was it the time it got so cold so fast that the "sunshine froze to the ground [and they had to pickax] chunks of it for the stove to cook on?" (p. 5) Was it the truth that his farm's land was "so amazingly rich [they] could plant and harvest two to three crops a day . . . or that when little Clarinda dropped her silver baby fork . . . by the time [they] found it the thing had grown into a silver pitchfork" (p. 11)? How about the eggs that flipped themselves over in the pan because the hens had eaten Mexican jumping beans? Could it be the cow that froze to death in a field of popped corn or growing tomatoes overnight in the middle of a dust storm? Read *McBroom Tells a Lie,* by Sid Fleischman, to tell the whoppers from the lie!

Spot the lie! "Telling the truth [is not the same thing as] telling the *whole* truth and nothing but the truth" (p. 7).

Read "The Donkey and the Carrots" from George Shannon's *True Lies: 18 Tales for You to Judge.*

Several fellows were swapping riddles as they sat around the potbellied stove.

Once, said Jim, there was a donkey tied to a rope that was eight feet long, and there was also a wagon of carrots thirty yards away. That donkey loved carrots more than words can say, and he got them, too! Any guesses how he did it?

Gnawed through a rope? said a man.

Nope.

It's impossible, said another.

Nope.

You're lying, said a third.

But Jim's best friend shook his head and smiled. He's telling the truth. I saw it myself. Even though the donkey was tied to a rope only eight feet long, he got those carrots in the wagon thirty yards away.

What's the truth, the whole truth?

And where's the lie?

The Whole Truth?

Jim never said that the other end of the eight-foot-long rope was tied to anything. The donkey just walked to the carrots. (pp. 11–12)

Or have your audience try to solve any one of the sixteen other brainteasers in *True Lies*.

There is another way to tell if someone is lying: ask him to take a lie-detector test. Here is an online polygraph machine that can tell if you are lying or not through a simple card trick. Do I have a volunteer?

For this trick you first need to carefully read the instructions on the website www.krazydad.com/ipolygraph/secret.php to learn how to set up the trick. This *is* a trick—if you do not follow the instructions exactly, the lie detector will not work. But don't let the children know that! The fun is in thinking that the computer can detect lies. Open the website www .ipolygraph.com. This will take you directly to the online polygraph machine. Follow the instructions from the Krazy Dad website as well as what is written on this one and you can do the card trick with an unsuspecting audience member.

Go to www.nodeception.com and let everyone watch the animation until the picture of an eye comes onto the screen. Then start the next booktalk.

Some lies are merely tall tales in disguise; others can cause the most terrible guilt that will stay with you for the rest of your days . . .

Play a few lines from the Sex Pistols song "Liar." The basic words are variations of the word *liar* sung in frenzied

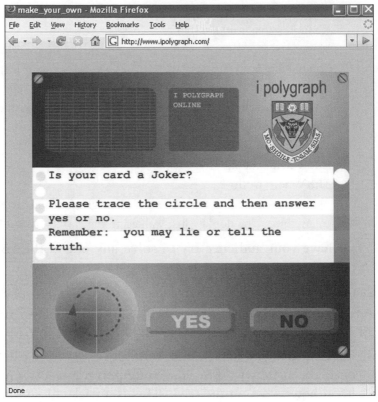

i Polygraph Machine. Courtesy of Jim Bumgardner,
http://krazydad.com/ipolygraph/secret.php.

**repetition. There are no objectionable words, so you may
decide to play the entire song.**

Joel promises his father, *On My Honor* (**raise right hand**), that he
and his friend Tony are only going to the state park on their bikes.
Instead he and Tony decide to ride to the Vermillion River and race
across. Tony has always found excuses not to swim, but when Joel
dares him to cross to the sandbar, he jumps right in the water. When
Joel comes home alone, the lie he tells will haunt him forever. Read
Marion Dane Bauer's story of a terrible truth revealed at last.

And then there'are lies that are planned and have a real purpose:

> **Project a picture of a naked mole rat from www.bio.davidson
> .edu/people/vecase/Behavior/Spring2004/lyons/lyons.html
> or a picture of many naked-mole-rat babies curled up together
> from www.shutterandpupil.com/99.html.**

Twelve-year-old Frankie accidentally reads her father's e-mail from Ayanna, a woman he met on a business trip. In order to undermine their relationship, Frankie e-mails the woman, among many other lies, that her two brothers have terrible diseases, that her father has severe allergies, "which makes him annoying to live with because his nose is always full of snot" (p. 13), and that he is especially allergic to small mammals. This is important because Ayanna (whose screen name is ratlady) works at the zoo with naked mole rats. Unfortunately Ayanna doesn't seem to believe Frankie's fibs, and she continues to communicate with both Frankie and her father. In desperation Frankie cuts school to intercept more e-mails, is grouchy with her brothers, and starts hanging with the wrong crowd. What happens when Ayanna (just when *does* Frankie stop calling her ratlady?) starts giving her good advice in *The Naked Mole-Rat Letters,* by Mary Amato?

Ayanna might have been able to use this test that parents are supposed to take about how to handle a child who lies. How would you like your parent to answer these questions? Try taking this honesty quiz.

> **Go to the honesty quiz at www.bblocks.samhsa.gov/family/
> activities/quizzes/honesty.aspx. If you don't have much time,
> just go to question number five.**

Sometimes grownups try to justify lying. Here's a scene from the movie *Liar Liar* where the father tries to explain why sometimes grownups need to lie.

> **Screen the scene toward the end where the father gives his
> explanation to his son.**

When grownups lie, how can children set things right? Adam Canfield dreams of being a reporter when he grows up. When he becomes coeditor of his elementary/middle school newspaper *The Slash,* a third-

Honesty quiz from the Substance Abuse and Mental Health Services
Administration's Building Blocks for a Healthy Future website,
www.bblocks.samhsa.gov.

grade reporter uncovers a major scandal: "Money that was supposed
to go to kids [paid] for gold plumbing in the principal's bathroom
[instead]" (p. 238). Read *Adam Canfield of the Slash,* by Michael Winerip,
and get your own nose for news.

Sometimes what sounds like a lie could actually be true . . .

Wanda Petronski always wore the same "faded blue dress that
didn't hang right" (pp. 10–12), but she claimed to have "a hundred
dresses all lined up in [her] closet" (p. 13). Every day the other girls
would tease Wanda about her clothing. It wasn't until Wanda's family
moved away that the children found out that she really did have *The
Hundred Dresses* she claimed to have. Read Eleanor Estes's book to find
out about Wanda's secret wardrobe.

Although sometimes when you tell the truth you are not believed,
telling the truth is always better than lying. And now, *honestly,* I really
had a good time telling you about all these books!

Storm: Chasing Storms with Warren Faidley, by Stephen Kramer, we meet a man who gets up close and personal with mammoth storms on purpose! The lightning strike that made him famous came within four hundred feet of where he stood. It "had the energy of a bomb blast and . . . lifted [his] body right off the ground" (p. 14). The picture he took was the clearest and nearest shot of a lighting bolt hitting an object ever taken. Now Warren Faidley makes a living taking pictures of Mother Nature run wild. If you too have a hankering to follow the awesome power of similar bolts from the blue, or if you just want to read about them from the safe, dry comfort of your bedroom, *Eye of the Storm* is for you.

Public moral standards prevent me from demonstrating another way of getting cozy with electricity. In both *Harris and Me* and *How Angel Peterson Got His Name,* Gary Paulsen warns us about the perils of peeing on an electric fence. Instead we are going to explain how to show only a slightly tamer example of the spectacular light show we know as lightning.

> From *Janice VanCleave's Electricity: Mind-Boggling Experiments You Can Turn into Science Fair Projects* you need only basic materials such as a wool scarf, a paper clip, a plastic report folder, and modeling clay to make a "bright spark of light leap between the plastic and the paper clip" (p. 16). Expect a sound-and-light show!

We couldn't talk about lightning without a mention of Benjamin Franklin, the man with the kite and the key . . .

In fact, in Philadelphia, there is a science museum called the Franklin Institute, which has a special exhibit dedicated to lightning and electricity. Other science museums also have lightning exhibits. The Museum of Science in Boston has online information, videos, and quizzes about lightning. Watch this video to see lightning striking a kite.

Show www.mos.org/sln/toe/kite.mov.

Now that you've heard so much about lightning (both fact and fiction), let's see how you do on this quiz.

> Show www.mos.org/sln/toe/safety.html, also from the Museum of Science in Boston.

Thank you for helping me have a *shockingly* good time. I hope I've *sparked* your interest in some of these books. If any of these *strike* your fancy, be my guest and check it out!

> **Fade out to the sounds of "Knock on Wood," by Eddie Floyd and Steve Croppe. Play the first verse and turn off the music after the lines "It's like thunder and lightning, the way you love me is frightening, You better knock, knock, knock on wood, baby."**

EXPANDING YOUR OPTIONS

Books for Use with Younger Audiences

Try keeping the peace with bolts of lightning instead of bullets. In *The Legend of Lightning Larry,* by Aaron Shepard, the western town of Brimstone is transformed by a very different kind of hero. Saddle up for a rip-roaring read. Yee-haw!

Aaron Shepard's *Master Man* will introduce you to a self-proclaimed superhero. He gets his just deserts when he discovers he's not the only superman in town—er, forest—while you get to learn how and why we have thunder and lightning. A Hausa tale from Nigeria. (**Suggested activity: Discuss other explanations for lightning and/or thunder, e.g., angels bowling.**)

Talk about a serious time-out! Ma Sheep Thunder and Ram Lightning are permanently exiled from earth all because of Ram's troublemaking. Don't get the wool pulled over your eyes; read Ashley Bryan's *The Story of Lightning and Thunder.*

"Lightning Bolt," in *Flicker Flash,* by Joan Bransfield Graham, is a concrete poem that shows Ben Franklin's discovery in all its high-flying glory. (**Suggested activity: For a dynamic presentation of this poem, scan it and show it on the big screen.**)

What vegetables do you hate the most? Sammy hates vegetables in general, but in particular, he loathes lima beans. He specializes in finding sneaky ways not to eat them, just as his mother keeps finding ways to tempt him into tasting them. One night he puts them in his sock and makes an excuse to go outside; he digs a hole in a vacant lot down the street and deposits them there. Once he shares his secret with the other neighborhood kids, the hole soon fills up with brussels sprouts and parsnips, too. One night during a terrible storm a bolt of lightning hits the mound of rotting veggies, not once, but twice, and *The Lima Bean Monster* is born! Read Dan Yaccarino's cautionary tale to find out if the creature gets to eat some human "beans," or not. **(Suggested activity: Here's an audience-participation opportunity! Ask audience members what vegetables or foods they hate the most. Then ask if they would rather eat their hated food or have a lightning-animated monster of that food come after them.)**

Additional Books for Older Readers

"The Great Cortado [has] devised a way of hypnotizing people with laughter, so he can get them hooked on a tonic that only he knows how to produce. He plans to gain control over the whole country" (p. 379). Facing this dastardly villain and his sinister circus crew are Miles Wednesday, an orphan with a mysterious past; Little, a Song Angel mistakenly fallen to earth; Tiger, who constantly threatens to eat the other characters; Lady Partridge, "mistress of a hundred cats" (p. 75), who lives in a tree house; and Silverpoint, a Storm Angel whose touch feels like a "distant cousin of the electric eel" (p. 306). Captured by Cortado and compelled to throw lightning bolts as part of the performance, Silverpoint's honor as a Storm Angel will not allow him to kill. Miles and company must figure out a plan that will turn the tables on the evildoers despite their overwhelming power. You will laugh until you cry when you read *The Palace of Laughter,* by Jon Berkeley.

Have you ever played a fantasy role-playing game like Dungeons and Dragons? When Max and his friends play the magical game Round Table, they realize that the characters on the cards they use are real and are out to destroy the world. Then Max himself begins to show real signs of special powers: "blue lightning crackle[d] over [his] body"

(p. 312). Read *The Revenge of the Shadow King,* by Derek Benz and J. S. Lewis, the first of a series, to see how Max follows in his grandfather's footsteps and takes measures to face a mortal enemy.

Caddy Ever After is the fourth book in the Casson Family series by Hilary McKay. Don't worry if you haven't read the first three. Just listen to one example of the hilarious predicaments of the Casson family and you will want to read them all. Here Rose, the youngest child, is irrationally afraid that her mother will be murdered as she sleeps in the backyard in her artist's shed during a thunderstorm. **(Read page 28 as breathlessly as possible, as Rose goes to her mother's rescue wearing her sister's sneakers, her brother's jacket, and pajamas.)**

Fourteen-year-old Leven Thumps didn't know he could control lightning. He had been living a miserable life in Oklahoma with his mean-spirited guardians, who barely tolerated him. But on the day the bullies pushed him into the stream, "he was remarkably calm . . . he pictured lightning coming down from the darkened, cloudy sky. And there, suddenly, was a bolt of it, striking the ground no more than a hundred feet away. The flash was blinding and the sound deafening, and Brick and Glen screamed and fell over on their backs in the stream bed . . . Leven envisioned lightning chasing them all the way home, and, amazingly, that was exactly what happened" (p. 58). Astounding as this was, Leven had already been astonished a few days earlier when he met Clover, a "twelve-inch-tall furry creature with wet eyes and a huge smile who was supposed to serve him" (p. 53). Clover wouldn't tell him much other than that something major was going to happen. Read *Leven Thumps and the Gateway to Foo,* by Obert Skye, to see how Leven—accompanied by Clover; Winter, a girl whose home life compares with Leven's in its neglect and abuse; and Geth, the rightful ruler of the land of Foo, whose body is trapped in a toothpick—sets out to save the world of Foo and thereby saves his own world as well.

Books for Use with Young Adult and Adult Audiences

Percy (Perseus) Jackson, a twelve-year-old New Yorker, is shunted from school to school and has difficulty making and keeping friends. When

(p. 91). So says eleven-year-old Ant (Antonia) MacPherson. Ant's family moves around a lot, but now that she has a dog, "Pistachio," a friend, Harrison, and a teacher, "Just Carol," who believes in her, the stakes are higher and her reasons for lying seem to take on a life of their own. Because she has felt little love or approval from her mother, lying has become second nature to Ant. She tells people that she is adopted; since her parents seem to care more about her two perfect sisters, she swaps her good report cards for Harrison's mediocre ones; because her parents hate dogs and she can't afford to pay, she has begun falsifying her address when taking Pistachio to the vet; when "Just Carol" gives Ant a chance to volunteer at the zoo she hides Pistachio in her pocket and almost gets them both attacked by a lion. Even though she brought him with her because she didn't know who else could give him his pill in the middle of the day, this is not just a little "green lie . . . the kind you have to tell to keep safe . . . like when chameleons change colors to camouflage themselves so predators don't eat them" (p. 90). "Just Carol" demands honesty. Ant must make amends to the vet and, when she finds out that they are moving once again, she must find a way to tell her mother what she really needs from her. Read *Notes from a Liar and Her Dog,* by Gennifer Choldenko, for a bracing dose of truth.

When thirteen-year-old Anastasia Krupnick decides she is ready for romance, she answers a personal ad that reads "[Single White Male], 28, boyish charm, inherited wealth, looking for tall young woman, nonsmoker, to share Caribbean vacation, reruns of *Casablanca,* and romance" (p. 6). Her responses are totally honest in every way, except that she doesn't mention her age. Oh, and when he asks for a picture, Anastasia doesn't send him a picture of herself; she sends a picture of her mother (whom Anastasia looks like) when she was twenty-two. When Mr. Single White Male wants to meet Anastasia, the facts she has left out make it very embarrassing indeed. Read *Anastasia at This Address,* by Lois Lowry, for a cautionary tale about lying and the Internet.

The first book in the Shamer Chronicles introduces us to Dina, who has inherited her mother's power/gift/curse of being able to look into people's eyes and make them face up to the truths in their lives and see through their lies. When her mother is called to confront the person accused in a triple murder (a shamer's duty), Dina goes with her to learn the trade. Read Lene Kaaberbol's *Shamer's Daughter* and see how a shamer might deal with someone who has no conscience and, hence, no shame at all.

Ailsa's mother runs an antique shop, but not very well. She always seems to be giving things away. No wonder they haven't enough money to pay the phone bill. Then Ailsa meets a curious young man in the library. Before they know it, MCC Berkshire is working for them, sleeping on the old bed in the shop and, miraculously, selling things, always by telling stories (Ailsa calls them *A Pack of Lies*) to the amazed customers. Would you buy a broken grandfather clock that caused a particularly fitting death, a roll-top desk with a hidden drawer that "was exhibit Number One . . . in The Case of the Bloodstained Blotter" (p. 106), or a bed from Transylvania whose owner and monster come to a grisly end? Are they lies within stories or stories within lies? Author Geraldine McCaughrean will have you fooled to the very last page.

"Most people think there are only two kinds of lies: 'little white lies' and all the others. But that isn't true. Lies come in a lot of different colors. White lies are the kind that protect other people's feelings. Yellow lies are the ones that tell only part of a story; they leave things out . . . Pink ones exaggerate. Green ones invent. Little kids like to use them . . . Blue lies are the ones that people use when they're desperately trying to get out of trouble" (p. 46); "A purple lie—diversion" (p. 90). Thea has the art of lying down to a fine art, and she only began lying five months ago. "One lie led naturally to the next. And eventually the lies started to feel like helium balloons: [she] could tie them to things [she] didn't want to think about, then watch them rise into the air and float away" (p. 12). On her way to stay with her grandparents for summer vacation, her mother gives her a notebook and tells her to write one hundred truths in it. But what is the difference between a truth and a fact? Perhaps that difference will help her come to terms with the horrible secret she has kept for those long five months. Meanwhile she is stuck babysitting her obsessively neat and snoopy seven-year-old cousin, Jocelyn, trying to find out the secret her aunts are keeping from the rest of the family, and continuing to watch as "lies slid[e off her tongue] like butter" (p. 10). It is only when she jeopardizes Jocelyn's safety that Thea realizes that "truth has a weight, a certain shape you can recognize. And it comes in only one color" (p. 176). Read Julie Schumacher's *The Book of One Hundred Truths* and find out why even one difficult truth is worth a thousand easy lies.

Would you lie for true love? When the king proclaims that his son must marry a village girl from Mount Eskel, the deception begins. All the girls who live and work there expect to follow in the footsteps of their ancestors and work in the quarry. Instead, to spiff up their manners, all Mount Eskel girls from ages twelve to seventeen are required to attend a *Princess Academy*. After a year's worth of training, the prince will decide who will be his bride. But it's not so simple . . . not all the girls are who they say they are, and the Academy sometimes seems more like a torture chamber than a finishing school. Does love really prevail? Read Shannon Hale's unpredictable fantasy and find out.

What happens when you find out that your whole life is a lie? It is 1840 and teenage Jesse lives with her parents and siblings in a log cabin in Clifton, Indiana. When a diphtheria epidemic strikes, Jesse's sister falls ill. Jesse's mother takes her on a hike and reveals a shocking secret: the year is really 1996 and a cure for diphtheria exists outside the village! Jesse's mom explains that the original founders of their village were people fed up with modern life who wanted to go back to the basics. They moved into a restricted area, went back to the old ways, and never told their children that a modern world existed. Originally, they thought they would have the option of leaving if they wanted. Instead, in the name of historical research, heartless scientists installed hidden video cameras all over and opened viewing stations where tourists, school classes, and researchers could watch what was going on at any time. Now, the scientists have sealed off all exit routes, surrounded the village with armed guards, and will severely punish anyone even referring to life outside the village. Jesse's mother shows her one possible escape route and begs her to enter the modern world to bring back the cure. If Jesse manages to outwit the scientists and escape the village, how will she deal with being thrust into a world with telephones, cars, and blue jeans and convince someone to supply the desperately needed medicine? To find out what happens in this fast-paced action story, read *Running Out of Time,* by Margaret Peterson Haddix.

The children at the Saints Peter and Paul School in Naperville, Illinois, liked *Running Out of Time* so much they created an entire website about it. If any of you have read the book, we can use their website to play Jeopardy. **(Suggested activity: Screen http://library.thinkquest.org/J0110073/. Go to "Activities," click on "Game," and play Jeopardy.)**

Books for Use with Young Adult and Adult Audiences

Always being honest can turn things upside down. Because his father never stopped lying, Wallace Wallace has vowed only to tell the truth. After Wallace[2] writes a book report giving a thumbs-down to his teacher's favorite book about a dog, published in 1951 (before the dinosaurs roamed), his punishment is daily detention until he rewrites the book report with a positive spin. Forced to sit through play practice of the very book he hates, Wallace finds his honesty responsible for creating major changes in the play. Will his devotion to the truth keep him off the football team and in detention forever? Read *No More Dead Dogs,* by Gordon Korman, to see if honesty is the best policy.

What if you can only tell the truth, the whole truth, and nothing but the truth? Radical honesty is not always the best policy, especially if you have been kidnapped by aliens. What happens when they want to know the identities of your friends, who have gone to great care to disguise themselves, and you are unable to lie? Will you be responsible for the death of everyone? *Extras,* by Scott Westerfeld, is the follow-up to the Uglies trilogy. Extra, extra, read all about it!

Additional Music

"Honesty," written and performed by Billy Joel, can be accessed at http://solosong.net/honesty.html.

Additional Poems

"Magical Eraser," by Shel Silverstein, from *Where the Sidewalk Ends,* p. 99.

Additional Films and Videos

Show an excerpt from the movie *The Village,* by M. Night Shyamalan, considered by some to be a direct rip-off of the book *Running Out of Time.* Give a bit of background, and screen the section in which the Land Rover appears.

Additional Websites

For pictures of different lie detectors, visit http://images.google.com/images and search for "lie detector." Choose a few of the most interesting ones to show the children.

Additional Activities

Consider purchasing a Pinocchio's nose tape measure. Do a Google search for "Pinocchio's nose tape measure." There are inexpensive ones available. Use the tape measure with the introductory passage about Pinocchio.

RESOURCES CITED

Books

Amato, Mary. *The Naked Mole-Rat Letters.* Holiday House, 2005.

Bauer, Marion Dane. *On My Honor.* Clarion, 1986.

Choldenko, Gennifer. *Notes from a Liar and Her Dog.* G. P. Putnam's Sons, 2001.

Demi. *The Empty Pot.* Henry Holt, 1990.

Estes, Eleanor. *The Hundred Dresses.* Harcourt, Brace, 1944.

Fleischman, Sid. *McBroom Tells a Lie.* Price Stern Sloan, 1999.

Fletcher, Ralph. *Spider Boy.* Clarion, 1997.

Haddix, Margaret Peterson. *Running Out of Time.* Simon and Schuster, 1995.

Hale, Shannon. *Princess Academy.* Bloomsbury Children's Books, 2005.

Kaaberbol, Lene. *Shamer's Daughter.* Henry Holt, 2004.

Korman, Gordon. *No More Dead Dogs.* Hyperion, 2000.

Lowry, Lois. *Anastasia at This Address.* Houghton Mifflin, 1991.

———. *Gooney Bird Greene.* Houghton Mifflin, 2002.

McCaughrean, Geraldine. *A Pack of Lies: Twelve Stories in One.* Oxford University Press, 1988.

McKissack, Patricia. *The Honest-to-Goodness Truth.* Atheneum, 2000.

Prose, Francine. *Leopold, the Liar of Leipzig.* Joanna Cotler Books, 2005.

Schumacher, Julie. *The Book of One Hundred Truths.* Delacorte, 2006.

Schwartz, Alvin. *Whoppers: Tall Tales and Other Lies.* Lippincott, 1975.

Shannon, George. *True Lies: 18 Tales for You to Judge.* Beech Tree, 1998.

Silverstein, Shel. "Magical Eraser." *Where the Sidewalk Ends.* HarperCollins, 2000.

Westerfeld, Scott. *Extras.* Simon Pulse, 2007.

Winerip, Michael. *Adam Canfield of the Slash.* Candlewick, 2005.

Music

Joel, Billy. "Honesty." *The Essential Billy Joel.* Sony, 2001.

Sex Pistols. "Liar." *Never Mind the Bollocks, Here's the Sex Pistols.* Virgin Records, 1977.

Films and Videos

Pinocchio. Directed by Hamilton Luske and Ben Sharpsteen. Walt Disney Productions, 1940.

Liar Liar. Directed by Tom Shadyac. Universal Pictures, 1997.

Truth. Fox Kids Network Totally for Kids PSA campaign. Produced by Churchill Entertainment, this clip won a Peabody Award for excellence in broadcasting in 1993. A good video can be found at www.youtube.com/watch?v=OVcmXCBpDYA.

The Village. Directed by M. Night Shyamalan. Touchstone, 2004.

Websites

Chevron Corporation. "Chevron Cars—Online Learning Corporation." www.chevroncars.com/learn/wondrous-world/tarantulas/.

Children at the Saints Peter and Paul School in Naperville, Illinois. "Running from Time to Time." http://library.thinkquest.org/J0110073/.

Google. www.google.com.

Google Images. http://images.google.com/images.

Krazydad.com. "i Polygraph—Computer Mentalist." www.ipolygraph .com and www.krazydad.com/ipolygraph/secret.php.

Leonard, Thomas J. "The Top 10 Ways to Tell if Someone Is Lying to You." http://topten.org/Content/tt.BG40.htm.

Long, Alec, photographer. "Shutter and Pupil—Spoon Me—naked _mole_rat." www.shutterandpupil.com/99.html.

Lyons, Gray. Spring "Naked Mole Rat—Animal Behavior—Davidson College." www.bio.davidson.edu/people/vecase/Behavior/Spring 2004/lyons/lyons.html.

Nodeception.com. "Welcome to nodeception.com—Lies, Deception, and the Truth." www.nodeception.com.

Solo Song's Place. "Honesty." http://solosong.net/honesty.html.

U.S. Department of Health and Human Services, Substance Abuse and Mental Health Services Administration, Center for Substance Abuse Prevention. "Building Blocks for a Healthy Future—Honesty Quiz." www.bblocks.samhsa.gov.

WGBH Educational Foundation. Teacher's Domain: Multimedia Resources for the Classroom and Professional Development. "From Seed to Flower." www.teachersdomain.org/resources/tdc02/sci/life/colt/lp_plantcycle/index.html.

Dreams

All You Have to Do Is Dream

Play the last stanza of the song "Dream a Little Dream of Me." There are many recordings, but the best-known one is by the Mamas and the Papas.

> Sweet dreams till sunbeams find you
>
> Sweet dreams that leave all worries behind you
>
> But in your dreams whatever they be
>
> Dream a little dream of me.

Recite the poem "Invitation," by Shel Silverstein, from *Where the Sidewalk Ends,* p. 9.

Dreams can be truth on a slant . . . Would they be friends if not for the dreams? Claudia is shy and scared of her shadow; Danger, also known as Mindy, is wild and, well, dangerous. Even though most of the things Danger tells Claudia are lies, they are so exciting Claudia doesn't care. Then the girls discover that every nine days they have the same dream! They had "3 types of dreams. The first dream . . . concealed some hidden information . . . the second set of dreams were exactly alike. And in the third type one girl started a dream, and the other finished it" (p. 29). They start to record the dreams in a dream book and eventually find that their dreams predict a plane hijacking, help them find out the truth about the mysterious doctor upstairs, and solve the mystery of Claudia's father's disappearance. Read *The Dream Book,* by Meg Wolitzer.

Dreams, by Larry Kettelkamp, will help you try to figure out some of your dreams:

> Look for a play on words and numbers in your dreams. Word puns are common and can often be discovered if you are on the lookout. For instance . . . one dream researcher tried an experiment to stimulate . . . dreams. Several volunteers were shown . . . two pictures [on a] screen. One was the number 10. The other was a picture of a hat. Many of the volunteers reported dreams in which an officer in uniform—a sailing captain or an army captain—played a part. Captain [is] a word combining *cap* and *10*! (pp. 90–91)

This is just the type of connection between something in real life and a dream that occurs in *The Dream Book*. One of the dreams that Claudia and Danger share involves jockeys racing on giant spheres and the number 999. It turns out that Claudia's father is a disc jockey at a radio station with 999 in the call numbers! If you like the idea of writing down your dreams to see if you can find connections between your subconscious and your real life, why don't you start a dream book of your own?

Some dreams reflect what really happened, except they leave important facts out. "It was . . . a *face*—a face that moved from one point of the darkness to another, a face that in some inexplicable, horrible way swung to and fro" (p. 7). Meg had been having the same nightmare since she was nine, right after her mother died and she went to live with her father. It was only at age nineteen, when she was engaged to be married and the dream began to come more often, that she decided to track down its source. In the part of England called Cornwall, where she and her mother had stayed long ago, a murder had never been solved. If only Meg can unlock her memories to find the clues beyond her dream before the murderer comes for her. Try *Night Fall,* by Joan Aiken, for a real nail-biter of a reading experience.

Most dreams are forgotten immediately, or at least we can put them behind us, but not this one.

"It was night; he was standing on the edge of a large empty field trying to move toward a glowing object floating over the center of the field . . . a relentless feeling of urgency . . . pulsed in the air around him. Something terrible was about to happen—something only he could prevent. His whole body was tense with fear. He knew he was being watched. He longed to look behind, he longed to run. But he could only move very very slowly. He inched his way painfully through the thick blackness as the terror all around him rose to a screaming pitch. And then suddenly there was a small figure in white dashing toward the light, pursued by a dark hulking creature" (pp. 1–2). Paul and Francine have the same dream. Although they weren't friends before, they are startled that they know personal information about each other that they had no way of knowing. When they investigate, they find out that they were both in Nevada on the same date that a UFO was sighted. They track down the woman involved in the sighting and discover her little boy is telepathic. Even their own unexplained knowledge of each other shows that they have the same ability! But who is sending them the dreams, and why? Who are the two men following them? Read *Into the Dream,* by William Sleator. It's one dream you won't forget.

The little boy in *Into the Dream* can't speak aloud, although his telepathy allows him to speak inside your mind. If he could draw the dream, it would not be any more remarkable than the dream drawings on this website.

> **Screen the Dream Art Gallery—http://dreamtalk.hypermart .net/gallery2005/index.htm—and show pictures by Bonnie Bisbee, Brenda Ferrimani, Thomas J. Dragavon, and Donna Fenstermaker. Play an excerpt from "Daydream Believer," by the Monkees: "Cheer up, sleepy Jean, oh what can it mean . . . to a daydream believer and a homecoming queen?"**

"When Peter was ten years old, grownup people sometimes used to tell him he was a difficult child. He never understood what they meant

Landscape portraying Jacob's dream: the angels' ladder,
by Michael Lukas Leopold Willmann, c. 1691.

. . . He didn't . . . tip ketchup over his head and pretend it was blood,
or slash at his granny's ankles with his sword . . . He wasn't noisier or
dirtier or more stupid than anyone he knew" (pp. 1–2). The problem
was that he liked to get lost in his thoughts. In *The Daydreamer,* by Ian
McEwan, you will find yourself inside eight of Peter's daydreams. For
instance, there is the dream where a naked doll incites the rest of his
sister's dolls to rebel against him; or three separate dreams in which he
trades bodies with a cat, a baby, and a grown man; and, my personal
favorite, when he uses vanishing cream to erase his entire family. They
may only take place in Peter's mind, but they seem so real.

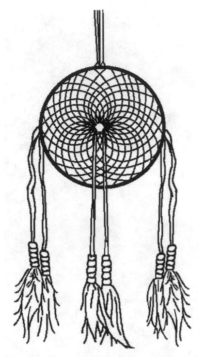

Native American Dream Catcher
copyright © 2004 PKelley
Enterprises, www.scissorcraft.com.
Used with permission.

Play the two-line chorus from "Dream Weaver," by Gary Wright: "Dream Weaver . . . I believe we can reach the morning light."

Dream catchers are traditionally woven by Native Americans. Typically, people put them over their beds to catch nightmares and protect themselves from evil things. If you would like to make your own dream catcher, check out this website. **(Project www.rivernen.ca/ build_dc .htm.)**

Even if you don't have a dream catcher, if you've got a dream giver, you are safe . . . "Dreamgivers are assigned to us. The act of dream insertion is called bestowal. It is very delicate. It requires absolute precision" (pp. 13–14). The dreamgiver collects fragments of memories from your possessions and returns them in the form of dreams. While Littlest One is learning her craft, she is assigned to practice creating dreams for an old woman and her dog. After Littlest One has been practicing for some time, the old woman takes eight-year-old John into her home as a foster child. John is so filled with anger at the horrible abuse in his life that he is easy prey for "sinisteeds." A sinisteed's only purpose is to inflict nightmares. "Sinisteeds rarely sleep . . . their energy is boundless . . . They prey on the most vulnerable [and] they have no mercy" (p. 47). Littlest One has only her gossamer touch to gather the filaments, made from strands of good memories and courageous words, to strengthen the boy against the sinisteeds' horror. Read *Gossamer*, by Lois Lowry. It will haunt your dreams.

Read the poem "The Child Who Cried," by Felice Holman, from *Bring Me All of Your Dreams*, edited by Nancy Larrick.

I found a cave
I found a cave
    deep
    deep
    deep
and went inside
and went inside
    to sleep
    sleep
    sleep
and dreamed a dream
and dreamed a dream
    deep
    deep
    deep
about a child who always cried
about a child who always cried
    weep
    weep
    weep
Then I awoke
    Then I awoke
        bright, bright, bright
    and climbed outside
    and looked about
    and saw the sky
    and shouted "I
am *not* the child who cried!" (p. 22)

But what do real kids like you dream about? Here are some examples from *Dream Makers: Young People Share Their Hopes and Aspirations*, by Neil Waldman. Some are fantastical:

> My dream is to have a lifetime supply of chocolate.
> I dream that someday I will make a car that can fly.
> I have a dream [that] I can even breathe underwater.

Some are serious:

> Now my . . . dream is that someday my children will grow up with no
>   violence in their heads.
> I'll find the cure for cancer.

To see an array of colorful tetrahedron pictures, which you can screen during the next booktalk, go to http://slffea .sourceforge.net/tetrahedron.html.

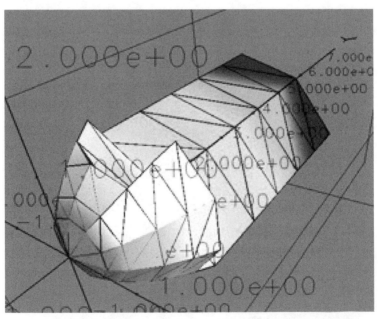

Tetrahedron designed by San Le, an artist and mechanical engineer.
Used with permission.

Some are *All of the Above,* by Shelley Pearsall. The middle school students in Mr. Collin's math class are mostly going nowhere fast. One day, out of desperation to shake things up, he challenges them to build a world-record-breaking tetrahedron. He begins an after-school math club that has only four consistent members: Sharice, who lives in a foster-care situation that goes beyond neglect; James, whose older brother's drug and gang leanings leave him with little to call family and only his artistic visions to give him hope; Rhondell, determinedly college-bound but with no real friends; and Marcel, who doesn't want to end up dishing out barbeque in his Vietnam-vet dad's carryout place. Then their months of labor are trashed by vandals, and "when you have a dream and you see it broken right in front of your eyes, it makes you think that maybe you never should have dreamed it in the first place. It makes you feel like not taking any risks or dreaming any dreams that are too big for you again, because you can't tell which ones to trust or what to believe in" (p. 172). Based on a true story, 16,384 pieces of rainbow-colored paper and the dreams of a teacher and his students come together to create a miracle of collaboration and hope.

Some dreams can come true if we all work hard at making them happen. After all, Martin Luther King Jr. said this in his speech at the Lincoln Memorial: "I have a dream that my four little children will one day live in a nation where they will not be judged by the color of their skin but by the content of their character."

> **Or show a film clip of Martin Luther King Jr. delivering those words.**
>
> **While the children are filing out, play the last few lines from the Everly Brothers song "All I Have to Do Is Dream," in which the word *dream* is repeated over and over.**

EXPANDING YOUR OPTIONS

Books for Use with Younger Audiences

Huey's falling-off-a-cliff dream made him feel like "[his] stomach climbed up into [his] head" (p. 3). He had the dream every night. His big brother, Julian, claimed that *his* dreams were scarier, but they didn't really bother him. Huey's parents tried to help, but it was his friend Gloria who came up with a plan to help even Julian face the dark after a bad dream. Read the first chapter of *The Stories Huey Tells,* by Ann Cameron, to lighten your bad-dream experiences. **(Suggested activity: Have audience members share scary dreams, or after the talk, ask listeners to write about their bad dreams.)**

When Julian and Huey can't decide what to get their father for his birthday, their friend Gloria suggests they ask him questions while he is asleep. "There are people who are sleep talkers . . . They always tell the truth. Afterwards, they don't remember that you asked them anything" (pp. 29–30). When they ask their sleeping father for his biggest dream, he answers, "Two snakes. Big ones" (p. 33). In *Julian, Dream Doctor,* by Ann Cameron, Julian and Huey are determined to deliver a birthday present their father will never forget!

"When you see a bee fly from someone's nose, good fortune will be yours." This Japanese saying comes true in a surprising way when Shin sees a bee fly from his friend Tasuke's nose while he is taking a nap. Tasuke dreams that he will find gold buried in a rich man's garden. But dreams go by contraries, and the gold is not what and where it seems. Read *The Bee and the Dream,* by Jan Freeman Long, to prove that "if good fortune is meant for you, no matter what happens it will be yours."

"In Kisana's village . . . every morning the women walked to a water hole an hour away to fetch water" (p. 1). Talk of a hidden spring was their only hope. In five days everyone was going to bring a special gift for the ancestors, and they were going to pray for water. Then Kisana saves a baby giraffe caught in a trap, and that night she dreams about a giraffe who says, "Because you saved me, I will save your people. I will show you where the hidden spring is . . . Find the fruit of the baobab tree, and you will find your spring" (pp. 8–9). The journey is long, dangerous (lions!), and full of disappointments. Read *Song of the Giraffe,* by Shannon K. Jacobs, to see how Kisana overcomes these obstacles and finds the spring, even though the last fruit of the baobab tree has been destroyed. **(Suggested activity: Show a picture of the unusual-looking baobab tree. For an impressive look at** the size of this tree, go to www.woodworkersauction.com/Trees/baobab.htm.)

Additional Books for Older Readers

Magpie Windwitch is alive because of a dream. She had been "*handmade by the Djinn King*" (p. 244) himself. And it's a good thing, because the fairies and, indeed all the world, are in need of a new champion. Blackbringer, the stuff of children's nightmares, has returned, but he is not just a story told to keep children from misbehaving. He is a "beast of night with flesh of smoke, wearing darkness like a cloak" (p. 275). And so Mags—with the help of the crows who had helped raise her; Talon, a fairy prince whose wings had never fully developed; and the Djinn King—must make the battle plans they dream come true. Read the first book in the Faeries of Dreamdark series, *Blackbringer,* by Laini Taylor, to see how they try to stop the unmaking of the world.

Dreams lead the former lost boys and Wendy (now all grown up) back to Neverland. After each dream they "woke to find leftovers in their beds—daggers or coils of rope, a pile of leaves or a hook" (p. 3). Something was not right! Read *Peter Pan in Scarlet,* by Geraldine McCaughrean, to see why as "Mrs. Wendy explained . . . dreams [were] leaking out of Neverland" (p. 6).

Chester Dumbello's mother is so embarrassing that he even lies and tells kids that she is his aunt. She manages the Dream Café, where she interprets dreams while drumming and singing, loudly. "One day a huge, white, one-eyed parrot with a blue head flies into the kitchen window of [the] restaurant" (p. 1). They name him Lorange. When Chester, in frustration with his lot, cries out, "Just get me out of [this loony bin]" (p. 28), he finds himself flying with Lorange to the planet of Alert, where sleep is forbidden. In fact it is a "five-letter word" (p. 31). When Chester is caught napping he is arrested on the charge of being a shuteye. To escape, he will need help from his mother, his strange M&M–popping neighbor Gower Pye, and, of course, Lorange. Read *The Shuteyes,* by Mary James, to find out why Chester is finally grateful to be home.

"Why [should] a house which felt like a house in so many ways
. . . feel so untrustworthy, so full of other people's dangerous spaces?"
(p. 58). **(Hold up *Dangerous Spaces*.)** Flora's house is haunted; it
is almost a family joke. But when her cousin Anthea moves in after
her parents' deaths, things change. Anthea is beautiful and "special"
because of her sorrow, and Flora resents her place in the family. Then
Anthea finds an old stereoscope and, in her dreams, she makes her way
to a world called Viridian, once imagined by Flora's great-uncle, Dead
Henry. Flora enters the dream world too and meets the family ghost,
who warns her that Anthea is being led by Dead Henry to a place from
which she will never return. Only Flora can reach out and bring her
back. Margaret Mahy knows how to send a chill down your spine!

In *The Serpent Gift,* the third book of the Shamer Chronicles, by
Lene Kaaberbol, Dina has already shown that she has some of her
mother's gift—the ability to see the truth in people's souls and shame
them into telling the truth. Now she meets her father for the first time.
Sezuan has the power to give people dreams, even to dream them to
death. Has Dina inherited his abilities too?

Thirteen-year-old Meryt-re lives in Egypt at a time when dreams
and the gods hold great power. As an orphan living with her aunt's
family, Meryt has little say in her life, but because she once predicted
a death, there are those who fear her. It is even said that Sekhmet, the
goddess of disease and destruction, controls her actions. When her
uncle wants her to marry someone she does not love, all she can do
is beg for time to consider and pray to the gods for help. When Meryt
starts having dreams she can't fully understand, she doesn't know who
to turn to until Teti, the village wise woman, helps her use *The Dream
Book,* an ancient guide to understanding dreams. Then her cousin
Baki falls deathly ill, and her uncle thinks Meryt has cursed his house.
Kicked out, she goes to stay with her friend Dedi. Next, Dedi's father
is accused of theft in a complex conspiracy with wide-ranging consequences for the whole town. Once again Meryt is set adrift. Teti is
sure that Meryt dreams true and that if she lets the gods lead her, she
will solve all the problems of her life and of those she has touched.
How will Meryt's dreams help her save Baki's life, prove Dedi's father's

innocence, and find out the truth about the man she is supposed to marry? Let Meryt's dreams take you back to ancient Egypt to find out in *Orphan of the Sun,* by Gill Harvey.

Fourteen-year-old Leven Thumps had been living a miserable life in Oklahoma with mean-spirited guardians who barely tolerated him. But then he met Clover, a "twelve-inch-tall furry creature with wet eyes and a huge smile who was supposed to serve him" (p. 53). Clover wouldn't tell him much other than that something was going to happen. *Leven Thumps and the Gateway to Foo,* by Obert Skye, takes Leven on a quest, accompanied by Clover; Winter, a girl whose home life rivals Leven's in its neglect and abuse; and Geth, the rightful ruler of the land of Foo, whose body is trapped in a toothpick. **(Hold up a toothpick.)** What is their quest? If they don't save the world of Foo, its destruction will mean the loss of all dreams in our world. No stress!

The Land of Foo sounds kind of ridiculous, but no more ridiculous than this limerick from *Bring Me All of Your Dreams,* edited by Nancy Larrick:

> There was an old man from Peru
>
> Who dreamed he was eating his shoe
>
> He woke in a fright
>
> In the middle of the night
>
> And found it was perfectly true.
>
> —Unknown author (p. 49)

Books for Use with Young Adult and Adult Audiences

Have you ever dreamed that you were in school in your underwear or being chased by a giant stalk of broccoli? How about falling off a cliff or being trapped? Psychologist and dream expert Patricia Garfield gives insights into dreams, what they mean, and how you control them. Dream on with *The Dream Book: A Young Person's Guide to Understanding Dreams!*

Additional Poems

"The Dream Keeper," by Langston Hughes, from *The Dream Keeper and Other Poems* (p. 2), is a classic poem that speaks to dreamers from every heritage.

Additional Music

"Any Dream Will Do" is the first song from *Joseph and the Amazing Technicolor Dreamcoat,* written by Andrew Lloyd Weber and Tim Rice. Listen to the soundtrack or screen the first part of the DVD that includes this song.

Additional Films and Videos

Screen the section toward the end of *The Wizard of Oz* in which Dorothy wakes up from her dream. You may also want to play Judy Garland singing "Somewhere Over the Rainbow."

Additional Websites

Use drop-down menus to record dreams and participate in a project at http://dreamer7.best.vwh.net/udreamkey_making.htm.

Find good questions and answers about dreams and dreaming at www.asdreams.org/subidxeduq_and_a.htm.

The website www.papermandalas.com/pages/natamerican/dream catcher.htm has templates for paper mandalas that younger children would enjoy coloring. The Native American dream catcher is used as an illustration.

Additional Activities

Dream Art Gallery

Revisit the Dream Art Gallery at http://dreamtalk.hypermart.net/gallery2005/index.htm. Look at the pictures by Bonnie Bisbee, Brenda Ferrimani, Evelyn Doll, Thomas J. Dragavon, and Donna

Fenstermaker. Then pass out art materials and have kids draw a picture of a dream that they have had and write a description to go with it.

Finger Painting

If you have the time and an appropriate physical setting, give each child a piece of colorful paper and a dollop of Dream Whip, and ask the group to finger-paint their own dreams. Older children don't often get the chance to finger-paint, and it can be great fun.

Poetry Writing

Use the book *Wishes, Lies, and Dreams: Teaching Children to Write Poetry,* by Kenneth Koch and Ron Padgett, to have the children write their own poetry about dreams.

Making Your Own Dream Catcher

Following the photographic instructions at www.dream-catchers.org/make-dream-catchers-kids.php will enable children to make simple but lovely dream catchers.

RESOURCES CITED

Books

Aiken, Joan. *Night Fall.* Holt, Rinehart and Winston, 1971.

Cameron, Ann. *Julian, Dream Doctor.* Random House, 1990.

———. *The Stories Huey Tells.* Alfred A. Knopf, 1995.

Garfield, Patricia L. *The Dream Book: A Young Person's Guide to Understanding Dreams.* Tundra Books, 2002.

Harvey, Gill. *Orphan of the Sun.* Bloomsbury Children's Books, 2006.

Holman, Felice. "The Child Who Cried." In *Bring Me All of Your Dreams,* edited by Nancy Larrick. M. Evans, 1980.

Hughes, Langston. "The Dream Keeper." *The Dream Keeper and Other Poems.* Alfred A. Knopf, 1994.

Jacobs, Shannon K. *Song of the Giraffe.* Little, Brown, 1991.

James, Mary. *The Shuteyes.* Scholastic, 1993.

Kaaberbol, Lene. *The Serpent Gift.* Henry Holt, 2006.

Kettelkamp, Larry. *Dreams.* Morrow, 1968.

Koch, Kenneth, and Ron Padgett. *Wishes, Lies, and Dreams: Teaching Children to Write Poetry.* Chelsea House, 1970.

Larrick, Nancy. *Bring Me All of Your Dreams: Poems.* M. Evans, 1980.

Long, Jan Freeman. *The Bee and the Dream: A Japanese Tale.* Dutton, 1996.

Lowry, Lois. *Gossamer.* Houghton Mifflin, 2006.

Mahy, Margaret. *Dangerous Spaces.* Viking, 1991.

McCaughrean, Geraldine. *Peter Pan in Scarlet.* Margaret K. McElderry, 2006.

McEwan, Ian. *The Daydreamer.* HarperCollins, 1994.

Pearsall, Shelley. *All of the Above: A Novel.* Little, Brown, 2006.

Silverstein, Shel. "Invitation." *Where the Sidewalk Ends.* HarperCollins, 2000.

Skye, Obert. *Leven Thumps and the Gateway to Foo.* Shadow Mountain, 2005.

Sleator, William. *Into the Dream.* Dutton, 1979.

Taylor, Laini. *Blackbringer.* G. P. Putnam's Sons, 2007.

Waldman, Neil. *Dream Makers: Young People Share Their Hopes and Aspirations.* Boyds Mills, 2003.

Wolitzer, Meg. *The Dream Book.* Greenwillow, 1986.

Music

Everly Brothers. "All I Have to Do Is Dream." *Everly Brothers' Best.* DCC Compact Classics, 2000.

Garland, Judy. "Somewhere Over the Rainbow." *The Wizard of Oz.* Rhino Movie Music—Turner Classic Movies Music, 1995.

The Mamas and the Papas. "Dream a Little Dream of Me." *Dream a Little Dream of Me: The Music of Mama Cass Elliot.* Universal, 2005.

The Monkees. "Daydream Believer." *Daydream Believer and Other Hits.* Rhino Flashback, 1998.

Osmond, Donny, and Maria Friedman. "Any Dream Will Do." *Joseph and the Amazing Technicolor Dreamcoat.* Universal Studios, 1999.

Wright, Gary. "Dream Weaver." *The Dream Weaver.* Warner Bros/ Wea, 1975.

Films and Videos

The Wizard of Oz. Directed by Victor Fleming. MGM, 1939.

Websites

Association for the Study of Dreams. "Dream Questions and Answers." www.asdreams.org/subidxeduq_and_a.htm.

Bearded Wolf. "Build a Dream Catcher." www.rivernen.ca/build _dc.htm.

Dream-Catchers.org. "Make a Dream Catcher for Kids." www.dream catchers.org/make-dream-catchers-kids.php.

Garfield, Patricia. The Universal Dream Key. http://dreamer7.best .vwh.net/udreamkey_making.htm.

International Association for the Study of Dreams (IASD). "IASD Dream Art Exhibition and Web Show." http://dreamtalk .hypermart.net/gallery2005/index.htm.

Kelley, Pat. "Native American Mandella Designs for Children to Color." www.papermandalas.com/pages/natamerican/dream catcher.htm.

Le, San. SLFFEA Tetrahedron Page. "Tetrahedron Images." http:// slffea.sourceforge.net/tetrahedron.html.

Sawdust Studios Enterprises. "Bar in a Baobab Tree: an amazing woodworking project." www.woodworkersauction.com/Trees/ baobab.htm.

6

Body Parts

*Missing, Extra,
and Just Plain
Strange*

Dr. Seuss didn't just write funny books. He actually wrote the story, screenplay, and lyrics for this feature film, *The 5,000 Fingers of Dr. T.*

> **Show a clip of the scene from *The 5,000 Fingers of Dr. T*, the musical fantasy written by Theodore Geisel, almost at the end of the film (between approximately 1:23:00 and 1:24:53), in which Dr. Terwilliker is just about to open his institute and is making a speech that starts with, "This is my day. Five thousand little fingers playing together on the piano." Try either the original 1953 version or the re-released 1991 DVD.**

Now let's find something else to do with those little fingers . . .

> **Recite the Shel Silverstein cautionary poem "Warning," from *Where the Sidewalk Ends*, p. 75, before giving your first book talk—they both take a humorous look at the implications of picking your nose!**

Harlan Atwater once told Kate that if for any reason a hair came out of her nose she would die within one week. This didn't sound right to Kate, but Harlan swore it was true, it was just not many people knew about it because it rarely happened. Nose hairs, he said, were attached very securely . . . anyway, she didn't think about it again until one Sunday afternoon in April, at 2:47 o'clock. She was sitting on her porch steps picking her nose and just happened to notice a tiny hair sticking out of the piece on the end of her finger. She sat there staring at it and she felt a little sick, because she was remembering what Harlan had said. How stupid, Kate thought as she rubbed her finger against the edge of the step. Harlan was just teasing me. But that was exactly what was worrying her. Harlan never teased . . . He was very smart and very serious . . . just then Kate saw Harlan . . . walk by . . . across the street . . .

"Hey Harlan, wait a minute . . . Do you remember what you told me about dying if you lose a nose hair?" Kate asked breathlessly.

"What?" said Harlan . . .

"You said a person would die if a nose hair came out. Was it true or were you lying?"

"Do I look like a liar?" asked Harlan. (pp. 3–6)

Spend *One April Vacation* (**hold up book**) with Kate while she waits to see what will happen in a week's time. Ruth Wallace-Brodeur will have you reexamining where you place your finger!

Would you like to see me remove the tip of my thumb?

Follow directions from *The Big Book of Magic Fun*, pp. 72–73, and have "Thumb Fun."

If you would like to try this trick with your friends, follow the instructions in *The Big Book of Magic Fun*, by Ian Keable-Elliott.

Talking about watching where you put your finger . . . This book tells you all you ever wanted to know (and even some things you might not have wanted to know) about the holes in your nose. Find out what happens when you pick your nose too hard and how your nose affects the rest of your body. This book gives all kinds of interesting information about the ways holes in the nose look, smell, and can even affect the way you talk. Let's try this exercise from the book: "Hold your nose and try saying, 'Na ne nu nay no, ma me moo may mo.'" The author of this book even asks his audience to look up at the ceiling so that the person reading his book aloud can see the holes in their noses. I'm not

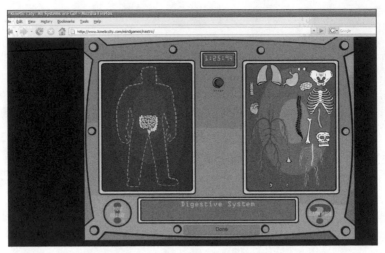

From "All Systems Go!" an educational module from the Kinetic City
project (www.kineticcity.com), produced by the AAAS, the Science Society
(all rights reserved). Used with permission.

sure that's a sight I'd want to see, would you? (**Tilt your head back
and show everyone the holes in your nose!**) When you read *The
Holes in Your Nose,* by Genichiro Yagyu, who knows (ha ha) what other
fascinating facts you might "pick up."

Now that you know where your nose is, let's see how quickly you
can find the rest of your body parts.

Try this next activity to the tune of "Side-by-Side."

Oh, Chester (**slap your chest**) have you heard (**cup hand to ear**)
    about Harry (**ruffle hair**)?
He just got back (**slap your back**) from the Army (**flap arm**).
I hear (**cup hand to ear**) he knows (**touch nose**) how to taste (**lick
    finger**) his toes (**touch toes**).
Hip Hip (**slap hips**) Hooray for Harry (**tousle hair one more time**)!

You may know your external anatomy, but do you know your
internal body parts as well? Let's take a quiz together!

**Go to the website www.sciencenetlinks.com/interactives/
systems.html, and ask at least one child to tell you which**

body parts match the system displayed. This can be surprisingly difficult.

Everyone who liked playing that game, please raise your hand.

Now, put them down out of harm's way because . . .

Barkbelly's adoptive father cuts his whole hand off accidentally while chopping wood. But, never mind! It grows back; Barkbelly is made entirely of wood and, along with having immense strength, he can regenerate his own body parts. Born from an egg and quickened in fire, he escaped slavery by accident and was adopted into a loving family. Although his first summer job prospect shows that his peculiar physical characteristics make him all but invincible against, for example, poisonous hedgehog spines, it does him no good after he is accused of murder. Barkbelly decides to run away to escape certain punishment by those who condemn his differences. Determined to search for his origins, he moves from job to job as he discovers his secret past, taking up with a circus and befriending some pirates. He finally makes his way to his homeland, where he learns the truth about his "real" family. Cat Weatherill's *Barkbelly* shows that even a heart in a chest made of wood needs a home.

But could Barkbelly do this?

How well do you know what your body can do? In Vicki Cobb and Kathy Darling's *Bet You Can't! Science Impossibilities to Fool You,* there are dozens of seemingly simple activities guaranteed to fail, complete with the scientific reasons to match. Here's one—all you need is a dollar bill and a wall:

> Bet you can't pick up a dollar bill that's right in front of you!
> The setup:
> Stand with your heels against a wall and your feet together. Place a dollar bill on the floor about a foot in front of your feet. Now . . . try to pick up the dollar without moving your feet or bending your knees.

If you want to find out why that dollar is as safe as if it were in a bank, finish reading page 14 in this book.

Don't try *this* trick, though!

Having a thirteen-pound iron rod shoot through your brain would ruin anyone's day. Phineas Gage was working on a railroad construction project in 1848 when he got a hole in his head that made medical history. While expected to die instantly, he lived another eleven years! If you want to be both fascinated and grossed out, read *Phineas Gage: A Gruesome but True Story about Brain Science,* by John Fleischman. Pictures available if you can handle them!

From real horrors to the kind that haunt your dreams, even if they aren't true . . .

"[Ezra] opened his mouth wide and leaned forward. We stared into a gaping, black hole. And then I realized that where his tongue should have been, there was nothing, nothing at all" (p. 18). Ezra is one of Weasel's victims. "Weasel . . . hunts by night and sleeps by day, and he kills not because he is hungry, but for the sheer sport of it" (p. 16). His job, according to the government, was to protect settlers moving into Ohio. Once he had driven the Native Americans out, he became a menace to everyone else too. In Cynthia DeFelice's *Weasel* read how eleven-year-old Nathan finds the courage to face a man who is pure evil.

A hand of glory.
Copyright © 2009 by Celia Yitzhak.
Used with permission.

Before the next booktalk, project the picture of a hand of glory from this website: www.mgol.net/Hand .jpg.

In *Hands On, Thumbs Up: Secret Handshakes, Fingerprints, Sign Languages, and More Handy Ways to Have Fun with Hands,* by Camilla Gryski, we find out that "a severed hand was a grisly part of a burglar's kit about 200 years ago. If the hand was taken from the right person—a hanged person was best—and prepared in the right way—preserved with saltpeter, salt and pepper, then dried in the sun—it was said to have magical powers. People believed this Hand of Glory could open locks and make thieves invisible. When the burglar lit a candle the hand was holding (or lit the fingers and thumb of the hand itself), all the people in the house were supposed to fall into a deeper sleep. If the thumb refused to catch fire, then someone in the house was awake . . . the flames on a Hand of Glory couldn't be blown out, or put out with water, lemonade or anything else you can think of—except milk" (p. 20).

See a photograph of a real hand of glory from a museum exhibit at www.citysnapper.org/chantrey/whitby/pics01/2002 0823012whitby.jpg.

When an American millionaire buys a Scottish castle for his daughter, Helen, and plans to move it to Texas, he insists that its ghosts be removed. "What kind of ghosts?" you might well ask. They included Krok Fullbelly, a Viking; Miss Spinks, a lovesick governess who was always soaking wet from throwing herself into the nearest body of water; an ancient vampire in a wheelchair; a five-year-old poltergeist; and a hellhound with an extra long body. Orphaned early, Alex, who was basically raised by this odd assortment of ghosts, agonizes over the decision to sell the family castle and tells his friends they must leave. When Alex is invited to the United States to oversee the reconstruction of the castle, little does he know that his faithful spirits have followed him. But then Helen is kidnapped, and even Alex and all his ghosts still need a hand of glory to foil the dastardly plot. Read Eva Ibbotson's *The Haunting of Granite Falls* to find out if they keep the upper hand!

The main character in this next book has a hard time keeping the upper hand. Let's find out why!

Throughout this booktalk you will call upon one or more volunteers to perform the specified actions.

Stretch your right arm high up to the sky. Now reach across the top of your head and touch your left ear . . . Do you see how [his/her] arm forms a kind of arch over [his/her] head like that? . . . Well, Georgie can't . . . It's not that Georgie's problems all started because he couldn't touch his left ear with his right hand, but the fact is that he can't. Even if he wanted to. You can let go of your ear now. (pp. 1–2)

The things about Andy are that he is Georgie's best friend and he is Italian and they have a dog-walking service together. **(Volunteer time.)**

> I need you to sit down on the floor . . . Now stretch your legs out in front of you, and pull your knees up to your chest. Wrap your arms around your legs, and rest your head on your knees for a second. Then take a couple of deep breaths, in and out. It's pretty relaxing to sit with your head on your knees like that, right? . . . You probably think that it's no big deal, that everyone can do it. Well, Georgie can't . . . Even if he wanted to. You can get up now. (pp. 7–8)

The things about Russ are that he is tall and "can make 11 free throws in a row" (p. 44), and he might be Andy's new best friend instead of Georgie. **(More volunteering: choose someone wearing shoes with laces.)**

> Untie both your shoes . . . Done? Good. Now, I want you to hold your hands out in front of you and curl your fingers, so you can't see past your knuckles. Then, with your fingers still curled up tight like that, I want you to tie your shoes. I'm serious. Tie your shoes . . . [I know.] It's really hard. Anyway, that's why Georgie's shoes are Velcro. Just thought you should know. You can straighten out your fingers now. (p. 67)

And retie your shoes. The thing about Georgie's parents is that they are musicians with a real symphony orchestra. Oh, by the way, Georgie can't play any musical instruments, not even with popsicle sticks taped to his fingers. The thing specifically about Georgie's mom is that she is pregnant. The thing about this unborn "Godzilla" (p. 45) baby is that someday soon it will be taller than Georgie.

The thing about Jeanie, other than that her nickname is "Jeanie the Meanie" (p. 2), is that ever since kindergarten she has been messing with Georgie. She even made up this song: "Georgie Porgie puddin' and pie / Too bad you're only two feet high" (p. 2).

Now that Andy and Russ are partners, Georgie and Jeanie have to work together to do a report on Abraham Lincoln, and she has signed Georgie up to *be* Abraham Lincoln in front of the whole school. One of the things about Georgie is that he is 42 inches tall; he is growing, but very slowly . . . and you know Abraham Lincoln was the tallest president. There are a few other things about Georgie you still don't know yet, but you will if you read *The Thing about Georgie,* by Lisa Graff.

Georgie may not be able to do many of the experiments from the *Super Science Book of Our Bodies,* by Graham Peacock and Terry Hudson, but we can. Here's how arm muscles really operate!

> **Try the simple science experiment on page 9, which shows how arm muscles work. Make sure to prepare in advance— all you need is some cardboard, five paper fasteners, and two rubber bands.**

Well, that's how your arm works, but the man known as the Arm in Nancy Farmer's *The Ear, the Eye, and the Arm* is not typical at all. In fact all three detectives show the mutations that occur when plutonium from a nuclear power plant gets in the drinking water. The Ear can "hear a bat burp in the basement; [the Eye] can see a gnat's navel on a foggy night" (p. 46); and the Arm can feel the world's emotions without even touching anything. He had a "long black snaky arm [that] far outreached anyone else's . . . the tips of his fingers were slightly sticky" (p. 46). And in the year 2194 they will need all of their unusual powers to find the three kidnapped children of Zimbabwe's chief of security.

Ear, Eye, Arm . . . Bend down and find your feet. (**Do so!**)

> **Play the song "Your Feet's Too Big," a jazz classic by Ada Benson and Fred Fisher that was performed by Fats Waller on the sound track of *Ain't Misbehavin',* or show and play it at the same time from YouTube: www.youtube.com/ watch?v=in1eK3x1PBI.**

If you are over five feet twelve inches tall (that's more than six feet!) before you are twelve years old, you're bound to get teased. And when your feet are so big you get nicknamed "Suitcase," the world can be a very unfair and unfriendly place. Alexander "Xander" Bingham prefers to draw, but his father wants him to excel in sports. How can he not trip over his size 13 shoes, succeed in baseball and basketball, *and* win the city art contest? Only Mildred Pitts Walter's *Suitcase* can draw you the whole picture without striking out.

Don't put your foot in your mouth; instead let's put all those parts to work. (**Ask audience members to stand up and then lead them through the following traditional song. The song is available on Mike Whitla's CD** *Early Morning Knee-Slappin' Tunes.* **A printable version can be found at www.teachervision.fen.com/performing arts/printable/6786.html.**)

> Head and shoulders, baby! One! Two! Three!
> Head and shoulders, baby! One! Two! Three!
> Head and shoulders, head and shoulders, head and shoulders,
>   baby! One! Two! Three!
> Shoulders, knees, baby! One! Two! Three!
> Shoulders, knees, baby! One! Two! Three!
> Shoulders, knees, shoulders, knees, shoulders, knees, baby!
>   One! Two! Three!
> Knees and ankles, baby! One! Two! Three!
> Knees and ankles, baby! One! Two! Three!
> Knees and ankles, knees and toes, knees and toes, baby! One!
>   Two! Three!

Let's do it again to see how fast you can do the song and the motions!

Now let's do one final exercise . . . As soon as I am done speaking, walk over, look carefully, and using only your thumb and forefinger (**mime a pincer effect**), select the book that you want to borrow today. Oh, by the way, if you don't return the book on time, the hand of glory will be put to good use . . .

EXPANDING YOUR OPTIONS

Books for Use with Younger Audiences

The village of New Auckland in Canada has not one person, but two who can remove their thumbs. "Little Charlie's thumb was cut off when he was working on a construction project . . . the doctors reattached it" (p. 23) . . . but he can take it off at will. All he has to do is unscrew the "tiny flesh-colored screws [that hold it] in place" (p. 24). If you have a strong stomach, perhaps you too can learn how to remove your thumb, just like Leon, who inherits *The Thumb in the Box,* by Ken Roberts. **(Suggested activity: Follow directions from *The Big Book of Magic Fun*, pp. 72–73, and have "Thumb Fun" again.)**

When Roxie Warbler's "magnificent, wonderful, round, pink, sugar-bowl handle ears" (p. 102) catch the attention of the worst bullies in the school, she knows she is going to need her Uncle Dangerfoot's favorite resource, *Lord Thistlebottom's Book of Pitfalls and How to Survive Them* (p. 2), to deal with them . . . especially if she is stranded with those same bullies on a desert island. Prick up your ears to catch all the details in *Roxie and the Hooligans,* by Phyllis Reynolds Naylor. **(Suggested activity: Tie in the following earlobe website: www .windows.ucar.edu/tour/link=/earth/Life/genetics_puzzle.html. Project the website and ask audience members to discover what types of earlobes are attached to their heads! Or you can also sing the song "Do Your Ears Hang Low?")**

In Warwick Hutton's *The Nose Tree* three good-hearted former soldiers befriend a little man they meet in the woods and are rewarded for their kindness with a cloak that grants wishes, a purse that is always full of gold, and a horn that can call an army when blown. When a witch princess tricks them out of their magic gifts, the little man shows them how apples from a nose tree can make her nose grow long enough to hang out the castle window. Which would you choose—the magic gifts or a nose you can blow yourself, instead of having someone wipe it for you a block away?

Willie McPhee is a fine bagpiper indeed, but times are hard and few people can pay for his playing. Struggling in the cold of winter with his shoes more holes than leather, he comes upon a dead and well-frozen body wearing a fine pair of boots. He doesn't hesitate to try to "borrow" the boots, but as he attempts to pull them off the body, the feet break off at the ankles! Well, Willie isn't too particular, so he takes the boots with the frozen feet inside and continues on to the nearest farmhouse, where he offers his musical skills for a hot meal and a place to sleep. The farmer rudely sends him to the barn to sleep with his cow. When the cow's warmth defrosts the feet, Willie decides to play a trick on the farmer he will never forget. Have you ever heard of a man-eating cow? Read *Cold Feet,* by Cynthia DeFelice, and feel the shivers start down at your toes.

From the beginning Clayton Bates was a dancing fool, but how can you tap-dance with only one leg? Clayton lost his leg in a terrible mill accident when he was only twelve years old. No one thought he would ever walk again, but he danced with his crutches. When his uncle carved him a wooden peg leg, he created his own tap-dance style that took him from vaudeville straight to TV, the movies, and a live performance in front of the king and queen of England. *Knockin' on Wood,* by Lynn Barasch, will have you tapping your feet in honor of Peg Leg Bates. **(Suggested activity: Search the Internet for a clip of Clayton "Peg Leg" Bates in action on the Ed Sullivan show. You may find one on YouTube.)**

If you were left with a three-eyed witch who had one daughter with one eye and another daughter with two eyes one on top of the other, and your own eyes were, oddly enough, placed above and to the sides of your nose **(demonstrate all locations)**, you might feel a bit, well, different. Larissa's father forfeited her freedom when he was captured by the witch. Her only companion is a little white talking goat who helps her perform the impossible tasks the witch sets for her. Eric Kimmel's Ukrainian tale *One Eye, Two Eyes, Three Eyes* will make you look twice and not even blink once until you see how Larissa wins her independence. **(Suggested activity: Have the children draw faces that have extraneous features.)**

In olden days, when people fought with swords, "it was not unusual for a person who had lost his nose in a duel or in battle to wear a gold or silver replacement" (copyright page). Assunta's two sisters are pretty, silly creatures who, one at a time, go off to work for *Count Silvernose* (**hold up book**) without a backward glance. Did no one ever tell them not to go off with a stranger? When he comes for plain Assunta, saying that her sisters have died, she agrees to go, but, unbeknownst to him, only to seek revenge. Upon arrival at his castle she smells something fishy indeed. Thanks to author Eric Kimmel, her payback is worthy of the most vile, vicious villains in all of Italian folklore.

Up in Yukon Territory, when you tell a tall tale it is called "yanking your toes." Gabe claims that Trapper Jack's big toe is "inside an empty tobacco tin behind the bar at the Sourdough Saloon." Josh doesn't believe him, so they go find Trapper Jack to see for themselves. Is that shriveled-up thing really his, and if so, why does he still have ten toes? Read *The True Story of Trapper Jack's Left Big Toe,* by Ian Wallace, for a toe-tally (pardon me!) satisfying tall tale that may indeed be true! (**Suggested activity: Read the author's note at the end of the book for a rather gross and unusual custom of toe kissing and drinking in the cold north.**)

Grandpa's false teeth have been stolen. Everyone in town is a suspect. Everyone who doesn't smile broadly at all times seems to be hiding something. The strain of mistrust begins to tell on the community, so they take up a collection to buy Grandpa new teeth. Who is the real culprit? Read *Grandpa's Teeth,* by Rod Clement. Sometimes the solution to a great mystery is right under your nose.

Perhaps *This Book Bites! Or, Why Your Mouth Is More Than Just a Hole in Your Head,* by Timothy Gower, will have some clues . . .

Let's play Dental Detective. All you will need is a "pack of chewing gum (in the stick form, preferably sugarless), a plate or paper towel, [and] three [volunteers]" (p. 46). Here is the gum (**hold up the pack of gum**), here is the paper plate/towel (**hold that up too**), and now all I need is three volunteers. Who would like to volunteer? (**Choose the volunteers.**) Come stand next to me and take this piece of gum. (**Give each volunteer a stick of gum and turn your back.**) While I'm not looking, unwrap your "gum and gently bite into it the long way—just hard enough to make an impression with [your] teeth. Then . . . put [your] gum on the plate, in no special order" (p. 46), but make sure to remember which is yours. (**Turn back around.**) Please open your mouths. I am now going to study your teeth to see if I can identify which piece of gum is yours. (**Study their teeth. Try to match the bite marks to each volunteer's teeth.**) "Crime does not pay—especially if you can't keep your teeth to yourself. Several notorious murderers have been convicted, in part, because they bit their victims. The police were able to make an impression from the bite mark and match it to the suspect's teeth" (pp. 46–47). Open wide and don't be afraid to bite into this book full of information!

Ned Mouse is in prison for protesting the government's unjust treatment of mice. Although he "would give [his] right arm to be out of [jail]" (p. 9), none of his escape plans work. Until, that is, he decides to literally give up more than just his right arm. Read Tim Wynne-Jones's *Ned Mouse Breaks Away* for the most heartless, brainless, and creative getaway in all of prison history.

When Gretchen injured her spine, she was able to pull herself around with her front legs inside the house, but the "custom-made, upholstered, padded cart" her family got her made her just about as mobile as any dachshund would want to be when braving the world outside. Now nothing can stop *Gretchen the Bicycle Dog,* by Anita Heyman. Ride along for a dog's-eye view of the challenges and possibilities when you've got wheels!

Additional Books for Older Readers

Whoever heard of a ballet dancer with flat feet? But *To Dance* is all Siena ever wanted. Her mother enrolled her in a dance class when she was six, and by the time she saw the Bolshoi Ballet at age nine, she was hooked. Siena lived, breathed, and dreamed ballet. Here is the magic of dance told in both words and pictures and, sometimes, with just pictures, as the music and movement fill the spaces of Siena's life. Read Siena Cherson Siegel's life story, *To Dance: A Memoir,* a graphic novel that will make anyone feel what it's like to dance in a first pair of toe shoes.

Primrose Squarp is an orphan, her parents lost at sea. Primrose herself is not convinced they are truly gone. While living with her uncle, she finds comfort eating at a restaurant called "The Girl on the Red Swing [that] serve[s] everything on a waffle" (p. 16; recipes included) and finds herself losing various parts of her anatomy. Yes, she got her little toe cut off when a truck driver almost ran her over. He felt so awful that "he kept sending chocolates. His wife made me chocolate-covered cashews . . . and they looked just like baby toes" (p. 71). Then the tip of her ring finger goes in a fishing accident. Quick! Read Polly Horvath's story *Everything on a Waffle* before Primrose loses any other body parts or relatives, or eats too many waffles!

> **Follow this with the Body Food game from *Mudluscious: Stories and Activities Featuring Food for Preschool Children*, by Janet Kay Irving and Roberta H. Currie. (You may need to explain what taffy is first, though; and don't worry, older kids like this challenge too!) Start . . . slowly. Then, after a few times through, get faster and faster . . .**

Banana peel,	**(Put arms above head, then lower to sides.)**
Taffy pull,	**(Clap and spread arms wide.)**
Pretzel twist,	**(Cross arms in front of chest.)**
Jelly roll!	**(Roll hands over each other.)** (p. 87)

"Ben mostly drew his left hand, because he was right-handed . . . It was hard to get a hand to look like a hand and not some weird sea creature or a row of sausages. When his drawing was going well, he often worked until his mother had to turn off the kitchen light and steer him toward his room. On those nights, he knew, the way he knew his name, that he truly was an artist" (p. 152). But the hand he is drawing is missing a finger. "When Benjamin Hunter was two and a half years old, the little finger on his left hand was cut off in an accident" (p. 13). His uncle Ian was babysitting, but since the accident neither of his parents had mentioned his uncle. On the eve of Ben's twelfth birthday, Uncle Ian invites him to visit him in Oregon. Ben, the artist and nephew, goes on a journey of discovery in Kevin Henkes's *The Birthday Room*.

Willy's eyes "glowed like stained glass windows with sunlight shining through them" (p. 6). Guy and Sarah immediately became great good friends with Willy when they met him on vacation in 1906. Why, they even tried to smuggle him home in their suitcase (after drilling air holes that would let him breathe) so they could see him after vacation was over! Every year thereafter vacation brought a deepening friendship between the three children. But eight years later, the reality that Willy was an Austrian and that Guy and Sarah were from France meant that they were on opposite sides of what we now call World War I. Fighting in the trenches, Guy finds an injured soldier with "dark eyes, deep set and almond shaped, eyes filled with pain. *Eyes like Willy's* . . ." (p. 117). Juanita Havill gives us a vision of friendship that crosses all boundaries and doesn't blink in the face of the horrors of war.

Not everyone has six toes on each foot, but orphan Lucy Wickwright, servant to the Baron of Cant's daughter, Pauline, does. She is a loyal partner in all sorts of schemes that Pauline devises, like catapulting wet underwear into the castle courtyard just as a royal execution is taking place. But it is Lucy who takes the blame when they get caught. When Lucy and Pauline uncover a serious rebellion, they must give much more thought to trying to foil the evil scheme than to their usual pranks. And when Lucy's "busy-toed" (*Secret,* p. 82) feet turn out to be proof of a very different heritage, the plot thickens. **(Try using Cheryl Bardoe's biography *Gregor Mendel: The Friar Who Grew Peas* to figure out why genetics explains who the real heir to Castle Cant is.)** Read both *The Secret of Castle Cant* and *Escape from Castle Cant,* by K. P. Bath, to find out why chewing gum can be the root of all evil and what the difference is between being "plain-toed, tongue-toed, and busy-toed" (*Escape,* p. 75).

Norm loses his hand in the meat grinder at his father's butcher shop. Now he has to relearn everything, like cutting his meat and tying his shoes—this is in 1946, after all, before there was Velcro. And what about baseball? Everyone keeps suggesting that he try another sport, but Norm is convinced that with enough practice, he can return to pitching, fielding, and hitting. After all, there was once a one-handed outfielder named Pete Gray in the major leagues. Then there is the racing bike he wants so badly. It has hand brakes, but one brake isn't enough to stop him. It's a good thing that Norm has his loyal and crazy best friend, Leon, for support and a mom who, believe it or not, refuses to make things easy for him. She still makes him take out the garbage! Read *One-Handed Catch,* by MJ Auch, to see how Norm figures out how to succeed in spite of the hand life has dealt him.

And don't forget Betsy Byars's Herculeah Jones Mystery series. Herculeah's hair serves as an early-warning system for danger; when it frizzes, watch out!

Books for Use with Young Adult and Adult Audiences

Have you ever wanted to change the way your face looks? In the Uglies series, Scott Westerfeld describes a society where everyone has an operation at the age of sixteen to become pretty. But when Tally learns that the operation affects her personality as well as her appearance, she decides to forgo it. This is not acceptable. Trying to keep one step ahead of the Department of Special Circumstances brings Tally into contact with unusual people who still have their own faces, the Rusties. Even if you're a fan of *Nip/Tuck,* you might think twice after reading *Uglies, Pretties, Specials,* and *Extras.*

Does anyone need a spare elbow? What about a new head? On the planet Treason, people who are injured can regrow replacement body parts. Some unlucky few become "radical regeneratives" (p. 6); when puberty ends, their bodies just keep growing extra parts, whether or not they are needed. Body-part harvesting can be big business, but it's not fun if you are one of the "rads." It could mean living through an ongoing series of operations to remove your extra dangling limbs. It is *not* something to look forward to. Meet Lanik, a member of the elite Mueller family, who expected to inherit Treason's leadership but whose plans change drastically when he discovers that he is a rad. Whether you need a leg up or not, you will enjoy *Treason,* by Orson Scott Card.

Additional Music

Play the refrain "Hands across the water, heads across the sky" from Paul McCartney's song "Uncle Albert/Admiral Halsey."

Listen to Marian Anderson sing "He's Got the Whole World in His Hands."

Additional Films and Videos

How long do you think you could keep your hand on a pickup truck? In 1995, a Nissan dealership held a contest to see who could keep his or her hand on a truck the longest when allowed only one five-minute break per hour. Twenty-three people took the challenge and were filmed in the funny, quirky documentary *Hands on a Hard Body*.

View a variety of tattoos, piercings, and body alterations resulting from cosmetic surgery in *Here's Looking at You: A Celebration of Body Art*. **(Suggested for use with young adult and adult audiences only.)**

Additional Websites

Here is an online find-the-word game about body parts: www.apples4 theteacher.com/word-finds/parts-of-the-body.html. Invite children to try this site on their own at home, in the library, or on the classroom computer.

Play artificial anatomy on this website run by the Smithsonian, the National Museum of American History, and the Belering Center: http:// americanhistory.si.edu/anatomy/bodyparts/nma03_bodyparts.html.

Additional Activities

If you have a small group or would like to select a small group of volunteers from your larger group, try the game Knots from *The New Games Book,* by the New Games Foundation. Ask players to form a circle and put their hands inside of the circle. With one hand, each player should grab onto to the hand of someone else—as long as it is *not* the person standing immediately to the right or left. With the other hand, each player should then hold a different person's hand. Once there are no free hands, the players must try to untangle themselves—without dropping hands—to form one big circle. For a more challenging game, try doing this without talking!

Have the group sing the following song several times, each time filling in the blanks with different body parts:

Sticky, sticky, sticky bubble gum, bubble gum, bubble gum.

Sticky, sticky, sticky bubble gum, stick your _____ to your _____.

UNSTICK! P-U-L-L

When singing this fun song, start with easy body connections, such as "Stick your finger to your nose," but work your way up to the impossible, such as "Stick your elbow to your ear." Watch the contortions multiply! A good recording can be found at www.nancymusic.com/Stickyplay.htm.

RESOURCES CITED

Books

Auch, MJ. *One-Handed Catch*. Henry Holt, 2006.

Barasch, Lynne. *Knockin' on Wood*. Lee and Low Books, 2004.

Bardoe, Cheryl. *Gregor Mendel: The Friar Who Grew Peas*. Abrams, 2006.

Bath, K. P. *The Secret of Castle Cant*. Little, Brown, 2004.

———. *Escape from Castle Cant*. Little, Brown, 2006.

Byars, Betsy. Herculeah Jones Mystery series. Viking, Puffin Books.

Card, Orson Scott. *Treason*. Orb, 2006.

Clement, Rod. *Grandpa's Teeth*. HarperCollins, 1997.

Cobb, Vicki, and Kathy Darling. *Bet You Can't! Science Impossibilities to Fool You*. Lothrop, Lee and Shepard, 1980.

DeFelice, Cynthia. *Cold Feet*. DK Children, 2000.

———. *Weasel*. Macmillan, 1990.

Farmer, Nancy. *The Ear, the Eye, and the Arm*. Orchard Books, 1994.

Fleischman, John. *Phineas Gage: A Gruesome but True Story about Brain Science*. Houghton Mifflin, 2002.

Gower, Timothy. *This Book Bites! Or, Why Your Mouth Is More Than Just a Hole in Your Head*. Planet Dexter, 1999.

Graff, Lisa. *The Thing about Georgie*. Laura Geringer Books, 2006.

Gryski, Camilla. *Hands On, Thumbs Up: Secret Handshakes, Fingerprints, Sign Languages and More Handy Ways to Have Fun with Hands.* Addison-Wesley, 1991.

Havill, Juanita. *Eyes Like Willy's.* HarperCollins, 2004.

Henkes, Kevin. *The Birthday Room.* Greenwillow, 1999.

Heyman, Anita. *Gretchen the Bicycle Dog.* Dutton, 2003.

Horvath, Polly. *Everything on a Waffle.* Farrar, Straus and Giroux, 2001.

Hutton, Warwick. *The Nose Tree.* Atheneum, 1981.

Ibbotson, Eva. *The Haunting of Granite Falls.* Dutton, 2004.

Irving, Janet Kay, and Roberta H. Currie. *Mudluscious: Stories and Activities Featuring Food for Preschool Children.* Libraries Unlimited, 1986.

Keable-Elliott, Ian. *The Big Book of Magic Fun.* Barrons Educational Series, 2005.

Kimmel, Eric A. *Count Silvernose.* Holiday House, 1996.

———. *One Eye, Two Eyes, Three Eyes: A Hutzul Tale.* Holiday House, 1996.

Naylor, Phyllis Reynolds. *Roxie and the Hooligans.* Atheneum, 2006.

New Games Foundation. *The New Games Book.* Dolphin Books, 1976.

Peacock, Graham, and Terry Hudson. *Super Science Book of Our Bodies.* Thomson Learning, 1993.

Roberts, Ken. *The Thumb in the Box.* Groundwood Books, 2002.

Siegel, Siena Cherson. *To Dance: A Memoir.* Aladdin Paperbacks, 2006.

Silverstein, Shel. "Warning." *Where the Sidewalk Ends.* Harper and Row, 1974.

Wallace, Ian. *The True Story of Trapper Jack's Left Big Toe.* Roaring Brook, 2002.

Wallace-Brodeur, Ruth. *One April Vacation.* Atheneum, 1981.

Walter, Mildred Pitts. *Suitcase.* Lothrop, Lee and Shepard, 1999.

Weatherill, Cat. *Barkbelly.* Alfred A. Knopf, 2006.

Westerfeld, Scott. *Uglies.* Simon Pulse, 2005.

———. *Pretties.* Simon Pulse, 2005.

———. *Specials.* Simon Pulse, 2006.

———. *Extras.* Simon Pulse, 2007.

Wynne-Jones, Tim. *Ned Mouse Breaks Away.* Douglas and McIntyre, 2003.

Yagyu, Genichiro. *The Holes in Your Nose.* Trans. Amanda Mayer Stinchecum. Kane/Miller Book Publishers, 1994.

Music

Anderson, Marian. "He's Got the Whole World in His Hands." *American Anthem.* RCA, 2001.

McCartney, Paul. "Uncle Albert/Admiral Halsey." *Wingspan.* EMI Records, 2001.

Traditional. "Do Your Ears Hang Low?"

———. "Head and Shoulders." (Can be found on Mike Whitla's *Early Morning Knee-Slappin' Tunes,* Rainbow Songs, 2005).

———. "Oh, Chester."

Waller, Fats. "Your Feet's Too Big." *The Very Best of Fats Waller.* Collector's Choice, 2000.

Films and Videos

The 5,000 Fingers of Dr. T. Directed by Roy Rowland. Stanley Kramer Productions, 1953.

Hands on a Hard Body: The Documentary. Directed by S. R. Bindler. J. K. Livin Productions, 1997.

Here's Looking at You: A Celebration of Body Art. Directed by Dick Bartlett. WGBH Boston, 2005.

Websites

AAAS, the Science Society. "All Systems Go!" www.sciencenetlinks .com/interactives/systems.html. See also www.kineticcity.com.

Apples4theteacher.com. "Printable Parts of the Body Word Search."
www.apples4theteacher.com/word-finds/parts-of-the-body.html.

Chantrey, Kay. "Hand of Glory." www.citysnapper.org/chantrey/
whitby/pics01/20020823012whitby.jpg.

Gardiner, Lisa. "Solve the Genetic Puzzle!" www.windows.ucar.edu/
tour/link=/earth/Life/genetics_puzzle.html.

Mother Goose on the Loose. "Hand." www.mgol.net/Hands.jpg.

National Museum of American History, Smithsonian Institution.
"Body Parts." http://americanhistory.si.edu/anatomy/bodyparts/
nma03_bodyparts.html.

Stewart, Nancy. "Children's Music by Nancy Stewart—Song of the
Month, August 2003—Sticky Bubblegum." www.nancymusic
.com/Stickyplay.htm.

TeacherVision.com. "Head and Shoulders, Baby! One! Two! Three!"
www.teachervision.fen.com/performing-arts/printable/6786
.html.

Waller, Fats. "Your Feet's Too Big." www.youtube.com/watch?v
=in1eK3x1PBI.

CHAPTER 7

Art

*Every Picture Tells a Story;
Every Story Draws a Picture*

Start out by playing a recording of the song "Vincent" while projecting Van Gogh's famous self-portrait on the screen. The song can be found on the *American Pie* album, by Don McLean, or you can play it from Rhapsody Online at http:// play.rhapsody.com/donmclean/americanpie/vincent/.

Has anyone heard of Vincent van Gogh? The song that you just heard is about one of his paintings, called *Starry Night*. He's probably the most famous painter who sold only one painting while he was alive! He also cut off his ear, but that's another story. Van Gogh was from Holland, where tulips bloom, people wear wooden shoes (or at least they used to), and windmills whirl.

Project on the screen a picture of a working Dutch windmill. You can find many on either Google Video or YouTube.

"If you're dead, it's not my fault" (p. 27) are the words that first greet Lizzy after she falls from a whirling windmill wing while trying to save a boy who had been hanging there himself. Twelve-year-old Lizzy is always getting into trouble. Orphaned only a month, she has been taken in by the Brewsters, who in 1608 have escaped to Holland, like her parents, to practice their religion freely. But Master Brewster is strict, and Lizzy can't seem to please him. She knows she must earn

Amsterdam windmill. Photograph © www.molendatabase.nl
(Bert Bulder). Used with permission.

her keep, so she takes a job cooking for the very family who owns the windmill. While there she forges a connection with a trouble-making, school-skipping eight-year-old boy who won't tell her his old-fashioned name but amazes her with his artistic talent. While trying to prove her cooking skills, Lizzy finds herself trying to keep her best friend from running off to sea to escape his life working on Stink Alley. They call it that because the cloth dyed there must be soaked in *urine* (**hold your**

nose while you say this) so the colors will set. She is also caught up in a threat from spies who are trying to capture Master Brewster and take him back to England for punishment. When Master Brewster sees the boy's sketches of Lizzy in some *very* undignified positions, he demands that she quit her job. Now Lizzie must decide which direction her life will take. And as for the boy? His own prediction that he will become the "most famous artist in the whole world" (p. 174) isn't far off the mark. I won't tell you what his real name is. You'll have to read *Stink Alley,* by Jamie Gilson, to find it out. Here's a hint . . . This is his face.

Show www.ibiblio.org/wm/paint/auth/rembrandt/self/self-1629 .jpg. (It is Rembrandt.)

In *Randall's Wall,* by Carol Fenner, there is a different kind of smell. It comes from Randall Lord in the fifth-grade classroom. "Even though his father had shaved his hair off and the . . . lice were gone, no one sat near Randall. 'He never takes a bath,' whispered Tiffany . . . 'He sleeps in his clothes and then comes to school,' hissed Lynda" (p. 2). Randall first found his wall in the middle of first grade, when he began to notice that "he could make other children go away just by getting close to them" (p. 5). Randall's wall grew higher after the incident with his picture. Randall loved to draw, and in the beginning his first-grade teacher praised his work, even though she never gave him hugs like she gave the other children. But the day he drew the picture of his mother when she was pregnant with his little brother, the teacher threw his picture away and made him sit in the hall. From that day on Randall hid behind his wall. But then comes fifth grade, and when Randall stands up to the two boys who have given Jean Neary a black eye, she actually thanks him and he gets the courage to ask her, "How do you get them to play? . . . How do you get them to stay on the swings [near you]? How do you get them to give you a black eye?" (p. 29) Jean is a girl who thinks for herself, and she decides Randall has friend potential. All he needs is a bath, even if she has to give him one herself. Once he is clean, though, Randall's wall won't be able to protect him anymore from the rejection and disgust he has come to expect. Is he ready to share his drawings with a world that can now really see him?

Here's someone who *is* ready to share her drawings . . . Twelve-year-old Annie finds comfort in the pulse of running, the steady same-ness of the way her bare feet slap the ground. She runs for the joy of it, not like her moody friend Max, who runs with the goal of eventually escaping the small-town life he says he hates. But the running also helps Annie in a year of wonder and change. Her mother is pregnant, and her beloved grandfather is becoming more and more forgetful. She is also finding the artist inside herself in an unusual drawing assign-ment. She must draw an apple one hundred times; she must get to know the apple, the "un-ordinary-ness" (p. 62) of it. Annie . . .

> love[s] drawing
>
> because if feels like running
>
> in your mind
>
> and on a blank page
>
> a picture appears
>
> straight out of your mind
>
> a phantom treasure (pp. 33–34)

With the hundredth apple you will see what she has discovered in the essence of the apple's *Heartbeat,* by Sharon Creech.

Have an apple with you and take a bite out of it as you hold up the book. Make sure to show the front cover with the picture of the apple, and then show the back cover with the picture of the core.

Apples come in many different colors. There are red ones, green ones, yellow ones, and a number of variations. Here is a quiz we can take about color and reading that has some very interesting results. First, I need a volunteer to read out loud. (**Choose someone.**) The experiment we are about to do illustrates the Stroop effect.

View http://faculty.washington.edu/chudler/java/ready.html. Invite the volunteer to read the words and colors aloud while you write down the time it took. Then ask the volun-

teer to read where the names of the colors are written in different colors while you time how long it takes. It should take longer. Do the comparison to see how your volunteer rates with others. Give out the website address above and encourage the children to investigate on their own afterward.

Although fun, this experiment won't work for anyone who can't read; the meanings of the words don't interfere with the names of the colors if you can't read . . . However, reading makes all the difference in *Saffy's Angel,* by Hilary McKay. "Other families had lullabies, but the Cassons had [always] fallen to sleep to lists of colors" (p. 1). When Saffron was finally able to read, she climbed up to look at the color chart in the kitchen. Because it was for a painter, it had every color an artist would ever need, with every possible variation of red, blue, and yellow; each tiny color had its name written below. Saffron found her brother, Indigo; the baby, Rose; and Caddy, the eldest—actually Cadmium—but she couldn't find her own name. Because their artist mother, Eve, had used the chart to name them all, Saffron finally learns that she was adopted after her birth mother, Eve's sister, was killed in a car crash in Italy. When Saffy is thirteen their grandfather dies, and he leaves something special for each of the grandchildren. For Saffy it is a stone angel in a garden, location unknown. Finding it will not be easy, but with the help of a very strong-willed new friend and her exceedingly unconventional family, Saffy finds her angel, a memento of her past; then, and only then, can she let her true color shine. How it comes about is a pleasure waiting for you to uncover.

But where do all the color names on the painter's chart come from? In *Naming Colors,* by Ariane Dewey, you'll find that "puce is the color of a flea's tummy" (p. 30), that cobalt blue is named for a trickster creature from German folklore called a Kobold, and that saffron (yes, it really is a color even though it wasn't on the Cassons' chart) comes from a flower, a crocus!

In addition to describing colors, words can also describe feelings. Let's make a caricature by using descriptions rather than paintbrushes!

Illustration from "Create a Caricature" (www.magixl.com/heads/
caricature-femme/). Used with permission from Magixl.com.

**Go to "You Are the Artist" at www.magixl.com/heads/poir
.html. Choose either the male or the female face, and use
the drop-down menus to create a caricature.**

Hollis Woods inspires worry, anger, and surprise. She longs for a
family. All the foster homes she has ever been in seem to run together.
She is a twelve-year-old "mountain of trouble" (p. 140) to her social
worker and every foster parent she has run away from. But now she has
found a safe harbor with Josie, a whimsical, elderly artist. The social
worker doesn't know it, but it's obvious to Hollis that Josie is forgetful and getting more so every day. But Hollis is learning so much from
Josie. Hollis looks at the world in terms of how she would draw it—the
kind of paper, brush, paint, and colors to choose. "Drawing is a language . . . [she has] to learn to speak" (p. 148). When the social worker

finally realizes that Josie isn't capable of being a foster parent, Hollis decides to run once again, but this time she takes Josie with her. And where does she go in the dead of winter? She breaks into the summer home of the one family that made her feel welcome and loved, the family she left because she felt she had torn them apart. Hollis can't seem to bury the memories of the happy times that ended in disaster. But "sometimes we learn from our drawings; things are there that we thought we didn't know" (p. 150). Read *The Pictures of Hollis Woods,* by Patricia Reilly Giff, and find the truth shining through Hollis's gift, the truth that will find her a home at last.

Hollis's life changed from one foster family to another. Let's watch as famous women's faces morph from one famous piece of artwork into another in "500 Years of Female Portraits in Western Art."

View www.youtube.com/watch?v=nUDIoN-_Hxs.

The most famous painting in the world is the *Mona Lisa,* by Leonardo da Vinci; I'm sure you saw her face just now among all the others. Da Vinci was a magnificent artist, but he was also a very secretive person. He studied human anatomy by performing illegal autopsies; he wrote his notes backward so others couldn't read them unless they had a mirror. (**Show an example of this by going to the Boston Museum of Science's website, www.mos.org/sln/Leonardo/write .html, where you can type in a phrase and have it shown to you in Leonardo's style.**) You can read more facts (mixed in with some good gossip) about him and many other artists in *Lives of the Artists: Masterpieces, Messes (and What the Neighbors Thought),* by Kathleen Krull. In fact his mirror writing could be very useful if you wanted to commit a crime with an accomplice or two . . .

Before the next booktalk, display a picture of the Teenage Mutant Ninja Turtles from www.ybfree.com/11TMNT1.jpg.

It's the perfect crime. No, not the time when the *Mona Lisa* was actually stolen and the authorities didn't even know it was gone for two whole days! The crime I'm talking about takes place in a tiny town in the country of Wales. Dylan is the only boy in the town. He loves soccer (but there's no one to play with) and cars (he keeps track of every vehicle that stops at his family's struggling gas station), but he doesn't know one thing about art. Then "the entire collection of paintings from the National Gallery of Art gets moved to a secret and secure location" (p. 57) at the top of the mountain overlooking his town. Dylan accidentally convinces the man in charge, Lester, that he is a brilliant authority on art when he tells him that he has named his two chickens Michelangelo and Donatello and makes comments about Leonardo and Raphael too. Of course *we* know he's talking about the names of the Teenage Mutant Ninja Turtles, but Lester is convinced that he is referring to real artists. Lester begins to invite Dylan up to look at the paintings because he thinks Dylan can really appreciate them. However, as the rest of the town sees the paintings too, they start to affect everyone in very peculiar and surprising ways. One painting makes Dylan's beautiful older sister lock herself in her room for two weeks, and another makes his mother buy fifty umbrellas. There is even a picture that makes the local butcher take a chainsaw to a mural of Elvis Presley! Meanwhile Dylan's younger sister, Minnie, who longs to be a criminal mastermind, is determined to steal a painting. "Big brothers are supposed to stop little sisters becoming involved in major robberies, aren't they?" (p. 296). Read Frank Cottrell Boyce's *Framed* to see how the right painting at the right time can "make you feel like nothing else matters" (p. 294), even if you'd rather be playing soccer.

> **Before the next booktalk, display a picture of a pentomino from www.fractalus.com/kerry/articles/uf-drawing/pentomino.gif.**

What "if you fell into a puzzle and couldn't get out" (p. 98)? Sixth graders Petra and Calder accidentally find themselves deeply involved in the theft of a valuable painting by the Dutch artist Johannes Vermeer called *A Lady Writing*. Calder likes to play with a set of mathematical puzzle pieces called pentominoes, like the ones on the screen. Petra is fascinated by a book that "collect[s] 294 records of showers of living things," like worms and frogs falling from the sky. Both of these interests play an important part in unraveling the clues. For, unlike most art thieves, this one seems to have stolen not for money but to prove that some of Vermeer's paintings were not actually his own work. In a series of letters to the newspapers the thief threatens to destroy the priceless work of art if museums around the world don't change the labels on their paintings. The artist "Picasso [once] said that art is a lie, but a lie that tells the truth" (p. 36). By the time you have finished reading *Chasing Vermeer,* by Blue Balliett, you will be dazzled by coincidence and confounded by the very truths that lie within the imagination and the realm of possibility. Oh yes, be on the lookout for clues in the pictures too!

Talking about clues in artwork, have your ever seen an optical illusion? This is art that is a visual game. Have a look at this optical illusion and see how many faces you can find.

View www.thebluething.com/media/Three-Faces/.

Of the thirty-four paintings in the auction, none are optical illusions, but sixteen are fakes. With just hours to go before the art auction begins, *you* must help find the crooked art dealer who is trying to pass them off as genuine. Four gangs of art forgers are at work. Each forger hides a symbol somewhere in the painting copied. You have all the clues at your fingertips. In the auction catalog you will find actual photos and descriptions of the real masterpieces; compare them with the items for sale and make your deductions. Investigate *Art Auction Mystery,* by Anna Nilsen, to see if you are cut out to be an art-fraud detective!

Now, let's see if you can detect how I do this magic trick. I can tell the color of a crayon even when I am blindfolded. Can I have a volunteer to come up and tie this blindfold around my eyes?

Follow instructions on pages 126 and 127 of Ian Keable-Elliott's *The Big Book of Magic Fun,* and do the magic trick. You will need a number of different colored crayons and a bandana or blindfold for this.

And remember, every picture tells a story, don't it? (**This is ungrammatical on purpose—it is a direct quote from the song below.**)

End by playing the final line that is repeated over and over in Rod Stewart's song "Every Picture Tells a Story."

EXPANDING YOUR OPTIONS

Books for Use with Younger Audiences

Imagine your father is the most famous artist in the history of the world. Titus, son of Rembrandt van Rijn, could honestly say this. He takes us into his world and helps us see how his father looked at the world . . . and how the world looked at him. Long the favorite artist in Amsterdam, the center of the Dutch artistic community, Rembrandt became unpopular when fashions changed. He went into debt, but he never compromised the honesty of his painting. There really was a Titus; just by showing you his father's paintings, he will demonstrate that "there is beauty in everything" (p. 10), even the old and ugly. Read and really look at *Rembrandt and Titus: Artist and Son,* by Madeleine Comora.

When James's mom was pregnant with twins she had to stay off her feet, so James was sent from his small town in North Carolina to visit his aunt and uncle in New York City. His uncle Romie was an artist, a big, bald-headed, grim-looking man who didn't have much time for James because he was getting ready for an art show. Aunt Nanette made up for it, though. She took James to see everything: the Empire State Building, Central Park, the Statue of Liberty, and Harlem, where Uncle Romie had grown up. Although James wasn't going to be home for his birthday, he was sure Aunt Nanette would make things special for him. But then Aunt Nanette's own aunt died and she had to go out of town for her funeral; James was left to celebrate his birthday with Uncle Romie. In *Me and Uncle Romie,* by Claire Hartfield, you will meet Romare Bearden, a man who could take scraps of this and bits and pieces of that and turn them all into a picture story. Read how Uncle Romie made James's birthday unforgettable and learn how to make your own story collage. (**Suggested activity: Give children a chance to make a collage or have one that you've already made so they can have a wonderful tactile experience. Or go to the website www.metmuseum.org/explore/the_block/guide.html. Begin the online guided tour with Romare Bearden and stop after two of his pictures are shown.**)

Tom Miller's life was filled with color from the very start. His "Mom paint[ed the] whole back yard . . . the tables orange, the benches red, the brick walk pink, and the fence bright green. The little side chairs were painted purple and yellow. She even painted the clothesline black to make it disappear." By the time Tom was ten, he and his big brother loved looking for "good stuff" in other people's castoff odds and ends. The day he found the dented coal scuttle, Tom knew he had something special. He turned that old black bucket into a magnificent bird. Tom was on his way to becoming an artist. He went to art school in another part of his hometown, Baltimore, where, at first, he felt out of place. But he continued to paint with the rich, glowing colors that were important to him. He eventually taught his students in the public schools that even with very few supplies they could still make art. "If you have no scissors, tear the paper. If you don't have the color you want in your paintbox, find the color in a magazine and paste it on your picture." Read *Can a Coal Scuttle Fly?* by Camay Calloway Murphy, to find out how "hope, love, hard work, and color" made a joyful artist whose wonderful paintings, murals, and painted furniture will make you tickled to see them. (**Suggested activity: Show the photo of Tom Miller from www.carlclark.net/tom.html and keep it displayed on the screen during your booktalk. Click on the picture of the cabinet on the website to enlarge it and use it as an example of Tom Miller's artwork.**)

"One day, Willy's papa put a painting in a golden frame in [his] shop window. It was called 'The Lady,' and she was so beautiful that when you smiled at her, she smiled back! 'Some things,' Willy's papa would remind him as they gazed upon The Lady's secret smile, 'are as precious as friends.'" Max's father must have agreed because when he came into the shop he bought *The Lady*. While their fathers were discussing the purchase, Willy, shy though he was, and Max got to know each other. Soon they became inseparable. It didn't matter to Willy that Max's family was Jewish, although he knew that there were people that were angry with the Jews. All that mattered was that Willy and Max would be friends forever. Soon, however, the war came to their town in Belgium and threatening soldiers came into Max's house, stealing anything they liked. One officer noticed *The Lady* and grimly declared he would be back for it. That night Max and his family left town, but first they brought the picture to Willy's family and asked them to hide it for them. Willy found what he thought was the perfect place to hide it, but then the soldiers came to *their* house because they had been seen talking to Jews. Ultimately Willy's hiding place turns out to be too good. Read *Willy and Max: A Holocaust Story,* by Amy Littlesugar, to find out what happens to *The Lady* and to Willy and Max's forever friendship.

Additional Books for Older Readers

Arduino comes from a family of tailors, but sewing fine seams is not for him. When he gets the courage to tell his father that he wants to be a painter, his father gives him one chance. Apprenticed to the famous artist Maestro Cosimo di Forli, Arduino must spend his time grinding pigments, cleaning the studio, fetching water, and enduring greasy, rancid food. The other apprentices are suspicious of him, and the maestro himself is impatient, demanding, and cruel. Is this the way to become an artist? Then Arduino discovers the unspeakable secret in the maestro's attic. If he tells the truth, he will have to give up his career before it has even begun. Travel back to the Italian Renaissance in Pilar Molina Llorente's *The Apprentice,* where dreams can come true with hard work and courage.

Eleven-year-old Noi and her fifteen-year-old sister, Ting, help their grandmother as she paints the delicate silk umbrellas she sells at market. "Ting was content to mix paint and wash brushes, but Noi always longed to paint. Sometimes [her grandmother] let her paint simple things like leaves. Noi's whole body came alive with the shades of green. Her hands felt magical when she guided the brush" (p. 2). But her family's life is hard, and Ting has to take a job making radios in a factory to help earn money. It is a mind-numbing job. Will this be Noi's fate when she leaves school next year? When Grandmother's hands hurt too much to paint, Noi begins to help her out; to every umbrella she paints she adds a little bit of herself. Read *Silk Umbrellas,* by Carolyn Marsden, and visit a Thailand where Noi's destiny lies either in the colors that animate her brush or in mindless technology.

Was Georgia named after the state her mother came from or after the painter Georgia O'Keeffe, "who painted flowers and bones so that you see them fresh, like they are secret worlds you can lose yourself inside if the real one gets too bad" (p. 15)? The real world is hard for Georgia. Her mother died when she was seven, and her father still turns away from anything that reminds him of her, even the artistic gift that Georgia has inherited. The school counselor gives Georgia a diary in which to write thoughts to her mother. Georgia plunges ahead, filling all the white pages with her day-to-day routine—walking her mother's old dog, her job at the horse farm, school, and her new (and only) friend Tiffany, wealthy, athletic, and ever the optimist. Then Georgia turns thirteen and receives a membership in the Brandywine River Museum from an anonymous donor. She doesn't tell her father, but several times a week she visits the museum and loses herself in the work of three generations of famous artists, N. C., Andrew, and Jamie Wyeth. Inspired by what she sees, she applies for an art scholarship, also behind her father's back. While Georgia becomes more involved in her drawing, Tiffany starts drifting into behavior that endangers her life. Can Georgia find the courage to help her friend and tell her father the truth so that she can have the freedom to "dance [her] fingers across a blank page and make something come alive" (p. 23)? Find out by putting together all the *Pieces of Georgia,* by Jen Bryant!

For the first time Kate's family is not going to spend the summer at her grandparents' farm. Her oldest sister is having a baby, her other sister is starting a new job, and her father is in need of serious back surgery, so Kate accepts an invitation from family friends, the Langs, to stay with them at the beach. It's Kate's first visit to the ocean, and she has to adjust to life in a small town, to the rhythm of the Lang family's life, and especially to their impulsive daughter, Alison. She and Alison sign up to take a beginning drawing class; their teacher finds ways to help them make magical transformations with just a few lines and a few simple techniques. Then, on a whim, Kate buys a fire-damaged painting at an auction. She gets instructions on how to clean it, and as she slowly, carefully uncovers the art beneath the soot, she gets caught up in the mystery of who painted it and whether she has bought a stolen masterpiece. As Kate learns in art class, "perspective is the effect of your point of view on everything you see" (p. 97). Read *The Vanishing Point,* by Susan Bonners, and discover with Kate the differences between "what the mind knows [and what] . . . the eye sees" (p. 266).

Books for Use with Young Adult and Adult Audiences

Did you ever visit a museum and wonder who the people were in the paintings? How the models were chosen and how they felt about being painted? Griet is a sixteen-year-old Dutch girl who found a job as a maid in the home of the artist Johannes Vermeer. When he notices the teen helping out with his children and household, he asks for her assistance running errands and mixing paints. She loves the chance to develop her own artistic talent, but trouble develops when Vermeer begins to paint her portrait. What do you think happens when his jealous wife discovers Griet wearing *her* pearl earrings in the painting? Although no one knows the real story behind the actual painting of the *Girl with a Pearl Earring,* Tracy Chevalier shows a believable and intriguing possibility of what might have been. **(Suggested activity: If it is available, you may want to screen a clip from the DVD of *Girl with a Pearl Earring*.)**

Although ignored by his father and bullied by the other students at his boarding/prep school, Carlton Dunne is a talented teen who draws a successful comic series. No one realizes that Carlton is the artist, because he avoids meeting his publisher in person and pretends to be a much older adult over the phone. When his father is kidnapped by a rival Scottish clan, Carlton sneaks out of school, sets off on a rescue adventure, and meets the girl of his dreams . . . or is she? Although this is not a graphic novel, snippets of Carlton's comics are included. His comic hero, Signy the Superbad, echoes his own story. Read *Drawing a Blank; or, How I Tried to Solve a Mystery, End a Feud, and Land the Girl of My Dreams,* by Daniel Ehrenhaft, to meet a boy who has never stood up for himself but finds the courage, like the superheroes he draws, to travel to Scotland to look for his dad and a lost dagger, the cause of an ancient Scottish feud. If you like a fast-paced story with a not-so-perfect hero, this story is for you!

Additional Websites

This site hosts a game of online Pictionary for budding artists: www .isketch.net.

Create a picture with different-colored grains of sand at "Sand Art": http://lovethosekids.com:80/playgrnd/sandart.htm.

If the children are intrigued by the Stroop effect, give out the website address http://faculty.washington.edu/chudler/words.html, and encourage the children to investigate on their own.

Cézanne's astonishing apple quiz from the Metropolitan Museum of Art can be found at www.metmuseum.org/explore/cezannes_apples/quiz.html.

RESOURCES CITED

Books

Balliett, Blue. *Chasing Vermeer.* Scholastic, 2004.

Bonners, Susan. *The Vanishing Point.* Farrar, Straus and Giroux, 2005.

Bryant, Jen. *Pieces of Georgia.* Alfred A. Knopf, 2006.

Chevalier, Tracy. *Girl with a Pearl Earring.* Plume, 2005.

Comora, Madeleine. *Rembrandt and Titus: Artist and Son.* Fulcrum, 2005.

Cottrell Boyce, Frank. *Framed.* HarperCollins, 2005.

Creech, Sharon. *Heartbeat.* Joanna Cotler Books, 2004.

Dewey, Ariane. *Naming Colors.* HarperCollins, 1995.

Ehrenhaft, Daniel, and Trevor Ristow. *Drawing a Blank; or, How I Tried to Solve a Mystery, End a Feud, and Land the Girl of My Dreams.* Harper Teen, 2006.

Fenner, Carol. *Randall's Wall.* Margaret K. McElderry, 1991.

Giff, Patricia Reilly. *The Pictures of Hollis Woods.* Wendy Lamb Books, 2002.

Gilson, Jamie. *Stink Alley.* HarperCollins, 2002.

Hartfield, Claire. *Me and Uncle Romie.* Dial, 2002.

Keable-Elliott, Ian. *The Big Book of Magic Fun.* Barron's Educational Series, 2005.

Krull, Kathleen. *Lives of the Artists: Masterpieces, Messes (and What the Neighbors Thought).* Harcourt Brace, 1995.

Littlesugar, Amy. *Willy and Max: A Holocaust Story.* Philomel, 2006.

Llorente, Pilar Molina. *The Apprentice.* Farrar, Straus and Giroux, 1993.

Marsden, Carolyn. *Silk Umbrellas.* Candlewick, 2004.

McKay, Hilary. *Saffy's Angel.* Margaret K. McElderry, 2002.

Murphy, Camay Calloway. *Can a Coal Scuttle Fly?* Maryland Historical Society, 1996.

Nilsen, Anna. *Art Auction Mystery.* Kingfisher, 2005.

Music

Stewart, Rod. "Every Picture Tells a Story." *Every Picture Tells a Story.* Mercury Records, 1971.

McLean, Don. "Vincent." *American Pie.* United Artists, 1971.

Films and Videos

Girl with a Pearl Earring. Directed by Peter Webber. Lions Gate Films, 2003.

Websites

Chudler, Eric H. Neuroscience for Kids—Colors, Colors. "Interactive Stroop Effect Experiment." http://faculty.washington.edu/chudler/java/ready.html.

Clark, Carl. "Tom Miller." www.carlclark.net/tom.html.

iSketch. www.isketch.net.

Johnson, Philip Scott. "500 Years of Female Portraits in Western Art." www.youtube.com/watch?v=nUDIoN-_Hxs.

LoveThoseKids.com. "Sand Art." http://lovethosekids.com:80/playgrnd/sandart.htm.

Magixl. "You Are the Artist." www.magixl.com/heads/poir.html.

Metropolitan Museum of Art. "Cézanne's Astonishing Apples." www.metmuseum.org/explore/cezannes_apples/quiz.html.

————. "Romare Bearden: Let's Walk the Block." www.metmuseum.org/explore/the_block/guide.html.

Mitchell, Kerry. Articles: "Using Ultra Fractal as a Drawing Tool—Pentominoes." www.fractalus.com/kerry/articles/uf-drawing/pentomino.gif.

Museum of Science, Boston. "Send in a Phrase—Leonardo: Right to Left." www.mos.org/sln/Leonardo/write.html.

Pioch, Nicolas. WebMuseum, Paris: Rembrandt. Self-Portraits. "Self Portrait 1629." September 19, 2002. www.ibiblio.org/wm/paint/auth/rembrandt/self/self-1629.jpg.

RealNetworks. Rhapsody. "Vincent." http://play.rhapsody.com/donmclean/americanpie/vincent/.

TheBlueThing.com. "Three Faces." www.thebluething.com/media/Three-Faces/.

Walford, Jennifer. Picture of the Teenage Mutant Ninja Turtles. www.ybfree.com/11TMNT1.jpg.

Mummies

Mum's the Word!

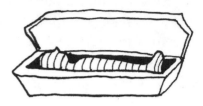

When the program begins, set a gruesome mood by screening the trailer for the original 1932 film *The Mummy* from www.dtrailer.com/watch/m/the-mummy/.

Have you ever seen a mummy? Not just a cartoon mummy or a mummy in a movie, but a real mummy? Mummies are dead people or animals that have gone through an ancient process to preserve their bodies after death. Some of their inside organs are removed, and a special formula helps to keep their skin from decomposing. Once the procedure has been done, the mummy is wrapped in cloth to preserve it. Read Joyce Milton's *Mummies* for a simple explanation that doesn't leave out any gruesome details.

Does anyone know how we got the word *mummy*? Would you believe me if I told you that people used to eat ground-up mummies because they thought it was a healing medicine? *Mummeia* was the name of a tarry substance that "just naturally oozed out of the ground. During the Middle Ages people used mummeia as medicine. They thought it would cure almost anything from headaches to diseases . . . ; there were lots of ancient preserved human bodies . . . [that] looked like they were coated with mummeia because they were usually black from a coating of hardened resin. So, creative businessmen started grinding up ancient bodies to sell as medicine. The name 'mummeia' which later became 'mummy' came to mean any preserved body" (p. 39). This book has great photos and a recipe for making your own mummifying solutions. You can follow directions for making a mummified apple head. All you budding scientists, check inside for X-rays and CT scans of mummies in *Outside and Inside Mummies,* by Sandra Markle.

After Matthew Martin's teacher makes him chair of the Mummy Committee for the class Egypt project, he wants to show how responsible he is. So when Brian Bruno gets picked to be the life-size model for the mummy, Matthew wants to be extra careful that nothing goes wrong. "Brian . . . stands on the porch . . . a giant garbage bag with a hole in the middle for his head has been placed over his body so that only his feet, neck, and head show. A bathing cap covers his ears and red hair. Vaseline is smeared over his freckled face. Joshua is holding a Milky Way bar to his mouth so that he can nibble on it. We're going to have to stop feeding you soon, Matthew informs him. We're almost up to your chest area and what if you start to choke? We won't be able to do the Heimlich maneuver on you because you'll be covered up with plaster . . . As they [continue to] work, Joshua holds up a glass of soda and a straw so that Brian can sip . . . [Brian says] Would you guys please hurry up? I'm beginning to have trouble standing here. This is getting heavy . . . and I think I'm going to have to go to the bathroom soon" (pp. 9–11). But even though they are finished wrapping Brian in plaster gauze, the plan to cut it off him and put it back together won't work if it is too thick to cut in the first place! *Make like a Tree and Leave,* by Paula Danziger, will make you want to get all wrapped up in a mummy project of your own!

OK, all you mummies watch and learn . . . Pay attention to this; you're going to be doing this in just a little while . . .

> **Play an excerpt from the Bangles' "Walk like an Egyptian" from their official website: www.thebangles.com/extras/ extras.asp. Start playing the music video near the end, at 2:46 minutes, where the singer repeats the words "Walk like an Egyptian" twice. End after the Statue of Liberty**

walks like an Egyptian. Or show the entire video of this song (with music and great shots of even more people walking like Egyptians). If you can't access the Bangles' website, try looking for this clip on YouTube.

Now that you've seen how to walk like an Egyptian, you can play the mummy-wrap game:

Divide the group into teams of three to five players. If space is tight, choose only three teams and let the other children watch. Give each team a roll of toilet paper. (Try to get the kind that does not break easily.) Ask each team to choose one teammate to be the mummy. Explain that you are giving the teams a three-minute time limit and that when you say "Go," the mummy stands or sits as requested by the team. Team members then wrap the mummy as quickly as they can in toilet paper (although remind them to leave mouth space for breathing). When time is up, see which mummy has been covered up the most. That team wins.

Many people think that mummies just come from Egypt, but mummies have been found in many other places, including Mexico and Peru. In *Discovering the Inca Ice Maiden,* by John Reinhard, you can see actual photos of mummies in Peru, frozen and preserved from the time of the Inca Empire. Have a look at this website to see mummies from around the world.

View http://community.webshots.com/album/3314781ANq DzZZgIg.

Because there is no one alive today who was an active participant in Egyptian mummy making, we need to rely on scientific methods and the deciphering of hieroglyphic writing to tell us how it was done. Scientific methods can also come in handy when solving crimes. In *The Bone Detectives,* by Donna M. Jackson, a woman is found dead and no one knows who murdered her. The Bone Detectives use science to discover the murderer.

You can also find out about mummies from a mummy himself. Maggie discovers that her yard-sale find is a real mummy of a cat, complete with golden toes. It turns out to be from the missing tomb of "Thutmose the Utmost" (p. 30). When Maggie actually meets the boy king's Ka—the part of the spirit that "stays . . . with the person's mummy and looks exactly like that person did during life" (p. 36)—he explains how he died of a scorpion's sting and how he

> lay in the embalmer's tent for sixty days . . . First they cut out my internal organs, and they took out my brain through my nose . . . They take out your liver . . . your lungs . . . and your intestines . . . and each of your organs gets preserved in its own special jar . . . Your heart stays in your body, though. Then after sixty days, you're done . . . I had the very best perfumes and salts, and I am wrapped in the most exquisitely woven linens . . . jewels wound in with my shroud cloths, because of course I am the pharaoh. (p. 85)

But Thutmose is afraid to go through the Underworld, where "there are . . . pits full of reptiles, each with seven heads and . . . bodies covered with scorpions" (p. 113). His uncle was supposed to teach him the correct answers to questions asked in the Underworld's Hall of Judgment, but he never got a chance to finish his lessons before Thutmose was killed. Maggie finds herself trying to help Thutmose move on, using spells she is taught by a man who tells her he is the curator at the museum. But although the spells start out working for her, she soon finds that she is being controlled as well. Can she help Thutmose and still survive herself? Read Catherine Dexter's *The Gilded Cat* with its solution to a murder that occurred thousands of years in the past.

And here are some pictures of actual cat mummies.

View the website of the McClung Museum at http://mcclung museum.utk.edu/research/renotes/rn-20txt.htm. Scroll down to see three different pictures of cat mummies and masks.

Do you have a pet cat at home? Do you ever feel that the cat thinks he's your master and you only exist to take care of his needs? The people in ancient Egypt considered cats to be sacred animals. They worshipped their cats, and held them in such high regard that when they died, some of them were also made into mummies. In Kelly Trumble's *Cat Mummies,* you can see real examples of cat mummies.

> *Warning:* **This website is not for the tender-hearted! Visit http: //kids.summum.us to see animals that have been mummified. There is background music to go along with this site.**

Summum is an organization that performs mummifications today. Some people want to preserve their pets when they die, so they ask Summum to mummify their birds, dogs, and cats. Close your eyes if this might make you sad.

The Egyptians didn't just mummify cats either; here's a different kind of animal mummy in a more modern-day story. The six children in Zilpha Keatley Snyder's *The Egypt Game* find a deserted storage area where they can pretend to be all things Egyptian. They wear costumes, hold sacred ceremonies, and use secret hieroglyphic codes. When Elizabeth's pet parakeet, Petey, is killed by a cat, they decide to have a Ceremony for the Dead to help her through her period of mourning. Their information about mummification, however, isn't quite complete. "Ken, who was assigned to bring the oil, [couldn't decide what kind to use:] crankcase, sewing machine, polyunsaturated, or bicycle" (p. 138); and when they discuss "'taking out the guts' [Elizabeth] felt so strongly about 'cutting holes in Petey' . . . that it was decided to dispense with that part of the procedure . . . Toby was disappointed, but . . . there was another way. Poor people, who couldn't afford the more expensive process, had been simply soaked in brine" (p. 139). "In the next few days, [after soaking,] he was anointed with spices and perfume and wrapped in thin strips of oil-soaked cloth, and laid to rest with a supply of birdseed . . . in a smallish pyramid made of old bricks" (p. 140). While the children become more and more involved in their private ancient world, the real world intrudes: a child is murdered and their secret hiding place is no longer safe.

How do people go about finding mummies, anyway? You can't just buy them in a grocery store! Generally, archeologists search through ancient structures to see if burial rooms can be found that

Egyptian Mummy, Third Intermediate, 945–722 BC, the Walters Art
Museum, Baltimore. Used with permission.

have mummies in them. *Egyptian Tombs,* by Jeanne Bendick, has photographs of an actual pyramid, and you can see this tomb room in
which a mummy was found **(display pp. 26–27)**.

   With the Internet, we can enter King Tut's virtual tomb and have a
look around. But be careful—don't let the curse descend upon you!

   View www.kingtutone.com/tutankhamun/enter/.

   Now it's time to put what you learned about walking like an Egyptian into practice with music! Everyone stand up and practice walking
the Egyptian way with right arm bent up and left arm bent down.

   **Play Steve Martin's "King Tut" from his *Wild and Crazy
   Guy* album, and, of course, encourage everyone to dance.
   The hysterically funny lyrics can be found on the Steve**

Martin website at www.stevemartin.com/world_of_steve/ television/kingtut.php. The song was written and performed by Steve Martin for a *Saturday Night Live* skit, backed by the Toot Uncommons. If you can find the video clip of this, it is worth watching. If you're singing a capella, try the first and last verses.

Perhaps you have heard stories about mummies that come with curses. Some people think that if you open a tomb with a mummy in it, you will be subject to terrible luck. It is said that there was a carving on Tutankhamen's tomb cursing those who disturbed the peace of the pharaoh. Despite that, the archeologist Howard Carter and his crew entered the tomb. As the first death occurred, all the lights in Egypt's capital, Cairo, went out. Many mysterious deaths followed. This convinced people that the curse was real, and it even inspired the creation of horror films like *The Mummy*. To find out many more mindblowing mummifying facts, read *Mysteries of the Past: Mummies,* by Paul Mason.

Or, if you want to hear about more curses, try *Curse of the Pharaohs* **(hold up the book)**. Like Indiana Jones, Dr. Zahi Hawass is an adventurer and explorer as well as an archaeologist. He's had harrowing reallife experiences. Once, he discovered some beautiful statues in a hidden tomb of a man named Inty-Shedu, but on the day that Dr. Hawass was going to announce his discovery, there was an earthquake, so the announcement was postponed. On the new date of the announcement, Dr. Hawass had a heart attack! Despite this, he lived to tell the tale. On another occasion he found a group of mummies and transported the boy and girl mummies to a museum in Cairo. **(Show photos on pp. 80, 81.)** After that, he started having nightmares. "The golden children had followed me to California, and they were haunting my dreams. I was having so much trouble sleeping that I could hardly wake up in the morning. The children, still wrapped in the white linen we had used to transport them to the museum, reached out their arms to me, trying to grab me. Another mummy we had put on display, a woman, also appeared in my dreams, looking at me with pleading eyes . . . In mid-

July . . . the children visited my dreams almost every night. In my worst nightmare, the little girl came for me. She reached her slender white arms toward me and tried to wrap them around my throat" (pp. 75, 79). After the nightmares got worse, Dr. Hawass "realized [he] could not ignore the golden children any more . . . [He] forced [himself] to remember every detail of the children's faces [and] suddenly [he] understood what they had been trying to tell him." To discover the way Dr. Hawass appeased the spirits of the mummies and see some more incredible photographs of mummies, tombs, and ancient Egypt, read *Curse of the Pharaohs,* by Dr. Zahi Hawass.

Now, I don't want you to have nightmares from all this talk about mummies, but I am going to read you one more thing: a poem called "The Mummy," from Jack Prelutsky's *The Headless Horseman Rides Tonight.* (**Read the poem aloud, pp. 6, 8.**)

To get away from the gruesome side of mummies for a while, let's tell some riddles.

Read riddles from *Mummy Riddles,* by Katy Hall and Lisa Eisenberg.

What did the mummy say when he looked in the mirror? "Who's the pharaoh of them all?" (p. 30)

What do you say about a terrible mummy movie? "It really sphinx!" (p. 22)

What do mummies like to listen to? "Wrap" music! (p. 46)

Here is a website with more lame mummy jokes.

View this site and tell some of the jokes: http://kids.sum mum.us/mummybear/jokes/.

What do you call a mummy who eats cookies in bed? A crummy mummy.

What happens to a mummy who eats too many archaeologists? It gets a mummy ache.

Plan at least ten days in advance, and mummify your own hotdog to show to the children.

What if you want to make your own mummy? You don't even need to find a dead body! All you need is this book **(hold up *Exploratopia*, by Pat Murphy, Ellen Macaulay, and the staff of the Exploratorium in San Francisco)** and a hotdog. Since we aren't allowed to bring real mummies into a library or school, I can do the next best thing . . . show you a hotdog mummy. **(Show the hotdog that you have mummified ahead of time.)** Or you can make one yourself, and I guarantee, it won't be beautiful. In *Exploratopia* there is an experiment called "Mind Your Mummy." Follow the directions and you can create your own mummy of King Oscar (pp. 97–99). Anyone want a bite? Actually, I wouldn't advise eating the hotdog afterward . . . you might get a mummy ache, too! Just be careful and don't put it back in the fridge, where your family might find it and eat it by mistake!

It's time to wrap things up; walk like an Egyptian right up to the front and select one of these books . . . I guarantee that none of them are written in hieroglyphics!

EXPANDING YOUR OPTIONS

Books for Use with Younger Audiences

First Joe's little sister Anna puts her Barbie doll in his King Tut's tomb diorama, then she bets him (and his friends Fred and Sam) that there was a woman pharaoh, and, inevitably, Joe's magic book transports them all back in time for some unplanned firsthand research for their ancient Egypt projects. When a bad guy priest named Hatsnat (that's right, it is pronounced "Hot Snot"; p. 14) accuses them of being grave robbers (punishment: "Look, Ma, no hands"), they are saved by King Thutmose III. But then Hatsnat, using Anna as bait, plans to turn them all into mummies—complete with using nose hooks to pull out their brains—and bury them alive. Where is that magic book when you need it? Read *Tut Tut*, by Jon Scieszka, and get wrapped up in all the fun, with or without your own sarcophagus.

Oh yes, Anna was right; there really was a woman pharaoh. She was Thutmose's aunt, Hatshepsut! Queen Hatshepsut is the ruler who rewards nine-year-old Nakht and his family when they help catch tomb robbers. "In the coffin [they saw] a shiny black face. [They] had ripped off the mummy's linen strips to get at the jewelry bound between them" (p. 24). Read Richard Platt's *Egyptian Diary: The Journal of Nakht* for a chance to see what life was like more than three thousand years ago, when robbing tombs would put you on ancient Egypt's equivalent of the FBI's most-wanted list!

What could be more innocent than a Cub Scout camping trip? They've forgotten their troop mascot (an owl), but when they find a statue of an ibis in a trashcan they adopt it as a substitute mascot. Things go downhill rapidly: a man is killed by an asp, a poisonous snake; their campsite is trashed; and a ghost is sighted in the woods. When Arthur creates his own clay ibis statue for his artist's badge, he finds it smashed, and then he is pushed into the river. Something is not right! *The Curse of the Egyptian Mummy* may keep you laughing so hard that you will have to wait until the end of Pat Hutchins's book to find out who, what, when, where, and why!

Merit serves "in the temple of the cat goddess Bastet . . . Her friend Bast, a small cat, keeps her company" as she works. When Bast accidentally angers Waha, the pharaoh's high priest, he drowns the cat. Merit, as witness to this dastardly deed, accuses Waha of killing a sacred cat. When Waha denies that he did it, the pharaoh sends them each to the Netherworld, where the gods will decide the one telling the truth. Merit may not know the magic spells from the Book of the Dead, but because she buried the little cat honorably, she does have the help of Bast's invisible and winged soul to help her face the twelve gates of the Netherworld and the Hall of Judgment. Take a memo: it's not nice to fool the judges of the dead, and *The Winged Cat: A Tale of Ancient Egypt*, by Deborah Nourse Lattimore, shows why.

Seymour Sleuth, wombat detective, and Abbott Muggs, mouse photographer, are called in to solve the mystery of a missing stone chicken. The hieroglyphics on the stone chicken lead to the lost treasure of King Karfu. Finding a mummy is exciting, but if you read *The Mystery of King Karfu*, by Doug Cushman, you will see that tracking down a missing treasure is even more challenging. **(Suggested activity: When you** have finished this booktalk hand out copies of the secret code and the key to the code.)

What would you do if the Bad Guy was after your best friend? In Tomie dePaola's *Bill and Pete Go Down the Nile,* find out how one friend rescued another using a very unusual mummy-making method! (**Suggested activity: Use this with the mummy wrap mentioned above. Or invite children to try this tongue twister: "My mommy's mysterious mummy-making method.")**

It's hard to be rescued from or to second-guess a curse. Some people say that the curse carved on Tutankhamen's tomb read, "Death comes on wings to he who enters the tomb of a pharaoh" (p. 14). This didn't scare archeologist Howard Carter, and he entered the Egyptian tomb with a team of men anyway. Shortly afterward, one member of his team died of an infected mosquito bite, one died from a fall, and still another died from a virus. Find out about these mysterious deaths and more in *Secrets of the Mummies,* by Harriet Griffey.

Additional Books for Older Readers

"Ladies and Gentlemen! Enter with me now into a world of vast darknesses, glittering heat, mysteries beyond your ken" (p. 3). It is 1855. Gideon and his father, the Mummy Professor, make their living traveling down the Mississippi River presenting a show about ancient Egypt. The center of their dramatic performance is a real mummy that Gideon calls George. Hot on their trail is a former colleague of the professor bent on stealing George. When they find a priceless emerald in George's linen wrappings, everyone seems to want a piece of the action. For not only is the emerald worth a fortune, but also the etchings on it are clues to the location of King Tut's tomb. *Gideon and the Mummy Professor,* by Kathleen Karr, takes you to New Orleans, where voodoo mixes with ancient Egyptian curses and ten-foot-long alligators sometimes have the last say.

Come along on a real archeological dig. In 1924 Will Hunt and his family help find a tomb a thousand years older than King Tut's.

They find the intestines, stomach, lungs, and liver, but the mummy of Queen Hetep-heres is missing. Based on a true story, *The 5,000-Year-Old Puzzle: Solving a Mystery of Ancient Egypt,* by Claudia Logan, will challenge your detective skills and, since the mystery is still unsolved, perhaps you will have a new theory about the missing queen yourself!

At age thirteen she is an Egyptian princess. By fourteen she is soon to be married and a queen thereafter. When her husband dies after thirteen years of marriage she supervises his entombment. After watching "the High Priest in his robe of leopard skin [touch] the sacred chisel to the lips of the face painted on the coffin . . . [to] open the mouth and [revive] Pharaoh's senses" (p. 50), she leaves the tomb resolved to solidify her own power and eventually make herself pharaoh. Who is this force to be reckoned with? For a story of a powerful woman in a man's world, read Dorothy Sharp Carter's *His Majesty, Queen Hatshepsut.*

Some museums have real mummies for you to see. Close your eyes and listen to one tell her story . . . (**To help the audience hear the thoughts of a mummy in a glass case as visitors are passing by, read the first page and the last line on the last page of Eve Bunting's *I Am the Mummy Heb-nefert.*)**

In *Discovering the Iceman,* Shelley Tanaka tells how the oldest mummy, nicknamed Ötzi, was found and recreates the hypothetical last few days of his life.

> The sun was hot that day, the sky was blue and clear. To Erika and Helmut Simon, the glistening white peaks of the Alps seemed to stretch forever. Like thousands of other hikers, the Simons loved to climb the craggy slopes of this magnificent mountain range . . . Today, the Simon's destination was the 11,535-foot peak known as the Finailspitze. They reached the summit just before noon and sat down to enjoy the spectacular view . . . That's when they saw it. It looked like a doll at first—a bare, brown head and bony shoulders sticking out of a slushy puddle of melting snow. (p. 4)

It *used* to be a man . . . (**Finish with a pregnant pause.**)

For a modern look at mummies, look at this photograph of a recent technique called plastination, which gives three-dimensional views of the blood vessels, bones, and muscles of real human bodies. It looks like it's straight from a horror movie! **(Show p. 37 in *Mummies: The Newest, Coolest, and Creepiest from Around the World,* by Shelley Tanaka.)**

Books for Use with Young Adult and Adult Audiences

Where can you find a group of adults from around the world comparing notes about mummies? At the Mummy Congress. Held every three years, this is the place to go to find out about "the arcane world of archeology" (p. 8). Discoveries such as that ancient South Americans were cokeheads and that the artist Peter Paul Rubens once used a "withered Egyptian mummy as a model for his drawings" (p. 11) are shared as scientists mingle and their egos collide. Join 180 experts as they promote their findings and expose their idiosyncrasies in Heather Pringle's *The Mummy Congress: Science, Obsession, and the Everlasting Dead.*

Additional Music

To hear background music from the soundtrack of *The Mummy,* go to www.amazon.com/Mummy-Original-Motion-Picture-Soundtrack/dp/B00000IWP1 and click on "Listen to Samples."

Additional Films and Videos

The Mummy, starring Boris Karloff, is the granddaddy (or should we say "grandmummy"?) of all mummy movies. Produced in 1932 this classic horror movie inspired many sequels.

> **For a bit of comic relief, screen a brief film clip from the 1999 version of *The Mummy.* Use the part toward the beginning of the film where the librarian's brother pops out of the sarcophagus and tries to frighten her.**

Additional Websites

Funny mummy images that can be used for personal or educational purposes can be found here: www.kidsturncentral.com/holidays/clip

art/hclipart9.htm (Wendy Hogan, Kids' Turn Central—Halloween Clipart—Mummies).

More funny mummy clip art can be found at www.clipart.com/en/search/split?q=mummy&PID=263489&nvc_cj=1&AID=10292438. Although you need to buy a subscription in order to download the graphics, they are still fun to view and viewing is free.

The Miami Science Museum has designed an easy experiment for cooling the mummy's tomb. You may want to print out the instructions as a handout so that the children can try the experiment in class or at home: www.miamisci.org/af/sln/mummy/coolingthetomb.html.

See if you can outrun the mummies in these colorful Halloween mazes on the Ben and Jerry's website: www.benjerry.com/fun_stuff/holidays/halloween/games/mummys_tomb/index.cfm.

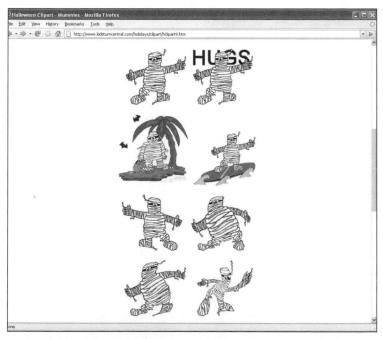

Find funny mummy clip art at www.kidsturncentral.com/holidays/clipart/hclipart9.htm. Used with permission from Kids' Turn Central.

In the Restless Mummy game, with Johnny Thunder and the Adventurers, return the Golden Snake to the mummy: www.lego.com/eng/orient/mummy/highband/default.asp?x=x.

Find your way through the mummy maze at www.channel4.com/entertainment/games/review.jsp?id=1028. This takes a long time to download, and you can only play one version of it for free, but it is challenging and fun. The maze can also be accessed through www.popcap.com/games/mummymaze/.

Younger children will enjoy this game in which they can place a mummy's body organs in the matching canopic jars or in the mummy himself: http://kids.discovery.com/fansites/tutenstein/mummifytut/mummifytut.html.

Additional Activities

Play the Freaky-Feely Game. Make canopic jars and have children identify the contents so that the jars can be labeled. To prepare, put the following in separate bowls: about ten large peeled grapes; some cooked and cooled spaghetti; some Jell-O, mashed with a spoon after it has set; and some cottage cheese.

Ask for a volunteer. Blindfold the child and then place the bowls on a table in front of the group. Ask the child to stick her hand into each bowl, and guess whether she is feeling eyeballs (grapes), intestines (spaghetti), brains (cottage cheese), or blood clots (Jell-O). Put a label on each canopic jar as she identifies the substance within.

RESOURCES CITED

Books

Bendick, Jeanne. *Egyptian Tombs.* Franklin Watts, 1989.

Bunting, Eve. *I Am the Mummy Heb-nefert.* Harcourt Brace, 1997.

Carter, Dorothy Sharp. *His Majesty, Queen Hatshepsut.* Lippincott, 1987.

Cushman, Doug. *The Mystery of King Karfu.* HarperCollins, 1996.

Danziger, Paula. *Make Like a Tree and Leave.* Delacorte, 1990.

dePaola, Tomie. *Bill and Pete Go Down the Nile.* Putnam, 1990.

Dexter, Catherine. *The Gilded Cat.* Morrow Junior Books, 1992.

Griffey, Harriet. *Secrets of the Mummies.* Dorling Kindersley, 1998.

Hall, Katy, and Lisa Eisenberg. *Mummy Riddles.* Dial, 1997.

Hawass, Zahi. *Curse of the Pharaohs: My Adventures with Mummies.* National Geographic, 2004.

Hutchins, Pat. *The Curse of the Egyptian Mummy.* Greenwillow, 1983.

Jackson, Donna M. *The Bone Detectives: How Forensic Anthropologists Solve Crimes and Uncover Mysteries of the Dead.* Little, Brown, 1996.

Karr, Kathleen. *Gideon and the Mummy Professor.* Farrar, Straus and Giroux, 1993.

Lattimore, Deborah Nourse. *The Winged Cat: A Tale of Ancient Egypt.* Greenwillow, 1983.

Logan, Claudia. *The 5,000-Year-Old Puzzle: Solving a Mystery of Ancient Egypt.* Farrar, Straus and Giroux, 2002.

Markle, Sandra. *Outside and Inside Mummies.* Walker, 2005.

Mason, Paul. *Mysteries of the Past: Mummies.* Raintree Steck-Vaughn, 2001.

Milton, Joyce. *Mummies.* Grosset and Dunlap, 1996.

Murphy, Pat, Ellen Macaulay, and the staff of the Exploratorium. *Exploratopia.* Little, Brown, 2006.

Platt, Richard. *Egyptian Diary: The Journal of Nakht.* Candlewick, 2005.

Prelutsky, Jack. "The Mummy." *The Headless Horseman Rides Tonight: More Poems to Trouble Your Sleep.* Greenwillow, 1980.

Pringle, Heather. *The Mummy Congress: Science, Obsession, and the Everlasting Dead.* Hyperion, 2001.

Reinhard, John. *Discovering the Inca Ice Maiden: My Adventures on Ampato.* National Geographic Society, 1998.

Scieszka, Jon. *Tut Tut.* Viking, 1996.

Snyder, Zilpha Keatley. *The Egypt Game.* Atheneum, 1967.

Tanaka, Shelley. *Discovering the Iceman.* Hyperion, 1996.

————. *Mummies: The Newest, Coolest, and Creepiest from Around the World.* Abrams, 2005.

Trumble, Kelly. *Cat Mummies.* Clarion, 1996.

Music

The Bangles. "Walk Like an Egyptian." *The Bangles—Greatest Hits.* Sony, 1990.

Martin, Steve. "King Tut." *A Wild and Crazy Guy.* Warner Bros., 1978.

Films and Videos

The Mummy. Directed by Karl Freund. Universal Pictures, 1932.

The Mummy. Directed by Stephen Sommers. Universal Pictures, 1999.

Websites

AG Interactive. Guanajuato, Mexico, and the Mummy Museum. "Webshots Travel, July 26, 2000." Uploaded by jimscrystals. http://community.webshots.com/album/3314781ANqDzZZgIg.

Amazon.com. *The Mummy—Original Motion Picture Soundtrack.* www.amazon.com/Mummy-Original-Motion-Picture-Soundtrack/dp/B00000IWP1.

The Bangles. "The Official Bangles Website." www.thebangles.com/extras/extras.asp.

Ben and Jerry's Homemade Ice Cream. "Halloween Mummy's Tomb Game." www.benjerry.com/fun_stuff/holidays/halloween/games/mummys_tomb/index.cfm.

Channel Four Television Corporation/4 Ventures Limited. 4 Games: Game Review. "Mummy Maze." www.channel4.com/entertainment/games/review.jsp?id=1028.

Clipart.com. Download Royalty-Free Clipart, Images, Fonts, Web Art, and Graphics. Keyword: "Mummy." www.clipart.com/en/search/split?q=mummy&PID=263489&nvc_cj=1&AID=10292438.

Discovery Communications. "Discovery Kids: Mummify Tutenstein: Put His Organs Where They Belong." http://kids.discovery.com/fansites/tutenstein/mummifytut/mummifytut.html.

Dtrailer.com. "The Mummy Trailer." www.dtrailer.com/watch/m/the-mummy/.

Evans, Elaine A. McClung Museum. "Cat Mummies." http://mcclungmuseum.utk.edu/research/renotes/rn-20txt.htm.

Hogan, Wendy. Kids' Turn Central. "Halloween Clipart—Mummies." www.kidsturncentral.com/holidays/clipart/hclipart9.htm.

KingTutOne.com—A Resource Center for Ancient Egypt. "Enter King Tut's Virtual Tomb." www.kingtutone.com/tutankhamun/enter/.

LEGO Orient Expedition. "The Restless Mummy Game." www.lego.com/eng/orient/mummy/highband/default.asp?x=x.

Miami Science Museum. The Atoms Family: The Mummy's Tomb. "Cooling the Mummy's Tomb." www.miamisci.org/af/sln/coolingthetomb.html.

PopCap Games. Mummy Maze. www.popcap.com.

SteveMartin.com. The World of Steve. "King Tut." www.stevemartin.com/world_of_steve/television/kingtut.php.

Summum Mummification. The Adventures of Mummy Bear. "Mummy Riddles and Jokes." http://kids.summum.us/mummybear/jokes/.

Summum Mummification. Kids Summum! "Mummy Images." 2007. http://kids.summum.us.

CHAPTER 9

Names

What's in a Name?

Play "Name Game" as your opening song. There are many versions of it, including the original by Shirley Ellis. Screen this website, which lets you type in the names of different audience members and shows how the verse of the Name Game should go: www.mathpower.com/namegame.htm.

Here's another site for playing the Name Game: http://cox-tv.com/namegame/.

Do you know the history behind your name? Let's see what we can find out. Can I have a volunteer or two?

Select one or two children and type each one's first name into the website www.behindthename.com to discover the name's etymology and history.

There's a funny song about a girl with a very funny name that you might already know. Some people call her Cathaline Magdalene Hootenstiner Wallaminer Hoten Boton Floton. This illustrator called her Catalina Magdalena Hoopensteiner Wallendiner Hogan Logan Bogan. **(Show cover of Tedd Arnold's *Catalina Magdalena Hoopensteiner Wallendiner Hogan Logan Bogan Was Her Name*.)** But when I went

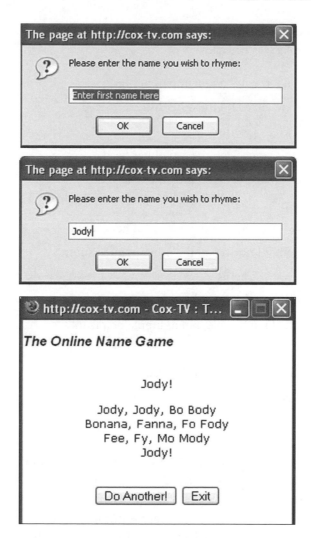

Play the Name Game
(http://cox-tv.com/namegame).
Courtesy of Randy Cox.

to camp, we called her Magalena Hagalena Ooka Takka Wakka Takka Oka Moka Poka. **(If you know this song already, please feel free to use your own pronunciation.)**

Chorus: Magalena Hagalena Ooka Takka Wakka Takka Oka Moka Poka was her name.

She had ten hairs on the top of her head,

Five were alive and the other five were dead.

Chorus

She had two eyes on the top of her head,

One eye was green and the other was red.

Chorus

She had two teeth in the middle of her mouth,

One pointed north and the other pointed south.

Chorus

She had a pimple on the side of her chin,

She called it a dimple, but a dimple points in!

Chorus

She raised her hand but the teacher said, "No!"

The joke was on the teacher 'cause she didn't have to go!

Chorus

Although Magalena Hagalena had a ridiculous name, at least she didn't have to risk her life to get it . . . . Over fifty years ago, at age thirteen, author Gary Paulsen and his friends tackled their versions of extreme sports, without real safety equipment like we have today. When Carl Peterson decided to try to break the world speed record on skis, all they needed to do was convince Archie, who was sixteen and had a car that would do 82½ miles per hour, to pull him. Carl "looked like a large leather ball with tinted green eyes" (p. 13) when he was fully dressed in his protective surplus army gear. By the time he came to a halt he was "a lump of snow and mangled sheepskin . . . snow . . . had been driven under his eyelids; it filled his mouth, was packed in his ears and jammed inside his jacket; it filled his pants; was packed into every opening and crevice of his clothes and his body"

Cover of *Catalina Magdalena Hoopensteiner
Wallendiner Hogan Logan Bogan Was Her Name,* by Tedd
Arnold. Reprinted by permission of Scholastic, Inc.

(pp. 32–33). Read the first short story in *How Angel Peterson Got His Name* to find out if he broke the world record and what he heard the angels sing when he thought he was a goner.

Everyone has to do it once . . . write an essay about what you want to be when you grow up. But not everyone has the pressure that Rod has. His teacher has promised the whole class pizza if no one gets an F in her class. But Rod doesn't know what to write about and thus is dangerously close to losing the pizza party for everyone. He doesn't want to be the typical doctor, police officer, astronaut, and the like. And then it hits him: he is surrounded by examples of the worst offenses known to humankind, and he is a prime example. Rod Curtain . . . can you guess his nickname? And his best friend, Lucas, is called . . . Mucus. And what about the girl who has a hyphenated last name? Her mom's last name is Pepper and her dad's last name is Mintz. Are you getting the picture? Rod decides he is going to be a "name expert" (p. 35). Find out how he plans to save the world from the horrors of thoughtless parental naming patterns in "Expert, Incorporated," by Sarah Weeks, found in the short story collection *Tripping Over the Lunch Lady, and Other School Stories,* edited by Nancy E. Mercado.

Perhaps Rod needs to read this book to find a way to keep his clients' names from becoming potentially embarrassing "things" . . .

Words may come from the names of people (eponyms) or places (toponyms). Where do you suppose bikinis (p. 55), polka dots (p. 57), and (shopping) malls (p. 75) got their names? Who were the inspirations for the Tootsie Roll and Baby Ruth candy bars—no, not Babe Ruth (p. 46)? You won't ever guess who or where gypsies (p. 37), sideburns (p. 33), and guinea pigs (p. 23) come from either. Read *A Chartreuse Leotard in a Magenta Limousine,* by Lynda Graham-Barber, and be "tantalized" (a Greek king; p. 14) by names!

Some places have *very* unusual names. Diane Siebert's poem "American Towns" will make you glad the name of your hometown doesn't make everyone laugh.

> **Read selected verses of the poem "American Towns," from *Tour America: A Journey through Poems and Art,* by Diane Siebert.**

Let's have a look at even more wacky town names at this Fact Monster website (**www.factmonster.com/spot/wackytowns.html**). Or later, find a map of the United States and see how many other crazy names you can discover.

Towns with weird names can overcome them or use them to attract tourists. But when you're in seventh grade, you don't want your nickname to make you stand out.

Some nicknames are given with affection, but not Jessica's. Her former best friend, Sheila, and Sheila's new camp friends, Cathy, Andi, Nancy, Tracy, and Amy, didn't tell her the outfit of choice for the first day of seventh grade. When Jessica showed up wearing a new dress with multicolored polka dots,

> Tracy said, "Looks like a Wonder Bread explosion!" . . . I knew when Mom pulled the dress off the rack it reminded me of something, and now I knew what—the wrapper of Wonder Bread, the shiny white plastic wrapper with the bright blue, yellow, and red polka dots. And there I was, trapped like a loaf of white bread inside it. (p. 5)

Will Jessica survive being a social reject? Read Rachel Vail's *Wonder* and stop wondering.

"It's a well-known fact that a nickname will never stick if it's not the right one" (p. 6). It is also a 100 percent certainty that you will get nicknamed by Jeff and Wiley if you go to their school, Old Orchard Public School, or "OOPS," as they call it. They call their new substitute teacher, Mr. Hughes, who looks like King Kong, "Mr. Huge." Peter, who has a white streak in his hair, is "Skunk"; skinny Christy Jones is "Crusty Bones." They have a sixth sense about the suitability of nicknames and are willing to bet on it. In fact they wager they can give Mike Smith, the most boring kid in the school, the name "Iceman" and make it stick. But when a new girl, Cassandra, joins their class, they are at a loss to give her a nickname. No name quite seems to fit for her. Meanwhile the nicknames they have been using start to go wrong. Mr. Huge is in danger of losing his job. Iceman becomes the coolest kid in school, and Cassandra has eyes only for him. And what do they finally call Cassandra? Read Gordon Korman's *The Sixth-Grade Nickname Game* to find out which nickname sticks.

Sometime athletes get nicknames that stick with them forever. How would you like to be called "Boom-Boom," or "The Owl without the Vowel," or "Refrigerator"? This website gives the background behind some of these crazy nicknames: www.factmonster.com/ipka/A0769826.html.

Athletes play video games just like the rest of us. How many video games have you played, and can you recognize them by their sounds? Who would like to volunteer to play Name That Game?

Choose a volunteer and screen this website: www.pbs.org/kcts/videogamerevolution/arcade/name/name_that_game.swf. Have the volunteer listen to the background music and try to guess the name of the game it's associated with.

I wonder what the sound would be for a game that involves underpants flinging. I think underpants flinging should be raised to an Olympic level. If you try it, maybe you too can earn a nickname . . . especially after reading our next book.

Who hasn't heard of Captain Underpants? **(Hold up a few of the books.)** In this series by Dav Pilkey, George and Harold rename their principal Captain Underpants, and the fun never stops. If you read the books in this series, you can also meet Professor Poopypants, the Lunch Ladies, and Dr. Diaper. If you would like to change your boring, ordinary name to one that would fit right in as a character in the series, try Professor Poopypants's Name Change-O-Chart!

Show www.scholastic.com/captainunderpants/namechanger .htm.

Although we have been busy coming up with nicknames, we haven't been as busy as Joe . . . Stand up and follow along with me as we chant another camp song mimicking the actions of Joe, who works in a button factory.

> Hi, my name is Joe,
>
> I've got a wife and five kids
>
> and I work in a button factory.
>
> One day my boss
>
> came up to me
>
> And said "Joe, are you busy?"
>
> I said, "No."
>
> "Then turn the buttons with your right hand." (**Move right hand palm up in circular motion.**)
>
> (**Repeat**) Hi, my name is Joe . . .
>
> "Then turn the buttons with your left hand." (**Move left hand palm up in circular motion while continuing the first motion.**)
>
> (**Repeat**) Hi, my name is Joe . . . (**Continue doing all previous actions as you add new ones.**)
>
> . . . right leg (**Pump up and down on right leg.**)
>
> . . . left leg (**Alternate pumping both legs.**)
>
> . . . hips (**Swivel hips.**)
>
> . . . head (**Nod head.**)
>
> . . . rear end (**Yes, wiggle your rear end.**)
>
> (**Repeat**) "Joe, are you busy?"
>
> I said, "YES!"

Working in a button factory (as you can see) can be a lot of hard work. It might just be easier to be a dog.

"I want to be a golden retriever when I grow up" (p. 28). Dogs don't care what color you are. Because Keath is the only kid in his fourth grade who is white, some of his nicknames are "Mayonnaise," "Vanilla," and "Ghost." His best friend, Lynda, gets called "Zebra" because her mother is black and her father is white. Too bad the school bully, "Toothpick," and his henchman, "Blob," have it in for them. Yes, Keath's a dog lover, and one of the reasons he and Lynda get along so well is her beagle, Leftovers. Minus a leg and an ear from a car accident, Leftovers is a survivor. Read *Nothing Wrong with a Three-Legged Dog,* by Graham McNamee, to find out how Leftovers shows Keath how "vanilla [can fit into] a chocolate school" (p. 27).

Bethany is a completely normal name. But Bethany's life turns abnormal when her parents pack her into a car, take her several states away to live with an aunt that she never knew she had, and then disappear. People in her aunt's town start calling her Elizabeth because she has an uncanny resemblance to a sister she never knew existed. Something odd and frightening is going on, and her father has forbidden her aunt to tell her anything. Then she finds out that her parents have changed their last names five times and that she herself has five birth certificates. Read Margaret Haddix's *Double Identity* to find out who Bethany really is.

John Jacob didn't have to change his name five times; he already had five names: John Jacob Jingle Heimer Schmitt. You may know this song already. Here are the words, sing along with me!

Show the lyrics at www.tushball.com/Jacob.html and sing the song a few times, getting softer and softer but always shouting out the "Da, da, da, da, da, da, da."

In a more serious vein, names can sometimes be political weapons. Name changes can be a matter of life or death.

"By order of the Emperor, all Koreans are to be graciously allowed to take Japanese names" (p. 5). All of their lives Sun-hee, whose name means "girl of brightness," and her brother, Tae-yul, whose name means "great warmth," have lived in a Korea under Japanese domination. But now it is 1940 and Japanese laws have become even more severe. Already forbidden to read and write in Korean, study Korean history, or fly the Korean flag, having to change their names is the ultimate disgrace. Their uncle, who has always secretly told them Korean folktales, is outraged: "Let them arrest me! They will have my body but not my soul—my name is my soul!" (p. 5) Their family begins risking their lives for the honor of their heritage. Uncle becomes involved in the resistance movement, and their mother secretly grows the Korean national tree despite laws requiring them to be burned. Even their quiet father's choice of their Japanese names is subtly subversive. Read *When My Name Was Keoko,* by Linda Sue Park, to see how, as the war continues, both Sun-hee and Tae-yul choose incredibly dangerous paths in order to be worthy of their family, their country, and the Korean names so carefully selected for them.

Raise your hand if you would like to find out what your name means.

Screen the name generator at Mystic Games, www.mystic games.com/names.htm, and use a few of your volunteers' names. End by entering "Rumpelstiltskin."

I didn't think that we were going to find Rumpelstiltskin's name at that website!

What if Rumpelstiltskin's name was really Herbert? In William J. Brooke's *Teller of Tales,* a storyteller and a young girl look at some of our favorite stories . . . on the slant. After the queen tricks the little man who helped her spin straw into gold and keeps her daughter, he retires to the woods. When the now-grown and runaway princess discovers him, he shares this bit of wisdom:

> A name is important. When everything else is taken away, it is the only thing that you still have. If you make up a name for your secret self, a name that no one else knows, then it can never be possessed by anyone else. And when you feel that you have been torn into little

pieces . . . you can still call your secret name and find the heart of you that no one can take away. (p. 70)

Read "Rumpelstiltskin by Any Other Name" and imagine, in your heart of hearts, a secret name for yourself to hold close for those times of greatest need.

> **Show a clip from the Faerie Tale Theatre version of *Rumpelstiltskin*. Start with the first time the queen is trying to guess his name and end after the second time she guesses funny names.**

There are other possibilities for the traditional story of Rumpelstiltskin. For example, what would have happened if the miller's daughter had married Rumpelstiltskin instead? His name is still Rumpelstiltskin (not Herbert), but she decides it's better to marry the guy willing to save her life than the man who locked her in the room and ordered her to spin straw into gold. Sixteen years later, meet their child, who isn't embarrassed by her father's name. In fact, she takes after her father when, like her mother, she is imprisoned by the king and forced to spin more gold. In *Rumpelstiltskin's Daughter,* by Diane Stanley, read about this resourceful daughter who lives up to her name and her father's reputation. And no, I won't tell you what her name is!

Some fathers don't think about the trouble they can cause by giving their child the wrong name. Shel Silverstein wrote a song (popularized by Johnny Cash) about a boy who was constantly teased about his name, Sue. The boy is so angry over his name that he decides to hunt down his father. When he finally finds him, his dad explains that he chose the name Sue to make his son strong. But in this last stanza, he rants and raves about the horrors of being named Sue.

> **Play the tenth/last stanza of the song, *but* make sure you start with the first line of that stanza and not a line before. In most versions of the song, the last line of the previous stanza contains inappropriate language.**

Whether you like your name or not, I guarantee that you will like these books, or my name isn't . . . Oops, that's confidential!

EXPANDING YOUR OPTIONS

Books for Use with Younger Audiences

Maria Isabel, new to her school, is the third Maria in her class, so her teacher decides to call her Mary. When the teacher calls on her, she doesn't answer because she doesn't recognize Mary as her name. Her full name, Maria Isabel Salazar Lopez, holds important meaning and memories of her Puerto Rican grandmothers, her grandfather, and her father. How can she explain to her teacher that a name is not just a label; it is a matter of pride? Read *My Name Is Maria Isabel,* by Alma Flor Ada. Where does your name came from?

Eight-year-old David is sick of his ordinary name; not only are there four other Davids in his class, but there are fifteen more in the phone book with his same last name too! When he changes his name to Ali Baba, exciting things begin happening right and left, such as finding a missing diamond earring, dealing with the threat of having to kiss a female frog, experimenting with a snail and a magic spell to remove warts, and, last but not least, inviting all the David Bernsteins in Manhattan to come to his ninth-birthday party. Read *The Adventures of Ali Baba Bernstein,* by Johanna Hurwitz, and then look in the phone book to see who else has *your* name.

Jo Louis is anxious about starting a new school because she knows she will be teased about her name. When she admits her fears to her grandfather, he tells her the history behind her name and how it ties in with the story of one of the greatest boxers of all time. Read *When Jo Louis Won the Title,* by Belinda Rochelle, and see how Jo's first day of school goes. **(Suggested activity: Display a picture of the real Joe Louis from his official website: www.cmgworldwide.com/sports/louis/photo1.htm.)**

Which is worse? To have a first name like Justin and have people say, "Like . . . 'Justin Time'?" (pp. 69–70), or to have a name like Amber Brown and have people call you a crayon? Amber Brown and her best friend Justin Daniels have always been there for each other. Now

Justin's family must move away, and out of nowhere the quarreling starts. When Justin decides to throw away the chewing-gum ball they have been building for a year and a half, it's the last straw for Amber. She calls him "Dirt Bag" (p. 72) and he calls her "Crayon Brain" (p. 73). Will name calling end their friendship even before Justin has to move away? Read *Amber Brown Is Not a Crayon,* by Paula Danziger, to see if picking a fight makes losing a friend any easier.

Judy Moody enjoys having a name that rhymes. When a new girl, Amy Namey, who belongs to the "My-Name-Is-a-Poem Club" (p. 73), moves to her school, Judy is jealous at first, but as they get to know each other more, Judy starts neglecting her other friends. Frank, now nicknamed "Frank the Tank," and Rocky, who doesn't "feel too talky," start calling her "Judy Snooty" (p. 103). This is a problem because the boys now refuse to work with Judy on their group project about Italy. Read *Judy Moody: Around the World in 8½ Days,* by Megan McDonald, to see if the whole class gets stuck-in-muck waiting for these ends-of-friends to seek-to-speak to each other. Okeydokey? (**Suggested activities: Spend a *limited* amount of time talking in rhyme. Or go to author Shel Silverstein's official website, www.shelsilverstein .com, and click on "Let's Have Some Fun," click on "Games and Puzzles," and click on "Name That Poem!" Listen to a few poems and see if audience members can guess the name of his poem. Is it "Easy Peasy"?**)

Since Clementine's name is also a fruit she insists on calling her little brother by vegetable names. In between calling him "Spinach," "Radish," "Broccoli," "Rutabaga," "Turnip," "Zucchini," "Lima Bean," "Pea Pod," and "Celery," she cuts off all of her friend Margaret's hair, colors the skin on Margaret's head red with permanent marker to fill in the gaps, cuts off her own hair and colors her skin green to make Margaret feel better, visits the principal's office more than anyone could think possible for a third grader (it's a paying-attention thing), tries to help her father fix the pigeon poop problem in their building, and, oh yes, tries to decide on a cat's name. How does this compare to her other troubles? Clementine thinks "the most exquisite words in the world are on labels . . . in a bathroom" (p. 20). In the past she has chosen "mascara," "fluoride," and "laxative." If you read *Clementine,* by Sara Pennypacker, you won't find out her little brother's real name, but you will find out which name she picks for her newest cat, and you will enjoy every minute of her semi-terrible, partly horrible, not-so-good, half-bad week. (**Suggested activity: Before the booktalk, play the chorus from "Oh My Darling Clementine" from** *Disney's Favorite Children's Songs,* **volume 1, or from any other recording.**)

Upsilimana Tumpalerado may have a long name, but it's not hard to pronounce, if you practice. When his grandmother challenges him to find out her name, he discovers it is even longer than his. Read the West Indian story *Turtle Knows Your Name,* by Ashley Bryan, and try to wrap your tongue around *her* name!

Bubba is the school bully. He's known for lying, cheating, stealing, and giving out nicknames. "Nolan Byrd is Byrd-the-Nerd . . . Jake is Bucktooth. Trey is Butthead. Marvin is Moron" (p. 5). You get the picture. All the kids in the school are totally defenseless against Bubba. When Nolan is assigned to write a newspaper article using any kind of computer technology he chooses, he has a brilliant idea. He will do his article on injustice, targeting Bubba. He creates a secret surveillance system by hiding his digital camera in his backpack and proceeds to document all of Bubba's evildoings. He even accidentally takes a picture of Bubba's butt. When he realizes that once he turns his project in, Bubba will beat him to a pulp, Nolan decides to create a website and a new identity for himself, Shredderman. Now he can let the whole world know about Bubba. Read *Secret Identity* (book 1 in the Shredderman series), by Wendelin Van Draanen, and meet the newest twenty-first-century superhero. (**Suggested activities: Display this colorful website with a list of characters in the Shredderman series: www.randomhouse.com/kids/vandraanen/shredderman/clean/ meet.html. Print and pass out the word jumble related to this book from www.randomhouse.com/kids/vandraanen/shredderman/clean/ activities/book1/id_jumble.pdf.**)

Additional Books for Older Readers

Ten-year-old Anastasia is confused about her life and spends her time making lists of things she loves and hates. She is particularly unhappy with her name. There are just too many letters—so many that if she was to put it on her T-shirt, the letters would run under her armpits. On top of that, she can't turn it into a nickname ending in *i* and thus join the "i club" (p. 51) in school. Babies immediately go into her "hate" column when she finds out her mother is going to have one. When her parents decide to let her chose his name, she spends a lot of time picking out the worst name possible, "One-Ball Reilly" (p. 95). Is there anything that could make her change her mind? Read *Anastasia Krupnick,* by Lois Lowry, to see how the baby earns his name and how Anastasia grows into hers.

Mary Margaret didn't respond well when a substitute teacher tried calling her just Mary for a while. "Later I told her I needed to go to the toy. 'Pardon me?' she said. 'You know, the toy,' I said, pointing to my bottom. 'The toy-let?' The other kids started saying stuff like that, too . . . Music was *moo,* and recess was *reese.* Then the principal came in, and someone said, 'Hey, prince!' After that, the substitute teacher called me Mary Margaret" (p. 94). When Mary Margaret comes up with a way to raise money so her teacher, Mr. Mooney, can put on a community play, she feels she will automatically be the first choice to get the part of Cinderella. When she gets only the understudy part, Mr. Mooney starts calling her "Cindy Two." He seems to have forgotten that Mary Margaret doesn't like to have her name abbreviated. When "Cindy Two" has to share the spotlight, she just might make a bigger name for herself than if she had been "Cindy One." Read *Mary Margaret, Center Stage,* by Christine Kole MacLean, to see what happens when the curtains rise.

Cluny Smith, named after a museum in Paris, decides to create her own magazine, *Cluny: The Magazine for People with Weird Names* (p. 51). She had planned to give copies only to her friends, who also have unusual names, but when the popular kids unexpectedly get to see a copy, they start to call her "Clue-less-Loo-ney" (p. 61). She even gets an anonymous letter:

> Dear Looney,
>
> I was so glad to see a magazine for people like us. My friend Frogetta wants to subscribe . . . Also my friend Frankfurter is interested . . . He's a real wiener. I hope you will have a joke section. Here's one. Q: How many people with weird names does it take to screw in a light bulb? A: None. They'd rather be in the dark. Ha. Ha. Ha. Anyway, have to run cos my boyfriend, Pizzaface, is at the door . . .
>
> Yours most sincerely,
>
> Lulu McDinkus-Puss (p. 59)

While the kids are loudly teasing Cluny, her school bus has a run-in with a train. On the train is a boy with the rather ordinary name of Harry, whose own story has been told in bits and pieces between Cluny's. Read "Strangers on the Shore," one of the stories in a collection by Tim Wynne-Jones called *Some of the Kinder Planets*. You will see why Cluny's mother may be right when she says that having an original name builds character and how Harry fits right into Cluny's universe.

Lillian's mother keeps reminding her that "sticks and stones can break my bones, but names can never hurt me. She's wrong about that . . . Names *can* hurt me. I'd much rather be hit with a stick than be called beanpole. A stick or a stone only stings for a minute. A name seems to hurt forever" (p. 9). Ever since she was in third grade and played the part of the maypole in the school pageant, Lillian has been called "Beanpole" because of her height. She's also been called "Giraffe Legs," "Olive Oyl," and "Jolly Green Giant." Read *Beanpole*, by Barbara Park, to see if Lillian, now starting seventh grade and turning thirteen, can leave all the names behind her.

Orville Rudemeyer Pygenski couldn't spell his name in first grade. No surprise there. He thinks his nickname, "Orvie," is even worse than his real name. By the time he is in sixth grade he decides to start an "I Hate My Name Club" (p. 23). Before he knows it, he has members with names like "Seymour Clear," "Heidi Ho," "Kitty Kat," "Anne Chovey,"

"Candy Kane," and "Robin Banks" (pp. 60–61). Read *ORP*, by Suzy Kline, to find out why the first meeting of Orville's club is also the last.

"When the last dragon and the last elf break the circle, the past and the future will meet, and the sun of a new summer will shine in the sky" (p. 61). So says the prophecy. The last elf is named Yorshkrunsquarkljolnerstrink, "Yorsh" for very short. When a man and a woman save Yorsh after he is orphaned, their intervention sets off a chain of events that keeps the prophecy alive. Yorsh lives in a harsh world of ignorance and superstition where elves are feared and hated. After he meets what he thinks is the last dragon, Yorsh discovers that in the final years of a dragon's life it lays an egg and in doing so forgets virtually of all its previously accumulated knowledge, including its own name. This is "the supreme knowledge, because one's own name is one's own soul, especially for dragons, who choose their own names when they are at the peak of their power" (p. 148). His dragon does indeed lay an egg, which, once hatched, helps Yorsh take on a second portion of the prophecy. In Silvana De Mari's *The Last Dragon* read how the smallest elf with the longest name finds his destiny.

Books for Use with Young Adult and Adult Audiences

In Bengali culture it is the custom to give two names to a child. The "pet" name is used only in a private, family context; the "good" name is employed as the official, formal identification for the outside world. As his parents, alone in the United States, wait for a letter from Calcutta bearing the chosen good name for their son, Gogol Ganguli's pet name becomes his good name purely by accident because the letter never arrives. Why Gogol? His father's life was actually saved by a book written by the Russian writer Nikolai Gogol. In *The Namesake*, Pulitzer Prize–winning author Jhumpa Lahiri introduces us to a family in which names are of sacred importance. We find that Gogol's mother has *never* spoken her husband's name aloud in his presence, and we marvel at this self-restraint even while their arranged marriage grows into a deeply loving relationship. On his fourteenth birthday, when Gogol's father gives him a copy of *The Overcoat*, the very book that saved his life, his inscription reads, "The man who gave you his name, from the man who gave you his name" (p. 288). Gogol so despises his name that when he turns eighteen, he changes it to Nikhil. With this change he tries to redefine himself in his choice of career and his often miserable romantic entanglements. When helping friends try to choose a name for their first child, Gogol's pronouncement that "human beings should be allowed to name themselves when they turn eighteen . . . until then, pronouns" (p. 245) gives us a window into the anguish his name has caused him. This novel of two generations and their struggle with immigration, assimilation, alienation, and universal longings will leave you with hope for the outsider in all of us. When we leave the adult Gogol/Nikhil, he has just begun to read the book his father gave him so many years ago, to pay tribute to his namesake and to the names of those who have gone before him.

Read the poem "The List of Good Names," by Robert Fanning, from his 2006 collection *The Seed Thieves*.

Additional Music

Display the lyrics for the song "Eddie Koochie Catchinary Toesinary Moesinary Sammy Gammy Wacky Brown" at www.boyscouttrail.com/content/song/song-471.asp and sing it with the group. A recording of the song "Eddie Coochie" can be found on Bonnie Phipps's *Dinosaur Choir*.

Have fun making up rhymes to match with your audience members' names in the traditional song "Hey Lolly, Lolly." This can be challenging and may require some poetic license. For example:

> I know a girl whose name is Maya, hey lolly, lolly-lo.
> She loves to eat her pizza-pie-a, hey lolly, lolly-lo.
> It's hey lolly, lolly, lolly, hey lolly, lolly-lo.
> Hey lolly, lolly, lolly, hey lolly, lolly-lo.

A good recording of this song can be found on *Wee Sing Sing-Alongs*.

Additional Films and Videos

From the comedy *Mrs. Doubtfire,* show the scene where Robin Williams chooses his alter ego's name after seeing a newspaper headline that reads, "Police Doubt Fire Was Accidental."

Screen the clip in *August Rush* where a passing truck inspires August to choose his new name.

Additional Websites

Read clues and play Name That Bug at www.orkin.com/learningcenter/ kids_and_teachers_games.aspx.

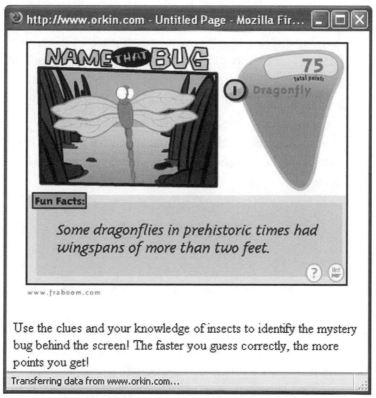

Name That Bug game from Orkin Pest Control Services,
www.orkin.com. Used with permission of Orkin, Inc.

Visit "What Was Her Name?" at www.geocities.com/~teddarnold/catalinaname.html, the part of Tedd Arnold's website where he solicits other verses for the song about Catalina Magdalena. Read the funny verses and different pronunciations of the same weird name.

Encourage your audience to try answering questions about the names of places from "Where the Name Fits the Place" at www.fact monster.com/ipka/A0770102.html.

Other Activities

"A My Name Is Alice" is an old jump-rope rhyme. While you are jumping, you have to think of two people's names, a place name, and the name of an object or activity that start with A—for instance, "A my name is Alice, my brother's name is Al. We live in Arizona and we sell apples." After finishing that verse, you have to make up a similar verse using the letter B and then continue through the alphabet, following the same pattern without pausing. This can be challenging, even without a jump-rope. Does anyone want to come up here and give it a try?

> **Take out a jump rope, and ask for a volunteer to jump and recite the rhyme, making up names starting with the appropriate letter as he goes. See how far down the alphabet he's able to get!**

RESOURCES CITED

Books

Ada, Alma Flor. *My Name Is María Isabel.* Trans. Ana M. Cerro. Atheneum, 1993.

Arnold, Tedd, illustrator. *Catalina Magdalena Hoopensteiner Wallendiner Hogan Logan Bogan Was Her Name.* Scholastic, 2004.

Brooke, William J. *Teller of Tales.* HarperCollins, 1994.

Bryan, Ashley. *Turtle Knows Your Name.* Atheneum, 1989.

Danziger, Paula, and Tony Ross. *Amber Brown Is Not a Crayon.* Puffin, 2006.

De Mari, Silvana. *The Last Dragon.* Trans. Shaun Whiteside. Miramax; Hyperion, 2006.

Fanning. Robert. "The List of Good Names." *The Seed Thieves.* Marick Press, 2006.

Gogol, Nikolai Vasilevich. *The Overcoat, and Other Stories.* Alfred A. Knopf, 1923.

Graham-Barber, Lynda, and Barbara Lehman. *A Chartreuse Leotard in a Magenta Limousine.* Hyperion, 1994.

Haddix, Margaret. *Double Identity.* Simon and Schuster, 2005.

Hurwitz, Johanna. *The Adventures of Ali Baba Bernstein.* Morrow, 1985.

Kline, Suzy. *ORP.* Putnam, 1989.

Korman, Gordon. *The Sixth-Grade Nickname Game.* Hyperion, 1998.

Lahiri, Jhumpa. *The Namesake.* Houghton Mifflin, 2003.

Lowry, Lois. *Anastasia Krupnick.* Houghton Mifflin, 1995.

MacLean, Christine Kole. *Mary Margaret, Center Stage.* Dutton, 2006.

McDonald, Megan. *Judy Moody: Around the World in 8½ Days.* Candlewick, 2006.

McNamee, Graham. *Nothing Wrong with a Three-Legged Dog.* Dell Yearling, 2001.

Mercado, Nancy. *Tripping Over the Lunch Lady, and Other School Stories.* Dial, 2004.

Park, Barbara. *Beanpole.* Alfred A. Knopf, 1983.

Park, Linda Sue. *When My Name Was Keoko.* Clarion, 2002.

Paulsen, Gary. *How Angel Peterson Got His Name, and Other Outrageous Tales about Extreme Sports.* Wendy Lamb Books, 2003.

Pennypacker, Sara. *Clementine.* Hyperion, 2006.

Pilkey, Dav. Captain Underpants series. Scholastic.

Rochelle, Belinda. *When Jo Louis Won the Title.* Houghton Mifflin, 1994.

Siebert, Diane. "American Towns." *Tour America: A Journey through Poems and Art.* Chronicle, 2006.

Stanley, Diane. *Rumpelstiltskin's Daughter.* Morrow Junior, 1997.

Vail, Rachel. *Wonder.* Orchard Books, 1991.

Van Draanen, Wendelin. *Secret Identity*. Alfred A. Knopf, 2004.

Wynne-Jones, Tim. *Some of the Kinder Planets*. Orchard Books, 1995.

Music

Cash, Johnny. "A Boy Named Sue." *Johnny Cash at San Quentin*. Columbia, 1969.

Ellis, Shirley. "The Name Game." *Shirley Ellis: The Complete Congress Recordings*. Connoisseur Collection, 2001.

Phipps, Bonnie. "Eddie Koochie." *Dinosaur Choir*. Wimmer-Ferguson, 1992.

Traditional. "Cathaline Magdalene Hootenstiner Wallaminer, Hoten Boton Floton."

———. "Hey Lolly, Lolly." (Can be found on *Wee Sing Sing-Alongs*, Price Stern Sloan, 1982.)

———. "John Jacob Jingle Heimer Schmitt."

———. "Oh My Darling Clementine." (Can be found on *Children's Favorite Songs*, vol. 1, Disney, 1991.)

Films and Videos

August Rush. Directed by Kirsten Sheridan. Southpaw Entertainment, 2007.

Mrs. Doubtfire. Directed by Chris Columbus. Twentieth Century Fox, 1993.

Rumpelstiltskin. Faerie Tale Theatre series. Directed by Emile Ardolino. Gaylord Productions, 1982.

Websites

Arnold, Tedd. "What Was Her Name?" www.geocities.com/~tedd arnold/catalinaname.html.

Boy Scout Trail. "Eddie Koochie Catchinary." www.boyscouttrail.com/content/song/song-471.asp.

Camp Timberlane, 1961–1986. Songs and Cheers. "John Jacob Jingle Heimer Schmitt." www.tushball.com/Jacob.html.

Campbell, Mike. "Behind the Name: The Etymology and History of First Names." www.behindthename.com.

CMG Solutions. The Official Site of Joe Louis. "Historical Photo Gallery." www.cmgworldwide.com/sports/louis/photo1.htm.

Cox, Randy. Cox-tv.com. "Name Game." http://cox-tv.com/name game/.

Freedman, Ellen. Mathpower.com. "Name Game." www.mathpower .com/namegame.htm.

Mystic Games. "Name Meanings." www.mysticgames.com/names.htm.

Orkin, Inc. Orkin—Bugs and Insects—Games for Kids. "Name That Bug." www.orkin.com/learningcenter/kids_and_teachers_games .aspx.

PBS. The Video Game Revolution. "Name That Game." www.pbs.org/ kcts/videogamerevolution/arcade/name/name_that_game.swf.

Pearson Education, publishing as Fact Monster. "Calling All Athletes." www.factmonster.com/ipka/A0769826.html.

———. "Wacky Town Names." Compiled by Holly Hartman. www .factmonster.com/spot/wackytowns.html.

———. "Where the Name Fits the Place—or Does It?" www.fact monster.com/ipka/A0770102.html.

Random House. "Shredderman Jumble: Secret Identity." www.random house.com/kids/vandraanen/shredderman/clean/activities/book1/ id_jumble.pdf.

———. "Shredderman: Meet the Characters." www.randomhouse .com/kids/vandraanen/shredderman/clean/meet.html.

Scholastic. Scholastic Kids. "Captain Underpants: Laffs." www.scholas tic.com/captainunderpants/namechanger.htm.

Silverstein, Shel. Shel Silverstein's Official Website. "Name That Poem." www.shelsilverstein.com.

10

Cats and Dogs

It's Raining Cats and Dogs

Project the image from the following website on the screen as children are entering the room: www.xmission.com/ ~email box/games/aquarium/aquarium.htm.

All over the world there are cats and dogs, but other countries don't always use the same words to describe the sounds cats and dogs make. In Chinese dogs say "Wang-wang," in Hebrew they say "Huf-huf," and in French they say "Wah-wah." Cats say "Nyan-nyan" in Japanese, "Yaong-yaong" in Korean, and "Me-yong" in Indonesian. Of course, even though we can try to give their sounds names, we still don't know exactly what cats and dogs are telling us, but at least in Hank De Zutter's *Who Says a Dog Goes Bow-Wow?* we can laugh at how we humans try to understand our animals.

Even if dogs and cats can't understand human language, they can still understand many sounds. Certain sounds get the same response from them no matter what country they are living in. If you want your dog or cat to think you are about to feed him, go to this website and click on the sounds of a can opening. (**Screen www.yuckles.com/dog sounds.htm.**) See your pet perk up! If your dog is feeling bored, ring doorbell 1 and see her come running. If your cat is in the mood to run, how about some puppy noise? Click on the "Puppy" button to see what happens. But of course, if you already can communicate with your pet, none of this is necessary.

John and his older brother, Tom, can both understand their dog, Mouse. They talk to her out loud or in their minds, and she answers inside their heads. They live in the north of England with their mom; their dad died several years before. When Tom is diagnosed with a life-threatening illness, the risk of infection is so great that Mouse must go. No neighbor will take her, so it will have to be the pound. Despite Tom's protests that he doesn't want to live without Mouse, their mother will not be moved. When their grandmother mentions that their dad's brother lives in the south of England, they know in a flash that he's the one to take Mouse. They haven't met him, but how can he say no? So "Operation Save Dog" (p. 26) is launched. Because John doesn't have enough money to pay for a complete train ride, he buys a ticket for as far as his money will take him (Thank goodness dogs are allowed on trains in England!) and walks the rest of the way. According to the newspaper reports of their adventures, along their way "[John] and Mouse . . . [rescue] a toddler from drowning in a swollen river, [fight] with savage guard dogs, [stop] half-starved wild ponies from going to slaughter, [save] a whole Gypsy family . . . from a mob who were setting fire to their camper, and finally [scale] a dangerous cliff to reach [their] uncle's house and safety" (pp. 164–165). Of course newspapers get everything wrong; the real story—which includes, of course, how Mouse is instrumental every step of the way—is even more incredible. Beyond a doubt, L. S. Matthews's Mouse is *A Dog for Life*. **(This story is available in CD format.)**

Jean Craighead George has written two books to help you understand what your dog or cat is trying to say. You may not be able to communicate quite the way John and Tom can with Mouse, but let's see how well you can translate. **(Call for two volunteers to demonstrate, or given that kids like to see adults in silly positions, do the demonstrations yourself. If you use volunteers, one will be the dog and the other will be the cat. Have the dog volunteer lie down on his back and draw up his legs.)** What is this dog saying? **(Pause and let your audience guess. Then give the answer:)** "I am your humble servant" (p. 10). **(Have the dog volunteer get down on his hands and knees and, with his rear end in the air, spank the ground with his hands.)** What is this dog saying? **(Pause to let your audience guess. Then give the answer:)** "Let's play." Learn six ways to read a dog's tail and five ways to read a dog's facial expressions in *How to Talk to Your Dog.* Pretty soon you and your "good dog" will understand each other without saying a word.

(Have the cat volunteer rub her head on your arm.) What is this cat saying? **(Pause and let your audience guess. Then give the answer:)** "Hello." Purring means a cat is content and happy, but did you know that a "purr is never given when [a] cat is alone[?] . . . [Purring] is communication, and cats are too smart to talk to themselves" (p. 13). There are as many as nineteen kinds of meows, each with its own meaning. Read *How to Talk to Your Cat* and you will soon be able to communicate with that furry creature who owns you.

Yes, cats own you . . . even if they are wacko! Here are some home videos of cats doing crazy things.

> **View www.funnycatvideos.net/funny-cat-video-compilation-1 .html, a funny cat video set to music. Stop after the scene in which the cat frightens itself in the mirror, or show the whole thing.**

Now let's get more serious. Cats don't exist merely to amuse us. Did you know that cats are able "to taste and smell the air when they open their mouths" (p. 47)? This enables them to smell smoke and other scents before humans can. In *Cats to the Rescue: True Tales of Heroic Felines,* by Marilyn Singer, you will meet Ringo, who saved twenty-two people from a gas leak and explosion. But having a keener sense of smell than humans have doesn't account for the actions of some other courageous cats: Wheezer saved his owner from a serious asthma attack by finding his inhaler for him; Gandalf pulled the alarm cord when his owner had a stroke; Sybil protected her nine-year-old owner from a stranger's abduction; Booboo Kitty saved her owner and five others from an armed gunman; even though she was blind, Aggie, "the attack cat" (p. 76), scared off a burglar; Sparky protected a poodle from a pit bull attack; and Puss Puss rescued a lamb from drowning in a swimming pool. Find out *how* they managed these daring deeds, and you will see how amazing cats can be.

Dogs are heroes too! Perhaps you've heard of Balto, who led a dogsled team through blizzard conditions to deliver lifesaving medicine to children in Alaska in 1925. More recently all kinds of dogs used their exceptional skills after September 11, 2001, to work with the human "heroes at Ground Zero" (p. 12) in search-and-rescue operations. Other dogs helped out because they had been trained to comfort people who were discouraged, exhausted, and sad. A guide dog was even able to lead his human to safety from the seventy-eighth floor of One World Trade Center. Not only can dogs help people who are blind, but they can also pull a wheelchair or alert people who are deaf. Some dogs are trained to sniff for bombs and other illegally smuggled things; others are trained to find people buried in avalanches. But even dogs that haven't been trained can save lives. Bullet was "just" a family pet, but he saved a three-week-old baby. *Hero Dogs: Courageous Canines in Action,* by Donna M. Jackson, will help you appreciate the warmth of a cold nose even more.

Let's stop briefly to see a clip of a famous and heroic dog of stage and screen . . . Here comes Lassie to the rescue now!

> **Show the clip from the very beginning of the movie *Lassie* where the hounds are chasing a fox and Lassie stands up to them so the fox can slip away.**

Wouldn't you reward a heroic dog with a bone? But maybe not until the dog has learned how to spell! Instead of playing Hangman, let's play Hang Dog.

> **Go to the website www.wolfweb.com.au/cgibin/hangman .cgi, and ask members of the audience to try guessing letters while you click on them.**

Remember Mouse? What if a dog really *could* talk . . . out loud, and unlike Mouse . . . to anyone!

> "Excuse me," the dog said . . . "I'm in trouble. Could you please help me?" Amy stopped, panicked . . . The last thing she would have expected a dog to say if it *could* talk was "Excuse me" and "Please." She wouldn't have guessed that a dog would be so polite . . . From what she had seen, dogs tended to eat out of garbage cans, bark all night, and poop where people were most likely to step. None of these struck her as indications of deep thinking. Yet here was this dog, speaking in a grumbly-barky but easy-to-understand voice, asking politely and intelligently for help. (pp. 2–3)

But this is not your average dog. F-32 is an escapee from a research facility at a nearby college where scientists have been attempting to increase human intelligence by first experimenting on dogs. Although it was lonely to be shut in the laboratory at night, F-32 had been relatively happy, until he heard the lead scientist planning "to cut open his brain to see how it [worked]!" (p. 30) And now it is up to Amy to save him. Although she is constantly picked on by the nastiest and most popular girl in the fifth grade, Amy's troubles can't compare to Sherlock's life-or-death situation. Yes, he wants a real name, not a letter and number, and naming him after the famous detective seems a natural choice. With the help of Sean, the smartest, shortest (he skipped a grade) kid in the class, and Minneh, who has also been rejected by the popular Kaitlyn, Amy has a fighting chance to help Sherlock lead a normal doggy life. But Sherlock keeps drawing attention to himself, the kids keep getting caught up in the web of lies they've been weaving, and the college students are starting to close in. What's a *Smart Dog* to do? Read Vivian Vande Velde's story; it may raise your IQ too!

Talking about raising your IQ, have you ever heard of Pavlov and his dog? Pavlov was a scientist who was able to prove that you can train a dog to act in a certain way. Pavlov rang a bell every time he fed his dog, and after a while he noticed that his dog expected food when the bell rang, even if there was no food around. Let's see if we can recreate Pavlov's experiment. Who would like to help?

Call for a volunteer to play the online Pavlov's Dog game from http://nobelprize.org/educational_games/medicine/pavlov/

Pavlov's Dog. http://nobelprize.org/educational_games/medicine/
pavlov/, © Nobel Web AB. Used with permission.

while it is projected onto a screen for everyone to see. Wait until the volunteer gets it right and receives a diploma before continuing.

Let's see how Lisa's dog, Penny, helps her with her math homework on measurement. Lisa is allowed to use nonstandard units of measure, for example, dog biscuits instead of inches and feet. She measures Penny's ears (with cotton swabs), how high she can jump (using her own body), and her weight (using the seesaw in the park). She measures how much time she spends taking care of Penny (guess how long it takes to clip her toenails?) and how long it takes for Penny to sprint from her bed to her food dish. She even measures how much Penny costs (having a pet *can* get expensive) and how much she is worth. Read Loreen Leedy's *Measuring Penny* and calculate the value of a good burglar alarm, exercise machine, live entertainer, and best friend.

Display Joel Sartore's photograph of a Siberian tiger grooming from http://animals.nationalgeographic.com/animals/en large/siberian-tiger-grooming_image.html.

When T.J. is ten weeks old his mother dies and he refuses to eat. He is already underweight because, due to her illness, his mother hadn't fed him enough. The staff at the Denver Zoo must try to raise him themselves. Using different kinds of math pictures they record how much T.J. eats and how much he weighs so they can track his struggle to survive. Ann Whitehead Nagda and Cindy Bickel introduce you to *Tiger Math: Learning to Graph from a Baby Tiger* and show you how big a ten-pound Siberian Tiger cub can grow. Here kitty, kitty!

Have you heard about cloning? Cloning is when you take the basic building blocks of life from one animal and use them to create another. Here's a game where you can guess which kitten was cloned.

> **View http://nature.ca/genome/04/041/0415_e.cfm. Explain that the cloned kitten is the one with the same DNA as the mother, but point out the fact that they don't look exactly alike.**

Copy Cat game from http://nature.ca.
Courtesy of the Canadian Museum of Nature, Ottawa, Canada.

All it takes is one scratch. Ever since the leopard cub scratched Charlie when he was little he has been able to speak "cat"; it's a good thing. His parents, who are scientists, have just been kidnapped, and it's up to Charlie to save them. With the help of an informal feline news network he starts to track them down. Their trail takes him onto a circus ship, where he uses his language skills to train some lions; they too offer him aid and comfort. His parents have been kidnapped because they discovered a cure for the cat allergies that seem to have struck most children around the world (but not Charlie). But this is bigger than just Charlie and his parents: if Charlie can save his parents, he can also save the world. Can Charlie do that and also honor his promise to return the lions to their homeland? Read *Lion Boy,* by Zizou Corder, the first in an exciting trilogy, and get in touch with your inner cat, lion, and even saber-toothed tiger!

On a lighter note, if you're talking to your saber-toothed tiger or house pet, here are some *Riddles to Tell Your Cat,* by Caroline Levine:

> What do cats eat for breakfast? Mice Krispies.
>
> What did the [cat] say when the doctor gave her a shot? Me-*ow*!
>
> What do you call an eight-sided cat? An octo-puss.
>
> Five copycats were sitting on a fence. One jumped off. How many were left? None.
>
> What was Egypt's most beautiful queen? Cleo-cat-ra.

Varjak Paw is not a descendent of Cleo-cat-ra; he is a descendent of Jalal, the mighty hunter. He is not much more than a kitten, a purebred Mesopotamian Blue, but not yet full grown. Because his Elder Paw has told him about his famous ancestor, Varjak yearns to explore beyond the house in which he has always lived. The Contessa owns the house and has always cared for his family, but now she is ill and hasn't been seen in many weeks. Instead a sinister man and his two coal-black cats have taken over the household. When the two black cats attack Elder, Varjak escapes over the wall surrounding the house. Before he dies, Elder tells Varjak to bring back a dog to defeat the man and his cats. But Varjak doesn't even know what a dog is. In the outside world he meets Holly and Tam, two independent cats who protect him and explain about the mysterious vanishings of cats throughout the city. Varjak starts having dreams in which he meets Jalal and begins his training in the seven skills of Jalal's Way, a kind of martial arts for cats. When Tam disappears, Varjak and Holly search for him and must confront the notorious gang leader Sally Bones, "a thin white cat with one ice blue eye . . . and an empty socket . . . around her was the smell of darkness, of dank and deadly things and places" (pp. 164–165). **(Show picture of Sally Bones on p. 165.)** Just as she is about to kill Varjak, their fight is interrupted by a giant, slobbering monster of a dog named Cludge. Varjak, Holly, and Cludge return to the Contessa's house, where they try to save Varjak's family, even if they don't want to be saved, and discover the truth behind the hundreds of vanished cats. What can they do against the soulless evil of the man and his two malevolent, machinelike cats? Read *Varjak Paw,* by SF Said, and learn how to "[move] faster than you can see" (p. 128) and other secrets of the Way.

Varjak Paw is a fictional character, but here are some real-life karate cats.

Show the YouTube video "Karate Cats" from www.youtube .com/watch?v=JwnpFTB8vPg.

In all honesty, Mesopotamian Blue Cats like Varjak Paw don't exist— they are a figment of the author's imagination. However, a Cornish Rex is a rare but real type of cat.

Project a picture of a Cornish Rex, a very unusual-looking breed of cat with big ears, from http://absolutelycats.tripod .com/24CornishRexGallery.html while you speak about the next book.

Purloom Popcorn is a grand champion Cornish Rex show cat with one blazing blue eye and one glittering golden eye. Before he became famous he was just an ordinary kitten, but he has forgotten what being a house cat is like. It has been a long time since he was "cuddled . . . , [had anyone tickle] his curly whiskers . . . , [or had a chance to sleep] at the foot of [anyone's] bed" (p. 2). Purloom is accustomed to constantly traveling on the cat-show circuit with his trainer, but his life changes course when his mistress dies and, in accordance with her will, he is sent back to her home, which Melinda's parents have inherited. Melinda thinks he is odd looking. She has always longed for a cat, but Purloom is "too long, too skinny, too wrinkled, and . . . [has] too little fur" (p. 12). "He certainly [isn't] a cat to trade a home, a neighborhood, a school, friends, a world for!" (pp. 16–17) Purloom is shocked at how Melinda treats him: she lets him run loose, drops him when he accidentally scratches her, and simply doesn't admire him. He decides to run away to the nearest cat show, but then he notices another cat blocking the stairs. When he closes his blue eye he is shaken to find that the cat has disappeared. Soon he finds out that there are five cats in the house that he alone can see with his "ghost eye." When he is able to see the ghost of his former mistress too, he thinks he may stay after all. But when he can't fit in his mistress's lap because he is alive, he convinces her and the other cats to help him become such an annoyance that Melinda's family will send him back to the cat-show circuit. He succeeds all too well at being a pain, but the family decides to send him to the pound instead. Keep your *Ghost Eye* on Purloom Popcorn to see if Marion Dane Bauer can find a way to change his fate.

Even if you don't have any cats in your house, they creep into your life through language. Who knows what the following expressions mean? **(Call for volunteers.)**

> Copycat
>
> Cat got your tongue?
>
> [To] let the cat out of the bag
>
> Curiosity killed the cat. (pp. 4–11)

These are from *There's a Frog in My Throat: 440 Animal Sayings a Little Bird Told Me,* by Loreen Leedy and Pat Street. And for equal time, here are some dog expressions:

> Doggie bag
>
> This place is going to the dogs.

His bark is worse than his bite.

It's a three-dog night (It's very cold [so you need three dogs in bed with you]). (pp. 4–11)

Remember Pavlov's dog, who was trained to slobber when he heard a bell ring? Here's a true dog story filled with slobber. Marley was a big goofball of a dog. He was a golden Labrador retriever who had inherited the "desire to fetch . . . [but] didn't quite get that he was supposed to return" (p. 23) whatever was thrown for him. He "always came on command—unless something caught his attention, such as another dog, squirrel . . . or floating weed seed. He always sat—unless he felt like standing. He always heeled—unless there was something so tempting it was worth strangling himself over, such as another dog, squirrel . . . Well, you get the idea" (pp. 46–47). Marley ate anything that came his way: "bath towels, sponges, socks, and used Kleenex" (p. 48); once even a gold necklace. Needless to say Marley flunked obedience school, or to be more honest, he was expelled. Of course, when he was more mature, he took a make-up class and passed—then he ate his diploma. Marley actually had a part in a movie once, but most of his life was just ordinary. He loved swims in the ocean, but wait until you read about the important law he broke at "Dog Beach." Like most dogs he loved his first encounter with snow, except you'll never guess what happened when he actually got on a sled. He also had ordinary dog fears; however, his response to thunderstorms was *way* over the top. *Marley: A Dog like No Other,* by John Grogan, will introduce you to 97 pounds of pooch who grabbed life by the paws and licked it up. (SLURP!)

> **For a real-life wacky dog, show the "Bike-Riding Dalmatian" video from Japanese television that's available on any number of websites, including www.coolanimalclips.com/view video.php?vid=76&sec=mr&cid=9.**

Wouldn't you love to hear the story from Marley's point of view? Well, this is the next best thing. *I, Jack* was written by Jack the dog (as told to Patricia Finney), a golden Lab that is loveable but foolish. Of course you will need to understand "dog" before reading Jack's story, but there just happens to be a handy word list at the back of the book to help you translate from "Jackspeak" (p. 82) into English. Here are some examples before I get started:

apedogs—dogs' name for humans

Big White Water Dish—toilet

NotFetch—you fetch the stick, and then forget to bring it back

talkbone—telephone

Terrible Hurty Kaboom—shotgun

weeeaw cars—police cars/ambulances

Wet Message—pee (pp. 82–85 [capitalization as noted in book])

Jack first introduces us to his pack, which is composed of five apedogs, including a Packleader, a Pack Lady, three apedog puppies, and three "normal-walking-with-fur-and-tail-type-dogs but small and hidden-claws" (p. 5). Yes, those are cats, and they help tell the story with comments at the bottom of the page. They call Jack "Big Yellow Stupid" (p. 10) because, among other reasons, Jack is good at playing NotFetch and he likes to drink from the Big White Water Dish. Jack spends most of his time trying to get something to eat, going for walkies, and getting to know the new dog next door. These might sound like ordinary doglike things to do, but whenever Jack gets interested in anything, his apedogs always seem to bark bad words at him. When Petra, the new dog next door, gets pregnant, Jack helps her run away to find a place to have her puppies; then he must bring her food. All this involves thinking, something that is hard for Jack to do, but every once in a while, he has a "head bubble" (p. 116) and acts. By the time Jack is done acting, he has had a run-in with a Terrible Hurty Kaboom, has broken his Packleader's talkbone just when his Packleader is in serious need of rescuing, and weeeaw cars have to be called in. And, oh yes, the puppies look just like Jack. If you could only read the Wet Messages Jack has left, you would know that he is a good dog and a hero besides!

And now, after hearing about all these great pets, wouldn't you like to buy one for yourself?

Listen to "Gonna Buy Me a Dog," by the Monkees, from their album *Monkees Music Box,* or check it out on YouTube.

Whether you are a dog person or a cat person, whether or not your parents will allow you to have a dog or a cat . . . at least there is a book here for you!

EXPANDING YOUR OPTIONS

Books for Use with Younger Audiences

"Mrs. Jane Tabby could not explain why all four of her children have wings . . . 'Maybe they [have] wings because I dreamed, before they were born, that I could fly away from this neighborhood,' said [their mother]" (p. 3). Thelma, Roger, James, and Harriet were born into an extremely bad area, with terrible traffic and less and less to eat. When Harriet gets away from a ravenous dog by flying over a wall, their mother realizes it is time for them to escape city life. But will country life, with predatory owls and coyotes, be any safer for them? How will they survive? Read *Catwings,* by Ursula K. Le Guin, and discover the purrfect book. (And it has sequels too!)

What's better to do when you are hiding in a storm cellar with a twister bearing down on you than listen to stories? As they wait out the storm, Peter the farmhand entertains the whole family with a story from his childhood: "Along about lunch, it hit. Only there was no warning . . . No funnel cloud, no nothing. One minute we were eating beans and biscuits at the table. Next there was roar—worse than a train— worse than a hundred trains. And then there came a terrible tearing sound, like the world was being ripped apart . . . I looked up and I saw sky. The ceiling was clean gone . . . The tornado had torn the roof off the kitchen and left the food on the table and us in our seats" (p. 7). But that wasn't all the tornado had left. In the yard he found an unknown doghouse and in the doghouse was a big black dog "shaking so hard, the doghouse was in danger of losing its boards" (p. 9). Well, they named the dog Tornado, and his arrival on the scene wasn't the only remarkable thing about him. He could do card tricks and had a most unusual technique for "saving" turtles. Read *Tornado,* by Betsy Byars, and you will also find out that Peter has the perfect solution to the problem of ownership when his original masters find him.

She looks Polish, acts Polish, speaks Polish, and secretly she is a Jew. She and her sister, Mira, the only other surviving member of her family, have a plan to sneak food into the Warsaw Ghetto for the Jews trapped there. The cats, once pampered and loved and now running wild, have shown her the way. Their bodies can find the narrowest crevices for sneaking in and out to catch the mice on which they feed. So she knows where to tell Mira and the smugglers she works with to hide the food. But the day before the plan is to be put into action they find out that the Gestapo, German authorities, will be waiting for them with dogs to track down the smell of food. Only the *Cats in Krasinski Square* can help outsmart the Germans. Read Karen Hesse's story based on an actual event during the dark days of World War II; you will never look at the age-old war between cats and dogs the same way again.

Meet Down Girl and Sit. They take their jobs protecting their masters very seriously. Down Girl, for instance, always wakes up her master well before the alarm clock goes off so it won't scare him; she shields him from the dangerous spanking weapon that the newspaper boy throws every morning. Both dogs guard the places where their families hide their wonderful, stinky food. This is a huge responsibility because humans haven't learned to bury their food the way dogs do. And, of course, they keep their world safe from squirrels and birds. Even if it means eating all the birdseed and acorns in the yard, no sacrifice is too great to keep these enemies away. But then they must face the worst menace of all, Here Kitty Kitty. Try *Down Girl and Sit: Smarter Than Squirrels,* by Lucy Nolan, to see if you can keep up with these two brilliant minds.

"Wimp" and "Scaredy Cat" are Martin's first two nicknames. He was different even from the beginning. Instead of pretending to fight like his brother and sister, he would hide behind his mother. Eating mice made him sick. He actually thought they were pretty. When he discovered that the girl on their farm kept pet rabbits, his mother explained that a pet is something that humans take care of and make a fuss over. The first mouse Martin catches he decides to keep as a pet in an old bathtub he has found in a junk pile. The mouse, "Drusilla," would much rather be a pet than dinner. Not long after, she has eight babies, who call Martin "Uncle." Martin is quite content. The mice are less so; the babies are growing up quickly, are bored with the limits of the bathtub, and are driving Drusilla crazy. Martin lets them go upon Drusilla's urging and then brings her a new husband. But before she can give birth to her second litter, Martin is sold to a lady in the city. All he has now is a litter box and a view from the fourth floor of an apartment building. Escape is all Martin can think about. How does Martin escape—and will he go back to his "mousekeeping" (p. 30) hobby? Read *Martin's Mice,* by Dick King-Smith, and get a unique perspective about life, liberty, and the pursuit of happy mice.

All it takes is an accidental bowl of alphabet soup. "The letters in the soup went up to Martha's brain instead of down to her stomach" and *Martha Speaks.* But, what starts out as fun gets out of hand; she begins ordering carryout (massive quantities of beef, of course), making embarrassing comments in public, and she simply doesn't ever stop talking. She is so hurt when her family tells her to be quiet that she totally stops speaking and, having lost her "appetite for letters," Martha is speechless. One night while her family is out she comes face to face with a burglar in the house. Martha still knows how to dial 911, but she can no longer communicate. It will take more than growls to save the day. Only the author, Susan Meddaugh, knows how Martha does it; that is, until *you* read her book!

Ike has been sent to sleep-away doggy obedience school. The last straw was either eating his mistress's chicken pie or chasing the neighbor's cats onto the fire escape. In either case Ike thinks his banishment is totally unfair and sends daily letters to his owner, Mrs. LaRue, begging her to rethink her decision. After all, since he won't sit or roll over, he has been placed in solitary confinement; he is also being starved and is wasting away from an unknown illness. How can any good dog learn under such conditions? On the ninth day of his prison term Ike escapes. Read *Dear*

Mrs. LaRue: Letters from Obedience School, by Mark Teague, but also read the pictures. The black-and-white pictures are very different from the pictures in color. Only by reading the pictures will you know the truth about what happened to Ike before, during, and after his jail break.

Avi and Hamudi both have a white cat with glossy long fur and blue eyes. Each saves scraps to feed her whenever she turns up at his doorstep. After she has been missing for many weeks Avi finally sees her. She is scrawny, shabby, and very hungry. After she eats and drinks ravenously he follows her until he sees her eat from another boy's hand. They quarrel over whose cat she is, but neither can prove true ownership. Their arguing scares her away. Then all of a sudden, it begins to snow. It is a rare thing indeed in Jerusalem. Both boys worry about their cat getting cold and wet, so they follow her to a box in an alley; there they find her kittens. Avi is a Jew and Hamudi is a Muslim, and their people know little of each other. The chance for Avi and Hamudi to find a compromise is as unusual as *Snow in Jerusalem.* Read Deborah da Costa's story to see how a cat named Snow works a miracle.

The devil sneaks into Noah's ark disguised as a mouse. He does everything he can think of to sabotage the ship. When he starts to gnaw a hole in the bottom of the boat, only Noah's cats can save what's left of the world. Read Arielle North Olson's *Noah's Cats and the Devil's Fire* to see how they do it—and, by the way, you will also find out why cats' eyes glow in the dark.

In 1925, the deadly disease diphtheria could easily have killed everyone in the town of Nome, Alaska. Everyone has heard of Balto, the famous sled-dog leader who delivered lifesaving serum to Nome with a run of 53 miles, but few have heard about Togo, who led his team for more than 350 miles as part of the antiserum run. "The temperature was 40 degrees below zero . . . [Togo's trainer, Leonhard Seppala, thought] about [how to run the] team: Too slow and the dogs would stiffen up. Too fast and just breathing would scorch their lungs . . . their stomachs were beginning to freeze where their fur was thin . . . [one dog's] eyes froze shut" and still Togo led them on. Robert J. Blake's *Togo* reminds us that heroes help every step of the way; Togo is a sled dog with heart and dogged determination. You will feel honored to have met him.

Born into a poor farming family the boy was too sickly to help in the fields, but he was clever. His mother offered him to the priests in the monastery in hopes that he could become a priest as well. He speedily absorbed everything he was taught, but he had one failing: he drew cats all the time and everywhere, even in the books. The priests could not allow this to continue. He was asked to leave but given one strange piece of advice from the oldest priest before he left: "*Avoid large places at night; keep to small.*" Setting his sights on applying for a position at another monastery, he reached that temple at night. The boy had no way of knowing that it was deserted except for a giant goblin rat that, having overwhelmed the priests, now occupied the holy place. When the boy entered the magnificent temple he was puzzled by its emptiness but delighted to see the large blank screens that made up the walls. They would be just right for drawing cats while he waited for the priests to return. What happened to *The Boy Who Drew Cats* when the goblin rat appeared? Since he followed the odd warning he was given earlier, only the cats he drew can tell you for sure; that is, once they have wiped the blood from their whiskers. Read Margaret Hodges's retelling of a legend based on a real Japanese artist who lived over five hundred years ago.

Additional Books for Older Readers

If you aren't from Vermont, they call you a Flatlander. And Josh feels that he doesn't belong anywhere. He dislikes his new stepfather and resents his new baby brother and having to leave his friends in Virginia. The school bully, Wes Rockett, has already targeted him. But one snowy day when he follows his dog, "Manch," he finds out that he can understand what Manch and the other dogs are saying to each other and that they too have a bully problem. When he meets Wes and his gang for an "initiation" rite he can't avoid, he is saved by the appearance of "a huge silver-gray dog with ice blue eyes . . . his teeth bared in a snarl" (p. 36), the leader of the River Gang dogs who have threatened Manch and his friends. This dog and his followers intimidate Wes's crowd, and, to help Josh escape, Manch starts a dogfight with them.

The next day in school Wes says that the initiation will be complete if Josh can bring him the silver-gray dog's collar. The only way out Josh can think of is to steal his stepfather's gun and shoot the vicious beast. This will solve his own problem with Wes and repay Manch for his help. The only hitch is that guns are just too dog-gone dangerous. Katherine Paterson's *The Field of Dogs* offers other options for handling bullies, the two-legged and four-legged kinds.

It's the age-old problem in the town of Hubcap. The elders of the town frown on the bored and restless teen crowd. Because these rowdy delinquents are setting a bad example for the children, they are driven out of town. The young son of the mayor wants to be part of the gang and follows them. Meanwhile bad guys take over the town and it's up to the exiles to save the day. Hold everything! This isn't your ordinary town. These characters are all dogs on wheels. For example, Digger is part retriever, part backhoe; Bull-worth is part bulldog, part bull-dozer; and Brake is part mastiff, part monster truck. Eager young Sparky, part Jack Russell terrier, part utility vehicle, alerts the Mongrel teen pack to the danger when Mr. Big, the leader of the Rottwheeler Gang of high-way bandits, threatens to drain all the town's fuel tanks dry. Fire up your engines and wag your tails as the TruckDogs stop their town from "going to the dogs" (p. 102).

By the way, *TruckDogs: A Novel in Four Bites* may have been written by Graeme Base, but it was actually "told to him by his dog Molly" (**who is featured on the cover at right**).

Cover of *TruckDogs*, by Graeme Base. Courtesy of Abrams Books for Young Readers/Amulet Books.

Whittington is no longer a house-pet type of cat; kicked out of his last home, he's got a torn ear and is definitely not cute anymore. Like all the other animals in the barn he is old and a leftover. Bernie, who owns the barn, has a soft heart. He and his wife are raising their grandchildren Abby, age ten, and Ben, eight. When Abby and Ben start coming to visit the animals, Whittington begins to tell all of them the story of his famous ancestor and his man, Dick Whittington. "[Dick Whittington] owed his wealth to his cat . . . [His] name survives but his cat's name is lost . . . If it hadn't been for his cat, no one would remember Dick. Now no one remembers his cat" (p. 35). But Whittington is determined to remedy this, if only for the residents of the barn—including the rats. As Whittington tells how Dick, born in poverty, tries to learn to read, it becomes clear that Ben too is struggling in school. Lady, the duck who is the leader of the animals, decides that Abby should teach Ben the way Dick learned. In between Whittington's episodes of Dick's amazing adventures, we see Ben's efforts to stay out of the special reading class so he can avoid the name calling he will undergo if he can't keep up. Each chapter of Dick Whittington's life shows how a boy can "take charge of himself" (p. 157) and earn riches beyond telling, while Ben takes his own painful steps to reach a different kind of treasure. Learning to read is "like being born" (p. 185) to Ben. Get cozy in the barn with Alan Armstrong's *Whittington,* a cat with a long memory, whose name you won't forget.

"The day I decided to steal a dog was the same day my best friend . . . found out I lived in a car" (p. 3). Georgina Hayes' father has left her family; when they are kicked out of their apartment, they are officially homeless. If Georgina can just get $500, she can help her mom make a deposit on another apartment. All she has to do is find a dog whose owner looks like he loves him enough and can afford to pay a big reward to get him back. So Georgina and her little brother Toby steal Willy, a little black-and-white bundle of energy. Stealing is the easy part. Once they meet Willy's owner, things get complicated. Barbara O'Connor gives you detailed advice on *How to Steal a Dog.* Make sure you don't skip any of the steps, or you will find out all the things that can go wrong with the best-laid plans.

Twelve-year-old Lily's family has "seven weeks . . . to move out, lock, stock, and barrel . . . [They] have to take everything with [them]: furniture, food . . . all [their] animals, farm machinery . . . Nothing [of] value must be left behind" (p. 37). Why? It is 1943, and the army will be using their land to practice "landings from the sea for the invasion of France" (p. 37). Three thousand people have to leave, but no one can explain the situation to Lily's cat, Tips. "She's out there somewhere in the night, cold and wet, hungry and lost, and I've only got one more day to find her before they close off the farm" (p. 72). Since Tips is still missing after the deadline passes, Lily keeps sneaking back through the barbed wire to find her, despite daily bombings. The American soldier, Adie, who befriends Lily, promises to keep searching too. Fifty years later, as Lily's grandson reads her diary, Michael Morpurgo's *The Amazing Story of Adolphus Tips* accounts for a good number of Tips's nine lives and includes one other miracle that will change Lily's life forever.

Additional Music

Play "Old Blue," a traditional song adapted by the Byrds in 1969 and recorded by many other artists.

Listen to Kirk Olsen's "The Dog Beach Boogie" from his CD *Dog Songs,* or view the music video on his website at www.dogsongs.net.

Additional Films and Videos

View Disney's *Lady and the Tramp.* Show the part where the cats are singing "The Siamese Cat Song."

Additional Websites

Here is a good site to visit if you want to adopt a cat; it could go with *Ghost Eye:* http://home.online.no/~mmera/.

Cats attacking toilet paper can be found at www.youtube.com/watch?v=cbRljNwZ7yU. This clip can be used in place of the silly cats video at the beginning of this booktalk.

Mr. Poodle Head, a fun dress-up game for younger children, can be found at www.yuckles.com/poodlehead.html.

Convert your age from human years to dog years at http://library .thinkquest.org/CR0211900/activities/human_to_dog_years.htm.

Take the "Name That Dog" quiz at http://library.thinkquest.org/ CR0211900/activities/name.htm to see if you remember famous dogs from books and movies.

Additional Activities

Recite some jokes and riddles from *Give a Dog a Bone: Stories, Poems, Jokes, and Riddles about Dogs,* by Joanna Cole and Stephanie Calmenson:

> Why does a watch dog run around in circles? To wind himself up.
>   (p. 74)
> Patient: I was bitten on the leg by a dog.
> Doctor: Did you put anything on it?
> Patient: No. He liked it just the way it was. (p. 75)
> What do you call a dog with the flu? A germy shepherd. (p. 76)

Read aloud some of the funny names of books in the chapter titled "Bow-Wow Bookshop Best Sellers for Dogs":

> *Puddles on the Floor* by Ima Puppy
> *Canine Cookbook* by O. Penn Accan
> *Dogs and Their Hobbies* by Chasen Katz
> *102 Dalmatians* by Seymour Spotz
> *Home Alone* by Chew N. D'Chaire (pp. 84–85)

Read more dog and cat expressions from *There's a Frog in My Throat: 440 Animal Sayings a Little Bird Told Me,* by Loreen Leedy and Pat Street, and ask your audience if they know what these mean:

> She's as sick as a dog.
> She's dogging my footsteps.
> Dog-eared page

This place is going to the dogs.

My dogs are barking. (My feet hurt.)

Putting on the dog

That dog won't hunt. (That idea won't work.) (pp. 4–8)

Fat cat

Kitty-corner

As weak as a kitten

Catnap

While the cat's away

To play cat and mouse

Who will bell the cat? (Who will face danger for the good
    of us all?) (pp. 9–11)

Here's a chance to see how much you know about cats and dogs.
Take this quiz from Patricia Lauber's *The True-or-False Book of Cats:*

1. Cats don't like to be stared at. Answer: True. "A stare is a
   threat." However, cats will like it if you look at them while
   blinking or with half-opened eyes. "Looking without staring
   is like blowing kisses—it's warm and friendly." (p. 6)

2. Cats have a hard time coming down trees. Answer: True.
   "The muscles of the hind leg are most suited to pushing
   forward and up." (p. 21)

3. Cats have nine lives. Answer: False. "Cats may seem to have
   more than one life because they are quick . . . nimble. They
   often escape harm when another animal might not." (p. 23)

And take this quiz from *The True-or-False Book of Dogs:*

1. Only some dogs are descended from wolves. Answer: False.
   Given the great variety we see in dogs—compare a bulldog
   to a greyhound, for example—"it's hard to believe that they
   are all the same kind of animal," but scientists have proven
   that they all originated from wolves. "Wolves var[y] in size,
   color, and behavior . . . they ha[ve] different traits," just like
   dogs. (pp. 8–9)

2. A dog treats a bone the way a wolf treats extra food. Answer: True. To hide its leftovers from other predators, a wolf will "dig a hole, . . . drop the [extra] meat in . . . and use its nose to fill the hole with loose dirt." Dogs can't carry dog food from a can around so easily, but they can carry a bone and will bury one in the same way that wolves do. (p. 16)

3. Dogs see what we see. Answer: False. "Dogs see some color, but can't see the . . . range of colors that we do." Like their "wolf ancestors . . . they don't need to see color. They need to see well in dim light . . . [and] don't need to see detail. They need to see movement—the fleeing prey." (p. 20)

RESOURCES CITED

Books

Armstrong, Alan. *Whittington.* Random House/Listening Library, 2006.

Base, Graeme. *TruckDogs: A Novel in Four Bites.* Amulet Books, 2004.

Bauer, Marion Dane. *Ghost Eye.* Scholastic, 1992.

Blake, Robert J. *Togo.* Philomel, 2002.

Byars, Betsy. *Tornado.* HarperCollins, 1996.

Cole, Joanna, and Stephanie Calmenson. *Give a Dog a Bone: Stories, Poems, Jokes, and Riddles about Dogs.* Scholastic, 1996.

Corder, Zizou. *Lion Boy.* Dial, 2004.

da Costa, Deborah. *Snow in Jerusalem.* Albert Whitman, 2001.

De Zutter, Hank. *Who Says a Dog Goes Bow-Wow?* Doubleday, 1993.

Finney, Patricia. *I, Jack.* HarperCollins, 2004.

George, Jean Craighead. *How to Talk to Your Cat.* HarperCollins, 2000.

———. *How to Talk to Your Dog.* HarperCollins, 2000.

Grogan, John. *Marley: A Dog like No Other.* Collins, 2007.

Hesse, Karen. *Cats in Krasinski Square.* Scholastic, 2004.

Hodges, Margaret. *The Boy Who Drew Cats.* Holiday House, 2002.

Jackson, Donna M. *Hero Dogs: Courageous Canines in Action.* Little, Brown, 2003.

King-Smith, Dick. *Martin's Mice*. Yearling, 1989.

Lauber, Patricia. *The True-or-False Book of Cats*. National Geographic Society, 1998.

———. *The True-or-False Book of Dogs*. HarperCollins, 2003.

Le Guin, Ursula K. *Catwings*. Orchard Books, 1988.

Leedy, Loreen. *Measuring Penny*. Henry Holt, 1997.

Leedy, Loreen, and Pat Street. *There's a Frog in My Throat: 440 Animal Sayings a Little Bird Told Me*. Holiday House, 2003.

Levine, Caroline. *Riddles to Tell Your Cat*. Albert Whitman, 1992.

Matthews, L. S. *A Dog for Life*. Delacorte, 2006.

Meddaugh, Susan. *Martha Speaks*. Houghton Mifflin, 1992.

Morpurgo, Michael. *The Amazing Story of Adolphus Tips*. Scholastic, 2006.

Nagda, Ann Whitehead, and Cindy Bickel. *Tiger Math: Learning to Graph from a Baby Tiger*. Henry Holt, 2000.

Nolan, Lucy. *Down Girl and Sit: Smarter Than Squirrels*. Marshall Cavendish, 2004.

O'Connor, Barbara. *How to Steal a Dog*. Farrar, Straus and Giroux, 2007.

Olson, Arielle North. *Noah's Cats and the Devil's Fire*. Orchard Books, 1992.

Paterson, Katherine. *The Field of Dogs*. HarperCollins, 2001.

Said, SF. *Varjak Paw*. David Fickling Books, 2003.

Singer, Marilyn. *Cats to the Rescue: True Tales of Heroic Felines*. Henry Holt, 2006.

Teague, Mark. *Dear Mrs. LaRue: Letters from Obedience School*. Scholastic, 2002.

Vande Velde, Vivian. *Smart Dog*. Sterling, 2004.

Music

The Byrds. "Old Blue." *Dr. Byrds and Mr. Hyde*. Columbia, 1969.

The Monkees. "Gonna Buy Me a Dog." *The Monkees Music Box*. Rhino Records, 2001.

Olsen, Kirk. "The Dog Beach Boogie." *Dog Songs.* Happy Dog Records, 2002.

Films and Videos

Lady and the Tramp. Directed by Clyde Geronimi, Wilfred Jackson, and Hamilton Luske. Walt Disney Productions, 1955.
Lassie. Directed by Charles Sturridge. Davis Films, 2005.

Websites

Absolutely Cats. "Cornish Rex Gallery of Cats and Kittens." http://absolutelycats.tripod.com/24CornishRexGallery.html.
Canadian Museum of Nature. "Online Games—Copy Cat—The Geee! in Genome." http://nature.ca/genome/04/041/0415_e.cfm.
Crunchmutt Studios. Cool Animal Clips. "Bike-Riding Dalmation." www.coolanimalclips.com/viewvideo.php?vid=76&sec=mr&cid=9.
FunnyCatVideos.net. "Funny Cat Video Compilation 1." www.funnycatvideos.net/funny-cat-video-compilation-1.html.
Mona. Schibboleths Cattery—British Shorthair. http://home.online.no/~mmera/.
Moore, Glenda. Catsuff: Games. "Aquarium." www.xmission.com/~emailbox/games/aquarium/aquarium.htm.
National Geographic Society. Animals. "Siberian Tiger Grooming." http://animals.nationalgeographic.com/animals/enlarge/siberian-tiger-grooming_image.html.
Official Website of the Nobel Foundation. "Pavlov's Dog." http://nobelprize.org/educational_games/medicine/pavlov/.
Olsen, Kirk. "Dog Songs." www.dogsongs.net.
Oracle Education Foundation: Think Quest. Man's Best Friend—Online Activities. "Human to Dog Years." http://library.thinkquest.org/CR0211900/activities/human_to_dog_years.htm.

————. "Name That Dog." http://library.thinkquest.org/CR0211900/ activities/name.htm.

Wolf Web Solutions. "Hang Dog." www.wolfweb.com.au/cgibin/ hangman.cgi.

YouTube. "Karate Cats." Posted by lesbrent. www.youtube.com/ watch?v=JwnpFTB8vPg.

YouTube. "Silly Kittens." Posted by Gingersdk. www.youtube.com/ watch?v=cbRljNwZ7yU.

Yuckles. "Mr. Poodle Head." www.yuckles.com/poodlehead.html.

————. "Sound Effects for Your Dog by Yuckles." www.yuckles.com/ dogsounds.htm.

Booktalking with Pizzazz

Using Science Experiments, Music, Magic, Crafts, Creative Dramatics, Video and Film, Role-Playing, Games, and the Internet with Booktalks

On Saturday, June 26, 2004, at the ALA Annual Conference, Betsy Diamant-Cohen, Blane Halliday, and Selma K. Levi presented a program called "Booktalking with Pizzazz," which was sponsored by the Public Library Association (PLA). The description in the conference catalog read:

> Today's library users, from preschool to seniors, are becoming increasingly media savvy. This program contains examples of "media talks," which are still rooted in the traditional book but use other media to add another dimension, e.g., science experiments, creative dramatics, videos, and magic tricks, to the traditional booktalk program. With these additions, short talks can easily be expanded into full-blown subject programs.

Equipment used included an audiocassette/CD player, a laptop with Internet connections, an LCD projector and screen, and a video player with projection capabilities. Below is a description of what was said and done. Because we wanted to stay true to our presentation, we have not updated it. This means that some websites mentioned are no longer viable. If you would like to use the material, substitute websites are easy to find through Google searches. In addition, please note that we realize comments such as waiting for the next Harry Potter book are outdated. But, since our program was not taped, we felt it was important to reproduce the original in its entirety. The handout that accompanied the program is reproduced in the appendix.

THE ALA PROGRAM

Blane started out with projecting the short film (with music) from *Rosie's Walk*. After about a minute, Selma began to speak and Blane muted the music.

Selma: Welcome to "Booktalking with Pizzazz." My name is Selma Levi. I am the supervisor of the Children's Department at the Central Enoch Pratt Free Library in Baltimore. With me, I have Betsy Diamant-Cohen, children's programming specialist at the Enoch Pratt Free Library, and Blane Halliday, former supervisor of the Sights and Sounds Department at the Enoch Pratt Free Library and currently senior AV specialist at the Collier County Florida Public Library. First I'd like to give you a feel for the genesis of this program. I was driving down the road one day listening to National Public Radio and it struck me just how the music they selected enhanced each segment as they segued from one story to the next. What a great way to pep up a booktalk!

I took my ideas back to the library and with input from Betsy and Blane, we not only added music, but we inserted Internet sites, science experiments, video clips, drama, and, as you will soon see, much more to the mix. Because Pratt also serves as Maryland's State Library Resource Center, we felt committed to using both older materials as well as new. By publicizing these oldies but goodies, our hope was to expose them to a new generation of users and give them new life. We also chose materials that would appeal to a wide range of ages. Because Betsy and I are both children's librarians, Blane is a bit outnumbered in the book department, but we feel very strongly that these techniques will be useful for all age programming! For example, you just watched and listened to *Rosie's Walk,* a film based on the book by Pat Hutchins. Normally, you would watch this film with preschoolers. But we have found that its humor appeals to everyone, and we encourage you to take a second look at films such as this.

The films we show you today have public performance rights, and we have copyright permission for all of the songs we use today as well.

A note of caution: There are three of us presenting today. Do not try to do everything at once all by yourself! A snippet of song, a touch of magic, one Internet site, will be more than enough to enhance your booktalk presentation without making you run around like a chicken without its head. And speaking of chickens . . .

Fowl Play

Selma: Dick King-Smith is most famous for writing about a certain pig named Babe, but my favorite of his books is *The Fox Busters.*

The foxes' depredations at Foxearth Farm were out of control. Farmer Farmer (yes, that was his name) had lost control of the situation, but, fortunately, three chicks hatched that changed the course of history. Now, I happen to be a farmer's granddaughter and I know that chickens can't fly very well, but I just wanted to make sure that you realize that most chickens can barely make it to the top of a fence. I do assume that you know that chickens normally lay their eggs in nests. These chicks were exceptional. Not only did they learn to fly, high, they learned to lay eggs in flight. Not only did they learn to lay eggs in flight, they learned to lay hard-boiled eggs in flight. Look out, foxes, bombs away!

> **Then Selma played the theme song of the movie *Ghostbusters* (striking a pose and snapping her fingers), but just when it came to the part that says "Who ya gonna call?" she turned off the music and substituted the word *Foxbusters!***

Moving right along with our chicken theme is *Some of the Adventures of Rhode Island Red,* by Stephen Manes.

> The first anybody ever heard of Red was when they found him in Mrs. Huckaby's henhouse. The Mrs. was gathering eggs and when she stuck her hand under Old Rhody, the queen of the flock, she felt something soft and squishy-like. Mrs. Huckaby squeezed her hand around it and all of a sudden there was a yell so bloodcurdling it fractured her spectacles.
>
> Well, Mrs. H. was pretty near-sighted . . . She could see a broken egg, but Mrs. H. never heard of a broken egg hollering like that. So she looked a little closer. There in the middle of the yolk was a little baby boy, no bigger than your toenail and nearly as pink, wearing a tiny little diaper and kicking like the hind end of a mule. (p. 8)

Young Red speaks chicken with a human accent and is immediately accepted into the family. On his first day of school, he beats up ten kids and an English teacher. Sent home, he convinces his parents that vacation has started early, and he sets off to seek his fortune. He advocates for chickens everywhere by leading a strike, convincing chickens to give no eggs without better food. Unfortunately, he falls in love with the daughter of the man running for mayor, whose election-year promise is to put "two chickens in every pot." You don't have to be big to be a hero. Red's brains show him the way to save his relatives without endangering a single feather. Read the most recent addition to the tall-tale hall of fame: after Paul Bunyan and Pecos Bill, there is now *Rhode Island Red*!

Selma and Betsy then mimed the Chicken Dance without using music and asked the audience to guess which dance they were doing. Then Betsy took over.

Betsy: One of the advantages of the Internet is that it enables you to travel all over the world from the comfort of your very own library. Since we were just talking about chickens, we can use the Internet to visit a website in the Netherlands, where we can see a live-time chicken coop and listen to the chickens squawking. Live from a chicken coop in Deventer in the Netherlands, here are some Dutch chickens, complete with noises!

> **Betsy showed the website www.kippenpagina.nl/kippenweb cam/.**

And since chickens come from eggs, have a look at this website (**Betsy showed www.rochedalss.eq.edu.au/chickens/experi ments.htm**). If you've ever wondered how to make an egg bounce, look at this bouncing-egg experiment from Rochedale State School. You can also try out some chicken jokes (**Betsy clicked on "Chicken Jokes" in the left column and read one of them out loud**). You can also play games with words that have *egg* in them by clicking over here (**Betsy clicked on "Egg Words" in the left column and read some of the words aloud**). Now, back to Selma . . .

Mad Scientists

Selma: We really haven't got a chicken fetish, but we couldn't resist starting our "Mad Scientists" segment with an eggs-periment story. Have you ever needed eggs-tra credit? *Egg-Drop Blues,* by Jacqueline Turner Banks, is about twin brothers Judge and Jury. Judge needs to earn extra credit for science in a big way. He's signed up for the egg-drop contest with his brother, but Jury has a reputation for being troublesome at the most inopportune times. How does Judge feel about his dyslexia and the conflicts with his brother? He'll need more than Styrofoam and duct tape to come to grips with this situation.

And now, Blane will scramble your brains a little bit more!

Blane: Hello! I am Blane Halliday, AV librarian for the Collier County Public Library here in beautiful sunny Florida! As Selma mentioned . . . we're here to show you how you can add some pizzazz to your booktalks, even possibly develop them beyond a booktalk into a complete themed program. I find the term *booktalk* to be very limiting. Today's library users, from the youngest preschooler to the eldest senior, are becoming increasingly media savvy with bombardment from TV, radio, the Internet, and myriad other access points. With that in mind, what follows are a few examples of what I call media talks, which are still rooted in the traditional book, but use other media to add another dimension to the endeavor. With the addition of the media, these short talks can easily be expanded into a full-blown subject program.

Here is a conceptual art piece that follows a Rube Goldberg–type experiment where there are chain reactions that just keep happening with no particular purpose, but they're fun to watch. I'm going to fast-forward through some of the slower parts just to give you a feel for what it is like. Please note that the only sound is that of the experiment itself.

Blane showed a clip of the big hanging trash-bag sequence from *The Way Things Go*.

Betsy: Perhaps you would like to encourage children and adults to enter the Rube Goldberg machine contest at this website.

Betsy showed www.rube-goldberg.com/html/contest.htm and scrolled down and read what some of the past challenges had been.

Selma: Children's literature has its own Rube Goldbergian (is that a word?) marvel in William Pène Du Bois's *Lazy Tommy Pumpkinhead.*

Those inventions may not have had any practical applications, but Lazy Tommy Pumpkinhead has a bed that has a definite purpose in his life.

> Lazy Tommy Pumpkinhead lived in an electric house. In the morning, when the sun rose over the hill and warmed his windowsill, his bed started to move . . . slid Lazy Tommy out, out of his nightshirt, into a bathtub filled with hot water . . . [A] water-spinning machine . . . made waves to splash and wash him. The bathtub then tipped over and slid Lazy Tommy out, water and all, through a trapdoor in the floor, into the drying room, into a harness which held him standing up . . . Lazy Tommy Pumpkinhead stayed standing to be dried . . . Hot air blew all over Lazy Tommy . . . A tooth-brushing

machine squeezed toothpaste on his teeth and scrubbed them. An electric comb and brush parted his black hair. Lazy Tommy found this made him tired . . .

It was soon over and he slid down a chute into his [clothes]. Still held up by his harness . . . rolling down a hall to the dining room, a sailor suit top fell on Lazy Tommy.

At the table, the eating machine played music and fed [him with] . . . cold cereal, hot cereal, five bananas, four apples, six scrambled eggs, ten slices of bacon, and eight pieces of hot toast and jam. The eating machine then poured one quart of orange juice and two quarts of milk followed by seven cups of cocoa into Lazy Tommy. [It] . . . then wiped Lazy Tommy's face . . . and turned itself off. After eating, Lazy Tommy was really tired . . . He wiggled out of his harness, pushed himself away from the table, and walked slowly to the staircase. He looked sadly at the terrible stairs, . . . [but] made himself start the BIG CLIMB because he knew that, hard as it was, when the sun set at night, he would at long last reach . . . his lovely electric bed. (pp. 1–12)

Well, all this is just fine and dandy, but one night there was a tremendous storm and the electricity went out. When he wasn't awakened by his bed, Lazy Tommy just kept sleeping. Seven days later the electricity was restored. The bathwater was seven days old and seven days cold, and the eating machine was filled to bursting with seven days' worth of food. As Tommy goes headfirst through the trapdoor, William Pène Du Bois's story will show you why labor-saving devices just aren't what they're cracked up to be.

Lazy Tommy's house is anything but ordinary, and neither is the result of this next experiment . . .

Allen Brewster, the hero of *Top Secret,* by John Reynolds Gardiner, doesn't want to do an ordinary science experiment for his science project. You've all heard about photosynthesis, when plants turn sunlight into food. Allen decides to try human photosynthesis. He ends up turning his teacher green and finds himself declared a threat to national security by the President of the United States! Don't try this at home!

But, then again, you *can* try this at home . . .

Amaze and delight your audience by demonstrating the results of a related experiment showing how water travels up the stems of plants. From *Plants: A Creative, Hands-On Approach to Science,* by Wendy Baker and Andrew Haslam (pp. 14–15), all you need is one white carnation and green food coloring in a glass of water. In just hours, if you put in enough drops, your flower will be exceedingly green. (We have also found that leaving the flower in a hot car will speed up the process.) Voilà! (And nobody gets grounded, or worse.) **(Selma showed a green carnation.)**

Blane showed a silent clip from *When the Lights Go Out* while Selma began talking about *Shoebag*.

Selma: Like all cockroaches, Shoebag was named after his place of birth. He was snoozing there now, in the open toe of a white summer sandal . . .

"Wake up, Shoebag," his mother shouted. "The jumping spider in the kitchen has let down his dragline! He'll be here soon!"

Of all their enemies, the black jumping spider was the fiercest . . .

"Shoebag!" his mother's voice again, this time from the top of a Reebok next to the sandal, "Hurry up! Get your cerci moving!"

A cerci is what cockroaches call their tails. Shoebag was anxious to get his cerci moving . . .

The trouble was, Shoebag couldn't get his cerci to go.

The reason was, Shoebag's cerci was missing.

So were his two back legs.

So were his two middle legs.

So were his two front legs.

And so were his antennae.

Something terrible had happened to Shoebag.

Shoebag's mother was named Drainboard. His father's name was Under The Toaster. When Drainboard took a good look at Shoebag . . . her shell quivered, and she called out, "Under The Toaster, come here immediately! Something's happened to Shoebag!"

"Something terrible happened to me!" Shoebag said. "I am changed!" . . .

"I have tiny hands," Shoebag said. "I have tiny feet! I have a tiny nose and tiny ears! I have a tiny head!"

"With hair!" Under The Toaster exclaimed.

"You have eyebrows and eyelashes!" Drainboard groaned.

"You have a neck and a chest and a stomach," Under The Toaster complained.

"I have become a tiny person," said Shoebag.

"You have become quite repulsive!" Under The Toaster told the truth, and the truth made Shoebag's father shiver with disgust.

"I cannot stand myself! Yeck!" said Shoebag. (pp. 1–4)

Well, Shoebag is adopted by the Biddle family, claiming amnesia when uncomfortable questions arise, and sets about being as real a boy as he can be. When he goes to school he has the usual problems of fitting in, being picked on by bullies, and making friends with other misfits. But he still misses his family and their late-night picnics in the kitchen. Read *Shoebag,* by Mary James, and find out if he will ever have six legs again.

If you are as interested in roaches as I am, the best way to study them is to make them feel cozy. You can make your very own roach motel. I didn't bring mine with me as it was too heavy to take on the plane, but you can find all the necessary equipment in *Cockroaches,* by Mona Kerby (p. 50). You can even throw in some shoes for all the comforts of home.

The Sights and Sound Department at Pratt is incredible. I came up with these ideas, and the Sights and Sounds Department was able to find media to match my topics. If they can find a clip of roaches to go with this booktalk, they can find anything! Cultivate a good relationship with your AV department, and watch your ideas blossom.

Just one more science experiment for the road . . . Betsy Duffey's book *Coaster* begins when Hart is ten years old. His dad has just picked him up for the first time since his parents' divorce, and he was supposed to be taking him shopping for back-to-school clothes. Instead he takes him for his first roller-coaster ride.

While Selma read from the book, Blane played a silent clip from *Here Comes a Roller Coaster!* starting when the boy and father get into the roller coaster and finishing just as Selma was done reading the quote below, when the roller-coaster ride is over and the father looks sick.

"You afraid?" his father asked.

"No," Hart answered. His voice cracked a little and gave him away. He wasn't good at lying.

His father's hand settled on Hart's thin shoulder as they hurried forward. "We die—we die together," he said.

Hart tried to laugh but it caught in his throat.

They walked up onto the ramp. The attendant opened a small gate and they got on the coaster side by side. The car was old and beat-up. It smelled of machine oil and hot metal and sweat . . .

"Here goes nothing," said his father . . . They rolled about twenty feet, then caught on the lift chain and jerked forward and upward. His father squeezed the back of Hart's neck as they were pulled up the lift.

No turning back.

They pulled up twenty feet.

Thirty.

Forty . . .

Fifty.

Sixty.

Seventy . . .

Then they dropped.

They plunged down the first hill out of control, screaming together. The cars jerked and bumped on the metal tracks, and they were thrown back and forth, beaten against the sides of the car. The metal restraining bar cut against their knees.

Going around a curve a hundred feet above the ground, Hart hit the wooden side once and felt it give a little. For a second he had an image of the side popping open and sending him flying out over the ocean like a watermelon seed squeezed between two fingers . . .

He heard his father beside him shouting, "Woah!" . . .

Hart screamed with him.

Halfway through the ride, at the point where the cars dipped toward a tunnel, there was a cross beam just above the track.

Hart felt the dip and heard the swish of air as the cross beam passed over his head, and he squeezed his eyes shut. He did not want to see. He gripped the restraining bar with both fists, knuckles white . . .

They rolled into the station and got out of the car on wobbly legs. Hart's throat was tight from shouting.

He looked at his father, who was resting his hands on his knees trying to catch his breath. His father returned his look with a grin. Hart grinned back, and without a word they both began to run out the exit to the back of the line to ride the Wild Side again. (pp. 3–5)

Well they never did get those school clothes, but Hart and his father did start a tradition of experiencing new roller coasters together every time they saw each other. Flash forward two years and Hart's mom is dating a crazy TV weather guy who wears silly hats and does embarrassing stunts. His dad has just stood him up for a roller-coaster outing. Behind Hart's house is a deep ravine. He decides to build his own roller coaster. *Not* a good idea.

You can convince your listeners to build their own roller coasters without risking life and limb by showing them how to "Make the Next Great American Scream Machine," found in *Roller Coaster Science: 50 Wet, Wacky, Wild, Dizzy Experiments about Things Kids Like Best*, by Jim Wiese (p. 39).

Betsy showed the website www.funderstanding.com/k12/ coaster/.

Betsy: Here is a website simulator that enables children to design their own roller coasters while teaching them some physics. As you can see, by adjusting the speed, mass, gravity, and friction of the

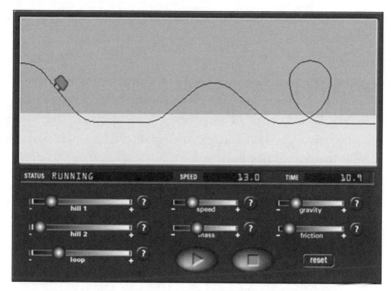

Roller-coaster simulation from www.funderstanding.com/
k12/coaster/. Used with permission.

roller coaster, as well as the height and length of the hills, you can
determine whether a roller coaster ride will be fun, dangerous, or
just plain boring!

Betsy then showed the website www.rcdb.com.

This website is a database all about roller coasters. You can find
out which roller coasters are the tallest, longest, or fastest around
the world. You can read facts about roller coasters—which ones are
made out of wood, if there are roller coasters in your state, which
ones are the highest, and what the names of the coasters are. Have
a look at some of the names . . .

Food, Glorious Food

Blane: Now I have a game for you. I'm going to show you a video
of a common object photographed in such a way that you won't
recognize it. Please feel free to call out what you think it is, and

whoever recognizes it first will get a special prize. If you are already familiar with this film, please do not give it away and ruin the fun for all the others.

> **Blane showed *Zea* and asked people to guess what it was *without showing the title*. After someone guessed that *Zea* is about a kernel of popcorn, Blane played the music to "Popcorn," by Hot Butter, and gave out the prize—a bag of microwavable popcorn.**

Selma: Leo's mother is on a vegetarian-cooking kick.

> Mrs. Nolan dished out bowls of soup. She handed one to Leo, who . . . looked at it closely. It was reddish-brown with some chopped-up green things floating in it and some squares of white stuff too . . .
>
> Leo watched as his father took a taste. He swallowed one spoonful and then another. "Delicious," he said.
>
> Leo eyed the bowl suspiciously . . . "What is it?"
>
> When his mother answered, Leo's mouth dropped open in surprise.
>
> "Measle soup!" he said. "Yuck! I'm not eating any measle soup. I don't want to catch measles." . . .
>
> "What are these white things?" Leo pointed to the little squares of white stuff.
>
> When he heard his mother's answer, he put down his spoon in a hurry.
>
> "Toad food!" he said in horror. "Toad food and measle soup! I'm not eating this. Not on your life. I'm not a toad." . . .
>
> The next night dinner was something new again. Leo examined his plate carefully . . . In the middle of the plate was a large round pocket of bread. Inside there was lettuce and tomatoes and crisp brown things shaped like meatballs . . . Leo poked his finger into the center of the bread pocket. The round balls were still warm.
>
> "Don't play with your food, dear," his mother said.
>
> "Mom? Do you think we'll ever have hot dogs again?"
>
> "We'll have them again sometime. But it's fun to try new things."

Leo wrinkled his nose. "Fun for you, maybe, but I'd rather eat stuff I know I like . . . What is this?"

"Just try it," his mother said.

"Tell me what it is first, then I'll try it," Leo bargained.

When his mother told him the name of the food on his plate, Leo thought she said, "Feel awful."

"That's not very nice, Mom," he said. "I don't want to feel awful. If that's what this is, then I'm not eating any." (pp. 5, 6, 8–10)

Selma turned to the audience and asked, "Who can identify these 'disgusting' dishes?" The answers were miso soup, tofu, and falafel.

With further negotiations Leo's family decides to rotate dinner preparations. Don't worry, Leo gets his own back. When it's his turn he creates chicken pox pie. Yes, food permeates just about everything in Christine McDonnell's *Toad Food and Measle Soup,* but even that doesn't sound as disgusting as this next song . . .

Selma sang her camp version of "Great Green Gobs of Greasy, Grimy Gopher Guts."

Great green gobs of greasy, grimy gopher guts
Mutilated monkey meat,
Little dirty birdy feet
Great green gobs of greasy, grimy gopher guts
And I forgot my spoon!

Blane: If you think that was gross, wait until you hear about this true book. Biographies of early fast-food entrepreneurs like Ray Kroc and Colonel Sanders are the starting point for Eric Schlosser's 2001 book *Fast Food Nation.* In it, Schlosser looks at the birth of the fast-food industry and quickly moves forward through the next fifty years to show how the fast-food industry has altered the American landscape, both literally and figuratively, for better or worse. He also examines how Americans themselves have been transformed by fast food. He concludes his book by examining the

American meatpacking industry, perhaps the most revealing look at it since Upton Sinclair's 1906 masterpiece *The Jungle*. Although meticulously researched and documented, it is an interesting read, and despite its grim view of the fast-food nation, Schlosser offers up a set of remedies, along with realistic steps for getting them accomplished. And currently in theaters is first-time director Morgan Spurlock's documentary *Super Size Me,* which looks at the subject of obesity in the United States, specifically zeroing in on the business and culture surrounding the nation's fast-food industry. Let's get our appetite back with this clip from the History Channel's documentary on the rise of American cuisine and the joys of the fast-food industry, *America Eats: History on a Bun.*

> **Blane showed a video clip from *American Eats: History on a Bun,* from the Chinese fortune cookies to the gigantic sub scenes.**

Betsy: Here is a reference book that is unusual and fascinating. It is called *Greasy Grimy Gopher Guts* (like the song you just heard), and it has songs in it that I used to sing in my childhood. Not the typical songs, but funny ones—parodies of commercials and of regular songs. Here is one example . . .

> **Betsy and Selma sang the parody of the McDonald's theme song from the book *Greasy Grimy Gopher Guts,* p. 151, "Restaurants," version two (to the tune of one of the old McDonald's themes).**

McDonald's is your kind of place,
Hamburgers smashed in your face,
French fries up your nose,
Pickles between your toes.

Before you get your money back.
You'll have a heart attack,
McDonald's is your kind of place.

And now from the ridiculous to the sublime . . .

Blane: Now we're going to watch a short video clip from Ang Lee called *Eat Drink Man Woman*. It's a beautiful movie that shows the relationship between Chef Cho and his family. Foreign language film screenings are often a big draw to the library.

Blane showed a clip from the beginning of the film, starting when one of Chef Cho's daughters starts to open the squid and ending when Chef Cho walks outside.

Betsy: Are you drawn to the taste of peppermints? Here is a book that I love, called *Peppermints in the Parlor*. It is a book about Emily Luccock. After her parents die, she is sent to live with her Auntie Twice. Emily expects to be greeted at the station by her plump and cheerful auntie, but instead she is greeted by "a strange woman . . . [wearing] a shabby brown coat [which] flapped wearily around her thin ankles. Her hair, of no particular color, straggled in drab, lifeless wisps from under a shapeless felt hat" (p. 7). It is Auntie Twice, but "she did not enfold Emily in her arms, and she explained nothing. Instead, she perched stiff and silent as a stone wall on the edge of her seat, moving her pale lips wordlessly from time to time" (p. 9). She takes Emily back to her home, Sugar Hill Hall, and warns her before entering, "Dear, darling child, will you promise me that no matter what happens, you will try to be a brave little girl, a *very* brave little girl?" (p. 10). Emily promises. When they arrive at Sugar Hill Hall, Emily meets Mrs. Meeching: "Her eyes rose slowly up, up, up past the waist of the deadly black skirt, past a gold medallion with a glittering ruby eye in its center, past a high black collar coiled around a white, serpent-thin neck, past a chin sharp as an ice pick, past thin bloodless lips under a pale nose so pinched it seemed air could never pass through it, and arriving finally at the meanest, wickedest, evilest pair of eyes Emily had ever seen in her whole life!" (p. 14). Mrs. Meeching looks Emily over and tells Auntie Twice that "she is puny for eleven" (p. 15). "There will be no need for silks and velvets in scrubbing sinks, scouring pots, and emptying slop jars, eh?" (p. 16) And finally she says, "Long golden braids take entirely too much attention . . . the scissors, please!" (p. 17). Mrs. Meeching cuts off Emily's braids. Emily realizes that Sugar Hill Hall has been converted into an old-age home and Mrs. Meeching is somehow in charge, with Auntie Twice working for her. Emily goes into the parlor, and sees "shadows . . . lurking everywhere. Shadows . . . huddling in every chair that lined the walls of the room . . . [But] what appeared to be shadows were not shadows at all. They were very old people sitting and staring silently ahead with pale, wrinkled faces as empty of expression as unmarked gravestones!" (p. 21). And in the middle of the parlor was a round table with a crystal bowl filled with peppermint candies.

Tilly, another girl who works at Sugar Hill Hall, is introduced to Emily and escorts her to her room:

> On they went, passing one door after another, all firmly closed. Except for the hollow sounds made by their footsteps on the stone floor and the bumping of the bag against Emily's knees, there was a deep underground silence all around them. But as Tilly started to turn at last through the open door of a very tiny room, a faint sound, as if something or some*one* were sighing, came from behind another closed door at the far end of the passageway. This particular door, unlike all the others, had a small square window in the center. The sound so startled and terrified Emily that she let go her bag and it fell to the floor with a jarring crash.
>
> Tilly whirled on her. "What was that for?" she said crossly. "You scairt me out o' my wits!"
>
> "Th-th-that room," Emily stammered, "I heard a *sound* come from there, I think."
>
> Tilly shrugged, "No doubts you did. That's the Remembrance Room. Someone in there remembering what it done wrong."
>
> "Remembrance Room?" Emily repeated dimly. There was a chilling sound about the words. "It did wrong? *Who* did wrong?"
>
> "One o' the old ones, o' course. Who did you thinks?" Tilly's flat nose wrinkled with disgust at Emily's stupidity . . .

"Took a peppermint most likely . . . That's what they always does." (p. 29)

If you would like to find out if Emily ever gets put in the Remembrance Room, and how she manages with Tilly and Mrs. Meeching, read *Peppermints in the Parlor,* by Barbara Brooks Wallace. (**Here Betsy paused for a minute or so.**) And . . . by the way . . . would anyone like some peppermints? (**Betsy held up a glass dish full of individually wrapped peppermint candies and passed it around the room.**)

Talking about candy, here is one of my favorite websites. (**Betsy showed www.smm.org/sln/tf/c/crosssection/namethatbar.html.**) It is from the Science Museum of Minnesota and has a fun game: Name That Candybar. You can see the insides of candy bars, and you get to guess which bar it is. (**She placed the pointer on one of the pictures.**) Does anyone know the name of this one? (**She clicked on the bar to show the name and read it out loud. She played the game for about four more candy bars and then stopped.**)

Name That Candybar game. Copyright © Science Museum
of Minnesota. Used with permission.

Isn't that fun?

Blane showed a clip from *The Making of Star Wars,* with Jabba the Hut, while Betsy continued talking.

Here is one of my favorite cookbooks, the *Star Wars Cook Book,* by Robin Davis. My children and I have tried many of the recipes and they are delicious. We especially like **(showing the pages with the pictures as she read the titles)** the Jabba Jiggle (p. 30), Yoda Soda (p. 22), Han Burgers (p. 36), and Wookie Cookies (p. 48). The Wookie Cookies are especially delicious!

Here's another book about food: *It's Disgusting and We Ate It!* This book gives recipes and tells stories about soup made from birds' nests, sun-dried jellyfish, garbage stew, live maggots, colonial squirrel pie with a side of milkweed shoots, and roasted spiders. Without being judgmental and in a humorous vein, the author describes delicacies around the world—illustrating that what would be gross to one person might be considered delicious to another . . .

Another fun book is *Play with Your Food,* by Joost Elffers. This book has wonderful pictures of fruits and vegetables showing human emotions. It seems like a coffee-table book—one that you might not ordinarily use in a program with children, but they love it. **(Betsy showed a few pictures.)** One of the cool things about this book is that there is a section at the end that shows you how you can make these characters. Through using beans, raisins, and other food items, you can make eyes, noses, and legs. Show the pictures in this book and then have a program where everyone decorates their own vegetables.

Here is a very silly website (**www.museumofhoaxes.com/ spaghetti.html**) that talks about the Swiss Spaghetti Harvest, a hoax that was perpetrated in Britain by the BBC on April Fool's Day. Read how knowledgeable people actually fell for this trick.

All of this talk of food is making me hungry. I think I am ready for some spaghetti. Now is a good time to make a Betty Spaghetti. Take a paper plate. Color in a face; it can be Betty or Eddie Spaghetti.

Make sure to draw the mouth around the two precut slits. Then take a piece of yarn with a tiny knot at each end, and stick one end through the slits. You can pull it up and down and show everyone how Betty is slurping her spaghetti!

> **Betsy passed out paper plates, crayons, and pieces of precut yarn. Everyone took a break to suck on their peppermints and make their Betty Spaghettis.**

In Other Words

> **Selma said the word *supercalifragilisticexpialidocious* forward and backward.**

Selma: Here's a book about a book with some really strange words in it, one of which is even longer than *supercalifragilisticexpialidocious* . . .

Have you ever ordered a book from a book club in school? Well, ten-year-old Howie Quackenbush sends off for *101 Pickle Jokes,* but when he receives his order he gets *The Secret Guide to N. Mellwood* instead. Bummer! N. Mellwood is where Howie lives, and he knows it like the back of his hand. But when he actually reads the book, he finds out that there is a lot more to his hometown than he could ever believe. The book teaches him that if you know the "true" words for places in town, you can go there instantly. He jumps from place to place by saying "Floccinaucinihilipilification"— the mall—or "Hurdy Gurdy"—the video parlor (p. 27). The only side effect seems to be a slight smell of rotten eggs. But when he experiments with a friend and they find themselves standing in two places at the same time, things start to get weird. Word to the wise . . . read Kevin Brockmeier's *City of Names.*

Blane: It's really hard to say some unusual words, but when you're learning a new language, everything is hard to say. *Destinos* is a big series for English speakers who want to learn Spanish. It is like a soap opera that teaches how to speak Spanish. Raquel Rodríguez, a lead character, is a Mexican American lawyer on a quest that takes her on a journey throughout Spanish-speaking countries. In each country, she hears different dialects and accents. There are fifty-two shows in the series. Although some of the earlier shows include English, by the end of the series they are all in Spanish. Accompanying the videos are a number of audiotapes and a textbook. **(Blane showed a clip in which a woman is doing a flamenco dance.)** What a great way to learn a new language—while being drawn into the lives and loves of a long-running drama!

Betsy: Sometimes foreign languages sound like you are talking backward. Palindromes are words that can be read backward or forward. Have fun with palindromes at www.niehs.nih.gov/kids/palindromes.htm or www.palindromelist.com. **(Betsy projected the websites and recited a few of the palindromes.)**

Selma: From palindromes to homonyms, we're still playing around with words. Here's "Homonyms," from *The Word Factory,* by Dan Crow.

> **Selma, Betsy, and Blane, wearing sunglasses, formed a chorus line. Betsy stepped forward and began reciting the words to "Homonyms" with the recorded version while Selma and Blane accompanied her softly in the background.**

Betsy: I saw Jim.
In the gym.
I heard him.
Singing a hymn.
Have you ever heard?
A cattle herd?
For words like this,
There is a word:

> **All three whipped off their sunglasses and pointed out to the audience each time the syllable *nym* was said:**

Homonym (nym, nym), homonym (nym, nym), homonym (nym, nym), homonym (nym, nym).

Sunglasses were put away and Blane took over . . .

Blane: Words are very powerful indeed. But combine those words with images and you can make an even more lasting impression. Just ask Michael Moore! His best-selling book *Stupid White Men* spent over a year near or at the top of the *New York Times* best sellers list. In it, he skewers the "Thief in Chief," George W. Bush, the 2000 election fiasco, the ongoing Iraq/Middle East mess, and Korean dictator Kim Jong-il. Although Mr. Moore can be quite polarizing, he presents his material in a humorous and highly readable, nearly conversational way. When he went on to combine this same satirical social criticism with video and interview images connecting the sitting president's family with the Bin Ladens in his new film *Fahrenheit 9/11,* his studio's parent company, Disney, dropped the film like a hot potato, despite the film's winning the Cannes Palm D'Or, making the United States the only country lacking distribution of this important film. Fortunately, Lion's Gate Films, in partnership with IFC Films and the Fellowship Adventure Group, did not find such censorship to be appropriate and released it themselves.

Those of you who saw Mr. Moore on the Academy Awards know that he can be quite polarizing, but even if you don't agree with his outlook, he presents it in a witty and readable way. Advertisers use words to convince people to buy things they don't really need, or to convince them to choose one product over another. Alissa Quart's *Branded: The Buying and Selling of Teenagers* is frightening for all of us who have been teenagers and remember how easily we were influenced. In this critical look at the advertising and marketing industries' influence on today's teens and tweens, Ms. Quart shows how product placement, strategically manipulated teen influencers, and other marketing tactics have made today's teens perhaps the most brand-conscious generation ever. It is definitely an ominous work on the future of teens and their place in our consumerist culture. Now there is no escape—it's coming at our own teens from all directions!

Betsy has another take on consumerism in her next book. Betsy?

Betsy: *Feed,* by M. T. Anderson, is a book for young adults about consumerism in the future. It is about a society where feeds are placed in people's heads so they have constant messages running through their brains. They can buy something by just thinking about it and communicate easily through their feeds. But is such constant technology a good thing? Listen to this excerpt from Titus, as he wakes up in a hospital bed one day:

> The first thing I felt was no credit.
> I tried to touch my credit, but there was nothing there.
> It felt like I was in a little room.
> My body—I was in a bed, on top of my arm, which was asleep, but I didn't know where. I couldn't find the Lunar GPS to tell me.
> Someone had left a message in my head, which I found, and then kept finding everywhere I went, which said that there was no transmission signal, that I was currently disconnected from feednet. I tried to chat Link and then Marty, but nothing, there was no transmission signal, I was currently disconnected from feednet, of course, and I was starting to get scared, so I tried to chat my parents, I tried to chat them on Earth, but there was no transmission etc., I was currently etc.
> So I opened my eyes. (p. 35)

And now for something else that will open your eyes . . .

Blane: Here's a parody on consumerism called "Affluenza." Note that the sound is supposed to sound like the speakers are talking through Jell-O!

Blane showed the beginning of the film *Affluenza* up until the words "Anyone you know?" came on the screen.

Also on the topic of consumerism, there is a series of videos for children called Buy Me That. I wonder where they got that name?

Flying High

Betsy: Here's a young girl just starting out on the road to consumerism. In *Mail-Order Wings,* by Beatrice Gormley, Andrea reads an advertisement for wings in the back of a comic book and actually orders them. When her package arrives, she follows the complicated instructions and puts together a set of wings. Although they are beautiful, Andrea "didn't see how she could put the wings on even to pretend to fly. There weren't any straps or pins or other fasteners in the carton" (p. 29). Once she figures out how attach them using Aero-hesive, she still doesn't know how to make them work. The wings "were gorgeous, still glowing red, blue, and yellow, and all the colors of the rainbow where the feathers overlapped. But they hung limply down her back like two big feather dusters" (p. 35).

> **Blane showed a silent clip of hang gliding from the 1973 tape of the video series Sensational '70s while Betsy connected all with a creative dramatic activity.**

Try this: Stand up and pretend that you are Andrea. You have just put together a pair of wings and are trying to get them to work. "[Andrea] jumped up and down and wiggled her shoulder blades— nothing. She stood at the edge of her bed and leaped, flapping her arms" (p. 35). Try jumping up and down . . . shrug your shoulders three times, twirl around . . . sway from side to side . . . Now sit back down and hear what happens . . .

Andrea notices a bottle of pink liquid labeled Aero-Joy Juice. "She unscrewed the cap and sniffed. Smelled like Hawaiian Punch. The directions seemed to mean that she was supposed to drink the Aero-Joy Juice. But should she? This mysterious bottle seemed like the kind of thing her mother had always warned her against. No thanks. She put the bottle down" (p. 36). But she kept thinking about it. She *really* wanted to be able to fly. She picked up the bottle again. "The juice wasn't poison . . . Andrea hesitated, then put the bottle to her lips and sipped. Yep, Hawaiian Punch. *Glug-glug-glug*" (pp. 40–41). But still, nothing happened. So Andrea went to sleep.

But later that night, Andrea woke up with two tingling spots on her back. "She was lying facedown . . . but her stomach was not pressing against the bed. Her cheek was not on her pillow. Her pajama top was pushed up under her arms, instead of covering her chest and back. Andrea opened her eyes. A square of moonlight lay on her rumpled sheets and blanket, two feet below her. The wings, flapping above her, loud as the wings of a startled goose, were her own" (pp. 41–43).

Although the wings seem impossible to take off, Andrea is excited about flying into all sorts of new adventures, at least for a little while . . .

Selma: Emeke's greatest wish is to fly, but it makes him the laughing-stock of his village. His grandmother has always told him that the Great Snake can make any wish come true, if one can but find him. Read on to see how the Good Snake and Emeke's belief in himself, despite humiliation, turn a goat herder into a *Brother to the Wind.* Mildred Pitts Walter will have you soaring right along with Emeke!

Betsy: Play the Internet Search Game! In order to find the websites for this program, all I did was choose the different topics and do a Google search to see what websites were available. I chose what I thought were the best sites and tested them out before this presentation started in order to ensure that they were still available. One way you can help your children to learn how to perform Google searches is to turn it into a game. Talking about flying, ask children to see how many websites kids can find with the myth of Dedaelus and Icarus. See if they can find out how many different ways the names are spelled.

Next, you may try to create a puzzle with words related to space and flight. Go to http://puzzlemaker.school.discovery.com. This is a free website for creating multiple kinds of puzzles. Let's try to create a crossword puzzle with words about flight. Choose "Criss-Cross." Fill in the title of your puzzle; since it's about flight, let's type in "Aviation." Skip steps 2 and 3; go straight to step 4. Can anyone tell me some words related to flight? (**Betsy listened to** audience suggestions and typed them into the computer. If no suggestions are forthcoming, you can use the following: plane, pilot, wings, soar, air, airlines, atmosphere, height, astronauts.) Press "Create my puzzle," wait a few seconds, and voilà! Here is your crossword puzzle. This site is great for creating handouts and activity sheets about a variety of themes.

In addition to flying with wings, there is another kind of flight, the kind you have when you are trying to flee, trying to run away from something bad.

> **Blane showed the clip from *Silence* of the baby girl flying over the Nazi. He turned it off when the audience could see the star on the old woman's dress.**

Blane: It's very hard to find material for young children on the Holocaust. This video in its entirety would not work, but this small clip helps to introduce a difficult topic.

Changing the World

Betsy: The Holocaust is a topic that some parents and teachers want to expose their children to, but there is not much appropriate literature about it. One book that I like is Jo Hoestlandt's *Star of Fear, Star of Hope.* This is the story of eight-year-old Helen, who invites her best friend Lydia to sleep over in celebration on the evening of her ninth birthday. During the night, Lydia gets the message that the Nazis are rounding up Jews and insists on going home to her parents; Helen gets angry at Lydia for abandoning her and shouts, "You're not my friend anymore." Lydia never returns. As Helen grows older, she often wonders what happened to Lydia and slowly understands that Jewish Lydia was probably deported along with her family. Without going into the gruesome details of the roundups, the stuffed cattle cars, and the mass exterminations, this simple tale of two friends succeeds at personalizing the story of one child, thus making the horror of the Holocaust understandable on one small level.

The famous legend of King Christian X of Denmark is recreated in this beautifully illustrated book: *The Yellow Star: The Legend of King Christian X of Denmark,* by Carmen Agra Deedy. During the Holocaust, one way that the Nazis were able to separate the Jews from all other people in order to identify them for punishments and death was to require them to sew a yellow star on their clothing. In countries under German jurisdiction, it was against the law for a Jew to leave his or her house without wearing a garment with a yellow star. Each morning King Christian X of Denmark used to ride his horse around the capital, Copenhagen, to say hello to his citizens. Just after the German edict went into effect in Denmark, when King Christian went out for his daily horseback ride, everyone saw a yellow star on his clothes. The Danish people realized that he considered all Danes equal and did not separate out people by religion; they responded by sewing stars onto their clothing, too. When the Nazis were unable to tell the difference between the Jews and the other Danes, they could not persecute the Danish Jews. Although there is no proof that this story is true, it is well known and gives a good example of how evil can be thwarted when people unite.

If you use this book, a website to go along with it is www.holo caustcenter.org/Holocaust/holocaustbadges.shtml. Here, children can see the actual yellow stars that Jews had to wear during the Holocaust. Each country had a different type of yellow star that Jews had to sew onto their clothing; a star from Germany is shown here. Looking at these patches, just a small symbol of what happened during World War II, helps to make the horror of discrimination much more than a concept for the viewers.

People don't always give in when there is pressure to do bad things. Kids can be encouraged to take a stand when something doesn't seem right to them. Although this true story takes place in the recent past and not during the Holocaust, it provides details about the Holocaust in an understandable way. *Hana's Suitcase* was an artifact that a Japanese teacher showed her students in order to make the Holocaust real for them. The suitcase was empty, but it had Hana's name on it. The Japanese students insisted on finding out who Hana was and what happened to her. While doing detective work to track down the former owner of the suitcase, they learned that Hana was exterminated in one of the concentration camps. Through their efforts to find Hana, the students eventually discovered her brother, living in Canada. From him, they learned more about Hana; at the same time, her brother was reassured that history would not repeat itself, since there were children willing to learn and take action. See what kind of significant things kids just like you can accomplish when they work together?

A yellow Star of David marked with the German word for Jew (*Jude*). Used with permission of the United States Holocaust Memorial Museum. The views or opinions expressed in this book and the context in which the images are used do not necessarily reflect the views or policy of, nor imply approval or endorsement by, the United States Holocaust Memorial Museum.

Selma: Speaking of taking action . . .

Roy has just moved from Montana to Florida and he is *not* impressed. He thinks Disney World is an armpit compared to his home state. On his first time on the school bus he sees a barefoot boy running away from the school. Intrigued, he finally tracks this elusive kid down and finds out that he is on a one-man campaign to stop a chain of pancake houses from building their newest franchise on the nesting grounds of a rare burrowing owl. And he doesn't play clean. This ecological avenger, also known as Mullet Fingers, puts alligators in the spot-o-pots and uses poisonous snakes to his best advantage. Read Carl Hiaasen's book to see if someone finally gives a *Hoot!*

Or perhaps we should say "Give a hoot" because . . .

Selma, Betsy, and Blane sang along with a recording of "All God's Critters Got a Place in the Choir," by Bill Staines, and used puppets for emphasis during the choruses.

Blane: Here's a short video clip about some cows who took a stand against the farmer.

> **Blane showed the part where the animals are typing a letter to the farmer in *Click, Clack, Moo.***

Betsy: Talking about animals, here's a website about a topic important to many kids besides Mullet Fingers, protecting animals. As you can see, there are opportunities from here to learn facts, play games, and become animal activists **(www.kidsplanet.org)**. Getting kids involved in important causes can be somewhat of a magic trick, given their addiction to video games and the television.

Abracadabra

Betsy: Speaking of magic, no booktalk would be complete without mentioning Harry Potter, defender of good against evil. For all those Harry Potter fans who need something to read while waiting for the next book to come out, I highly recommend books by Tamora Pierce. The first book in her Song of the Lioness series is *Alanna: The First Adventure*. Alanna always dreamed of becoming a knight, and her twin brother, Thom, wanted to be a sorcerer. That does not matter to their traditional father, who arranges to send Alanna to study magic and Thom to the palace to become a knight. But Alanna and Thom switch places. A forged letter is all that Thom needs for the switch; since girls are not allowed to be knights, Alanna has to adopt the identity of "Alan." How long can she keep up the charade? What will she do when all the knights-in-training go swimming? There are four books in this particular series; each book has stories of magic, intrigue, friendship, and determination with familiar characters. And when you are done reading these, there are other books by Tamora Pierce about the same kingdom with the same characters, even though they are parts of different series. With so much material, these books are sure to keep your Harry Potter fans busy!

A different kind of magic is optical illusions. Let's have a look at some of these optical illusions and see what you think!

Betsy went to the website www.eyetricks.com/illusions .htm and clicked on "Gallery 1—Eye Tricks" and "Gallery 2—Faces."

Selma: *Stringbean's Trip to the Shining Sea,* by Vera B. Williams and Jennifer Williams, has nothing to do with magic, but as it is written solely on postcards you will see the connection soon enough. Stringbean and his big brother, Fred, are on their way across the United States to the Pacific Ocean. Each page shows the front or back of a postcard telling about their adventures. They start off alone, but as you can see their dog, Potato, insisted on following them (**showing picture of dog and Stringbean**). Along the way they stay at a buffalo ranch, eat in a restaurant shaped like a boot (**showing each picture**), see bears swimming, and find a clown's shoe. The circus has just left, so all along their route, they keep trying to catch up with it. Like most brothers they don't always get along.

> Dear Ma,
>
> I miss you. And Daddy too.
> I miss Grandpa too. I miss Lily too.
> The Ocean is still far away.
> Fred is VERY mean.
> He made me let my lizard go.
>
> Love, Stringbean
>
> p.s. I have given up on finding the clown
> and giving him back his shoe.

Read the postcards and look at the hand-drawn postcard pictures and stamps, and find out what happens when Stringbean, Fred, and Potato reach the Shining Sea and whether that clown ever gets his shoe back!

And now the pièce de résistance! I will take an ordinary postcard, just like the ones in this last book, and I am going to walk through it. Yes, a 5 × 8 inch card versus a size 12 adult female. Can it be done with just a pair of scissors? This is actually an oversize note card—still the size of a large postcard—after all, why waste a pretty postcard? Now as I carefully follow the instructions in Caroline Feller Bauer's *Leading Kids to Books through Magic* (pp. 10–12), I will demonstrate how easy it is to do the impossible. **(Selma cut the postcard while speaking.)** You too can use music, websites, film, crafts, science experiments, creative dramatics, puppets, food, and, yes, magic to enhance your booktalking presentations. You may not be able to use all of these ideas at the same time, but unlike most magicians, we have shown you the tricks of the trade!

Selma climbed through the postcard, bowed, and gestured for Betsy and Blane to join her for the end of the program. All held hands and bowed together.

CHAPTER 12

Trials, Tribulations, Testimonials, and Tips

ONE OF OUR FIRST PRESENTATIONS WAS IN HAGERSTOWN, Maryland. When we arrived, we were told immediately that the Internet in the presentation room was not working but that there was a small technology lab downstairs that we could use. There were many participants, and the room downstairs was small. So, we reorganized our booktalk, taking out all of the integrated websites and putting them at the end. Our intention was to do the general booktalk in the main room and to take the crowd downstairs to finish with the websites.

Selma and Blane started out the booktalk in a room full of librarians, and in the middle of it, there was a short in the fire alarm. Everyone sat in the room covering their ears until the alarm was fixed. This happened three times, and each time the alarm went off for at least five minutes. Not only that, making things even more challenging, there was a high-powered lawn mower outside that kept making swipes past the windows of the presentation room. When we finally went downstairs to the media room so Betsy could show the websites, the Internet connection was not working there either. Luckily, she had prepared handouts with the website addresses; instead of actually showing the websites, she directed people to the web addresses on their handouts and described in detail what they would have seen if the addresses were accessible online. We learned two things from this: *what can go wrong will,* and *being able to punt is a must.*

Despite this, the evaluations from that session were off the charts. This indicated both sympathy for circumstances beyond our control and recognition of our ability to be flexible without losing our cool. We were able to make on-the-spot, unusual accommodations because we had practiced together numerous times and knew our material inside out. Of course, our presentation was multifaceted because we were trying to show every possible way to add pizzazz to a booktalk. Booktalks for students given by just one librarian should not be so complex. However, the failure of even one website can be disconcerting if you are not prepared.

If you are going to be using technology that requires Internet connections, LCD projectors, and even CD players, you must be prepared for the possibility that something might not work. You may have to sing a cappella, describe websites rather than using them, or literally and figuratively cut and paste your presentation based on time constraints and room considerations.

It is important to work within your means; don't try to do too many techie things unless you have the setup for it. Although each chapter in this book mentions a few different websites, some film clips, and recorded music, integrating even one or two of our ideas will make a difference in pepping up your booktalks. These additions will make your presentations more exciting and relevant to today's technology-savvy children.

We have presented "Booktalking with Pizzazz" in big rooms and small rooms, in rooms with automatic screens that come down from the ceiling at the press of a button, on portable screens, and on walls that are almost white and *almost* OK for screening an image. We have had people sitting on the floor, around tables, and in rows. We have had audiences of over a hundred and as small as fourteen. No matter what the circumstances, we try to keep our energy level high and put the emphasis on our love for the books rather than on frustration with the surroundings. Enthusiasm breeds enthusiasm, whatever your audience.

Despite the sometimes adverse conditions, we have found that librarians are always happy to have new ideas. All of us have to do booktalks, and new ideas give us inspiration and energy. As a testimonial, after one training workshop for librarians, we received a CD from Kris Buker, a teen specialist from the Howard County Library system in Maryland, who was motivated to create a PowerPoint presentation combining music with book covers for a teen booktalk.

There are many good books about booktalking, so rather than include general how-to instructions, we focus on tips for adding pizzazz to your presentations. Once you've chosen a book to booktalk, look for themes that jump out and are easy to track as website subjects, in films, and as musical themes. See if a topic can be translated into a piece of realia (such as the mummified hotdog). Look for websites that are interactive and fun, but make sure that there are no links to sites of questionable content. If you are planning on using a song from YouTube, make sure to view it in its entirety before you screen it for the students. Make sure there are no raunchy lyrics or visuals. You may decide to use just the opening few seconds or the last few bars of a song. YouTube is a wonderful tool, but be careful to use the right version of your chosen song in order to prevent unwanted surprises.

A recent development on YouTube has been the posting of clips with people booktalking their favorite books. Students, teachers, and even facilities staff have used the technology to promote books. The quality of these booktalks varies, however. We recommend the following two examples that were available at the time that this book went to press:

> "The Teacher's Funeral: A Comedy in Three Parts," by Richard Peck, is a digital booktalk done through PowerPoint. Funny and short, with creative narration, it can be found at www .youtube.com/watch?v=UWCXkSercQc.

> "Show Way," by Jacqueline Woodson, at www.youtube.com/ watch?v=J9QsdhIfu1c, starts with realia by using a Peruvian blanket to lead into the story of the Show Way quilts that helped lead slaves to freedom.

Once you have given your booktalk, you may want to encourage children to make their own YouTube booktalks. By encouraging children to choose a favorite book and use technology to share it with others, you may be igniting an interest they might not previously have felt. You may want to link some of their better attempts to your library website. Adding pizzazz to your booktalks and giving children the opportunity to make their own completes a cycle. Posting some of the booktalks on your website melds books with technology and social networking to create a satisfying whole. We have come full circle; the possibilities are endless.

Booktalking with Pizzazz

An Audiography, Bibliography, Filmography, and Webliography

Including science experiments, music, magic, crafts, creative dramatics, puppets, videos, role-playing, and games

THE TERM *BOOKTALK* CAN BE VERY LIMITING. TODAY'S LIBRARY users, from the youngest preschooler to the eldest senior, are becoming increasingly media savvy, accustomed as they are to bombardment from TV, radio, the Internet, and myriad other access points. With that in mind, what follows are a few examples of materials to be used in media talks, which are still rooted in the traditional book but use other media to add another dimension to the endeavor. With the addition of the media, these short talks can easily be expanded into full-blown subject programs.

FOWL PLAY

Books

King-Smith, Dick. *The Fox Busters.* Delacorte, 1988.

Manes, Stephen. *Some of the Adventures of Rhode Island Red.* Stephen Lippincott, 1990.

Compiled by Betsy Diamant-Cohen, Blane Halliday, Selma Levi, and Michael Rios.

ALSO USE WITH

Angelou, Maya. *My Painted House, My Friendly Chicken, and Me.* Clarkson Potter, 1994.

Karr, Kathleen. *Great Turkey Walk.* Farrar, Straus and Giroux, 1998.

King-Smith, Dick. *Pretty Polly.* Crown, 1992.

Maguire, Gregory. *Three Rotten Eggs.* Clarion, 2002.

Naylor, Phyllis. *The Great Chicken Debacle.* Marshall Cavendish, 2001.

Pinkwater, Daniel. *Hoboken Chicken Emergency.* Aladdin Library, 1999.

Films and Videos

Rosie's Walk. Directed by Gene Deitch. Weston Woods, 1970.

Music

Broadway Kids. "Ghostbusters." *At the Movies.* Lightyear Entertainment, 1997.

"Chicken Dance." *Drew's Famous Party Music.* Turn Up the Music, 1994.

Websites

While talking about chicken books, you can show chickens around the world: www.kippenpagina.nl/kippenwebcam/. Live from a chicken coop in Deventer in the Netherlands, complete with noises!

Learn about breeding the Seney chicken at www.capital.net/~intranet/chickens.htm.

Provide some background music to your booktalks at www.classical.net/music/rep/lists/baroque.html.

MAD SCIENTISTS

Books

Baker, Wendy, and Andrew Haslam. *Plants: A Creative, Hands-On Approach to Science.* Macmillan, 1992.

Banks, Jacqueline Turner. *Egg-Drop Blues.* Houghton Mifflin, 1995.

Du Bois, William Pène. *Lazy Tommy Pumpkinhead.* Harper and Row, 1966.

Duffey, Betsy. *Coaster.* Penguin, 1994.

Gardiner, John Reynolds. *Top Secret.* Little, Brown, 1984.

James, Mary. *Shoebag.* Scholastic, 1990.

Keller, Charles. *The Best of Rube Goldberg.* Prentice-Hall, 1979.

Kerby, Mona. *Cockroaches.* Franklin Watts, 1989.

Wiese, Jim. *Roller Coaster Science: 50 Wet, Wacky, Wild, Dizzy Experiments about Things Kids Like Best.* Wiley, 1994.

ALSO USE WITH

Branzei, Sylvia. *Hands-On Grossology: The Science of Really Gross Experiments.* Penguin Putnam, 1999.

Cook, Nick. *Roller Coasters; or, I Had So Much Fun, I Almost Puked.* Carolrhoda, 1998.

Domke, Todd. *Grounded.* Alfred A. Knopf, 1982.

Frazee, Marla. *Roller Coaster.* Harcourt, 2003.

Hicks, Clifford B. *The Marvelous Inventions of Alvin Fernald.* John C. Winston, 1960.

Hodge, Deborah. *Simple Machines.* Kids Can Press, 1996.

James, Mary. *Shoebag Returns.* Scholastic, 1996.

Mahy, Margaret. *The Girl with the Green Ear: Stories about Magic in Nature.* Alfred A. Knopf, 1992.

McArthur, Nancy. *The Plant That Ate Dirty Socks.* Avon, 1988.

Torey, Michele. *The Case of the Graveyard Ghost.* Dutton, 2002.

Turner, Megan Whalen. "Leroy Roachbane." *Instead of Three Wishes.* Greenwillow, 1995.

Yep, Laurence. *Cockroach Cooties.* Hyperion, 2000.

Ziefert, Harriet. *Egg-Drop Day.* Little, Brown, 1988.

Films and Videos

Here Comes a Roller Coaster! Directed by David Hood. Kid Vision, 1995.

The Way Things Go. Directed by Peter Fischli and David Weiss. First Run Icarus Films, 1987.

When the Lights Go Out: Cockroaches, a Domestic History. Directed by Tony Gailey and Julian Russell. Landmark Media, 1994.

ALSO USE WITH

Earth Science for Children. Series produced by Andrew Schlessinger. Schlessinger Media, 2000.

Energy in Action. Series produced by Andrew Schlessinger. Schlessinger Media, 2000.

Mechanical Universe and Beyond. Series produced by Peter F. Buffa. Annenberg/CPB Project, 1985.

Roller Coaster! Directed by Graham Moore. WGBH Educational Foundation, 1993.

Roller Coaster Physics. Directed by Mark Everest. Discovery Channel School, 2000.

Websites

Design your own roller coaster! At www.funderstanding.com/k12/coaster/, kids can design their own roller coaster and educators can simulate the application of physics. (Requires Java applet.)

At www.rcdb.com, find statistics on the fastest, tallest, or longest roller coasters with the interactive Roller Coaster Database. Some of the names of the newest roller coasters are Hot Tamale, Marvel Mania, Canyon Blaster, Fiesta Express, Batflyer, and Asteroid.

Learn about an invention contest in 2004 at the official Rube Goldberg website: www.rube-goldberg.com/html/contest.htm.

ALSO USE WITH

See examples of roach anatomy, read from the diary of Ralph Roach, learn about roach removal, and take the roach quiz: http://yucky.kids.discovery.com/noflash/roaches/index.html.

An archive of edible and inedible science experiments for teachers and librarians can be found at www.madsci.org/experiments/.

FOOD, GLORIOUS FOOD

Books

Davis, Robin. *The Star Wars Cook Book.* Chronicle, 1998.

Elffers, Joost. *Play with Your Food.* Stewart, Tabori and Chang, 1997.

McDonnell, Christine. *Toad Food and Measle Soup.* Puffin, 1982.

Schlosser, Eric. *Fast Food Nation.* Houghton Mifflin, 2001

Sherman, Josepha, and T. K. F. Weisskopf. *Greasy Grimy Gopher Guts: The Subversive Folklore of Childhood.* August House, 1995.

Solheim, James. *It's Disgusting and We Ate it!* Simon and Schuster, 1997.

Wallace, Barbara Brooks. *Peppermints in the Parlor.* Atheneum, 1980.

ALSO USE WITH

Corbett, Scott. *The Hateful Plateful Trick.* Little, Brown, 1971.

dePaola, Tomie. *The Popcorn Book.* Holiday House, 1978.

Horvath, Polly. *Everything on a Waffle.* Farrar, Straus and Giroux, 2001.

Sandburg, Carl. *The Huckabuck Family.* Farrar, Straus and Giroux, 1999.

Films and Videos

American Eats: History on a Bun. Produced by Ted Schillinger. A&E Home Video, 1999.

Eat Drink Man Woman. Directed by Ang Lee. Central Motion Pictures and Good Machine, 1994.

The Making of Star Wars. Directed by Robert Guenette. Twentieth Century Fox, 1977.

Zea. Directed by Andre Leduc and Jean-Jacques Leduc. National Film Board of Canada, 1981.

ALSO USE WITH

Classic Creatures: Return of the Jedi. Directed by Robert Guenette. Films, Inc., 1984.

Ray Kroc: Fast Food "McMillionaire." Produced by Greg Weinstein. A&E Home Video, 1998.

Music

Hot Butter. "Popcorn." *Super Hits of the '70s: Have a Nice Day.* Vol. 9. Rhino, 1990.

ALSO USE WITH

Little Richard. "On Top of Spaghetti." *Shake It All About.* Walt Disney Records, 1992.

"Chicken Lips and Lizard Hips." *For Our Children.* Walt Disney Company, 1991.

Websites

Name that Candybar—Science Museum of Minnesota: www.smm .org/sln/tf/c/crosssection/namethatbar.html.

Scroll down to see pictures from *Play with Your Food* at http:// calendars.vendimus.com/play-with-your-food-2004-mini-wall -calendar-200400002761.html.

Read about the Swiss Spaghetti Harvest at www.museumofhoaxes .com/spaghetti.html.

ALSO USE WITH

Visit the Wonka factory at www.wonka.com for the joke of the day.

Visit the Flavor Mausoleum at www.benjerry.com/fun_stuff/ to view Ben and Jerry's Dearly Departed Flavor List!

For fun with kids and food, visit http://familyfun.go.com/recipes/ kids/.

Learn about mints at www.candyusa.org.

Craft Projects

Betty Spaghetti craft project with paper plates, crayons, and yarn (see chapter 11 for instructions).

IN OTHER WORDS

Books

Anderson, M. T. *Feed.* Candlewick, 2002.

Brockmeier, Kevin. *City of Names.* Viking, 2002.

Moore, Michael. *Stupid White Men and Other Sorry Excuses for the State of the Nation!* ReganBooks, 2001.

Quart, Alissa. *Branded: The Buying and Selling of Teenagers.* Perseus, 2003.

Van Patten, Bill. *Destinos: An Introduction to the Spanish.* (Textbook to accompany episodes on video.) McGraw-Hill, 1991.

ALSO USE WITH

B., David. *Epileptic.* Pantheon, 2005.

DeGross, Monalisa. *Donavan's Word Jar.* HarperTrophy, 1994.

Graham-Barber, Lynda, and Barbara Lehman. *A Chartreuse Leotard in a Magenta Limousine.* Hyperion, 1994.

Kelly, Katy. *Lucy Rose: Here's the Thing about Me.* Delacorte, 2004.

Kerr, P. B. *The Akhenaten Adventure.* Orchard Books, 2004.

Korman, Gordon. *The Sixth-Grade Nickname Game.* Hyperion, 1998.

Skolsky, Mindy Warshaw. *Hannah Is a Palindrome.* Harper and Row, 1980.

Films and Videos

Affluenza. Produced by John DeGraff. Bullfrog Films, 1997.

Buy Me That! A Kids' Survival Guide to TV Advertising. Directed by Jim Jinkins and Mike Tollin. Films, Inc., 1989.

Buy Me That 3! A Kid's Guide to Food Advertising. Directed by Edd Griles. Films, Inc., 1992.

Destinos. Television series. WGBH Educational Foundation, 1992.

The History of the Comics. Directed by Alejandro Vallejo. White Star, 1990.

ALSO USE WITH

The Ad and the Ego: Truth and Consequences. Directed by Harold Boihem. California Newsreel, 1996.

All the Right Stuff. Directed by Connie Littlefield. Bullfrog Films, 1997.

The Awful Truth. Complete first season. Directed by Michael Moore. Docudrama, 2000.

The Awful Truth. Complete second season. Directed by Michael Moore. Docudrama, 2001.

Clio Awards: 40th Anniversary Reel. Hosted by Neil French. Films for the Humanities and Sciences, 2000.

Douglas Coupland: Close Personal Friend. Directed by Jennifer Cowan. Bullfrog Films, 1995.

Fear and Favor in the Newsroom. Directed by Beth Sanders. California Newsreel, 1996.

How to Draw Comics the Marvel Way. Produced by John Gates. New World Video, 1988.

The Myth of the Liberal Media: The Propaganda Model of the News. Directed by Sut Jhally. Media Education Foundation, 1997.

Roger and Me. Directed by Michael Moore. Warner Brothers, 1989.

Tell the Truth and Run. Directed by Rick Goldsmith. New Day Films, 1996.

The 30-Second Seduction. Produced by Allan A. Goldstein. Films Inc., 1985.

Music

Crow, Dan. "Homonyms." *The Word Factory.* Sony, 1992.

"Supercalifragilisticexpialidocious." *Disney's Classic Sing Along Collection.* Vol. 2. Walt Disney Records, 1996.

ALSO USE WITH

Crow, Dan. "Madam, I'm Adam." *The Word Factory.* Sony, 1992.

Websites

Find some amusing illustrated English words that are derived from Latin and Greek elements at www.wordphiles.info/image-word -unit1/image-word-set1.html.

Have fun with palindromes at www.niehs.nih.gov/kids/palindromes .htm.

See more palindromes at www.palindromelist.com.

FLYING HIGH

Books

Gormley, Beatrice. *Mail-Order Wings*. Dutton, 1981.

Walter, Mildred Pitts. *Brother to the Wind*. Lothrop, Lee and Shepard, 1985.

ALSO USE WITH

Green, Susan Kohn. *Self-Portrait with Wings*. Little, Brown, 1989.

Le Guin, Ursula. *Jane on Her Own: A Catwings Tale*. Orchard Books, 1999.

McCaughrean, Geraldine. *The Kite Rider*. HarperCollins, 2001.

Munsch, Robert. *Angela's Airplane*. Annick Press, 1996.

Myers, Christopher. *Wings*. Scholastic, 2000.

Ryan, Pam Muñoz. *Amelia and Eleanor Go for a Ride*. Scholastic, 1999.

Films and Videos

1973—The Year of Watergate. The Sensational Seventies. Series directed by James Orr. Cinema Guild, 1993.

Silence. Directed by Orly Yadin and Sylvie Bringas. Filmmakers Library, 1998.

ALSO USE WITH

There Goes an Airplane. Directed by David Hesson. Kid Vision, 1994.

Websites

Use Google or other search engines to challenge children to see how many websites they can find about the myth of Dedaelus and Icarus. How many different ways are the names spelled?

A great website for creating all types of puzzles is http://puzzlemaker .school.discovery.com.

ALSO USE WITH

Here are some fun space songs with lyrics and music: www.geocities .com/bourbonstreet/2690/glazer/tomglazer.html.

Play Harry Potter Quidditch games at www.surfnetkids.com/games/ broomsticks/.

An actual training manual on the basics of space flight by NASA's Jet Propulsion Laboratory can be found at www.jpl.nasa.gov/basics/. For serious students only!

CHANGING THE WORLD

Books

Deedy, Carmen Agra. *The Yellow Star: The Legend of King Christian X of Denmark.* Peachtree, 2000.

Hiassen, Carl. *Hoot.* Alfred A. Knopf, 2002.

Hoestlandt, Jo. *Star of Fear, Star of Hope.* Walker, 1995.

Levine, Karen. *Hana's Suitcase.* Albert Whitman, 2002.

ALSO USE WITH

Bridges, Ruby. *Through My Eyes.* Scholastic, 1999.

Cooper, Susan. *Green Boy.* Simon and Schuster, 2002.

D'Adamo, Francesco. *Iqbal: A Novel.* Atheneum, 2003.

Earth Works Group. *Fifty Simple Things Kids Can Do to Save the Earth.* Andrews and McMeel, 1990.

Fine, Anne. *My War with Goggle-Eyes.* Little, Brown, 1989.

Going, K. L. *Fat Kid Rules the World.* Putnam, 2003.

Joseph, Lynn. *The Color of My Words.* Joanna Cotler Books, 2000.

Powell, Pamela. *The Turtle Watchers*. Viking, 1992.

Weizmann, Daniel. *Take a Stand*. Price, Stern, Sloan, 1996.

Films and Videos

Click, Clack, Moo: Cows That Type. Directed by Maciek Albrecht. Weston Woods, 2001.

ALSO USE WITH

Anne Frank: The Life of a Young Girl. Produced by Brooke Runnette. A&E Home Video, 1998.

Blue Eyed. Directed by Bertram Verhaag. California Newsreel, 1996.

The Earth at Risk. Environmental video series directed by Michael Pearlman. Schlessinger Video Productions, 1992.

Forget Me Not: The Anne Frank Story. Directed by Fred Holmes. Grace Products, 1996.

A Painful Reminder: Evidence for All Mankind. Directed by Sidney Bernstein. First Run, 1986.

Rebels: A Journey Underground. Directed by Kevin Alexander. Filmwest Associates, 1998.

Music

Staines, Bill. "All God's Critters Got a Place in the Choir." *The Whistle of the Jay*. Folk Legacy, 1985.

ALSO USE WITH

Rosenshontz. "Garbage." *Share It!* Lightyear Records, 1992.

Thomas, Marlo, and Friends. "On My Pond." *Free to Be You and Me*. A&M Records, 1988.

Websites

A website with different yellow badges from World War II is www .holocaustcenter.org/Holocaust/holocaustbadges.shtml.

Here's a website about protecting animals: www.kidsplanet.org.

ALSO USE WITH

Youthvoice.net, sponsored by the Civic Literacy Project in Indiana, offers a handbook that helps students become involved in social action: www.indiana.edu/~ythvoice/socialtools.html.

ABRACADABRA

Books

Bauer, Caroline Feller. *Leading Kids to Books through Magic.* ALA, 1996.

Pierce, Tamora. *Alanna: The First Adventure.* Random House, 1983,

Williams, Vera B. *Stringbean's Trip to the Shining Sea.* Greenwillow, 1988.

ALSO USE WITH

Brisson, Pat. *Your Best Friend, Kate.* Bradbury Press, 1989.

Hest, Amy. *Travel Tips from Harry.* Morrow, 1989.

Leedy, Loreen. *Postcards from Pluto: A Tour of the Solar System.* Holiday House, 1993.

Pattison, Darcy. *The Journey of Oliver K. Woodman.* Harcourt, 2003.

Websites

A different kind of magic is optical illusions: www.eyetricks.com/illusions.htm.

If you are looking for magic tricks, try checking out this website: www.conjuror.com/magictricks/free_tricks1.html.

INDEX

Note: Page numbers in italics refer to the resource lists at the end of each chapter. The topics of booktalks appear in bold type.